Dying, Death and Grief

Praise for the book

This book bridges the gap between the overly simplistic self-help type book and the more academic research-based one. For students, this will introduce research without overwhelming.

Jan Hawkins, Independent Practitioner

Full of common sense, wisdom and warmth ... it is a book about theory and skills, which is unique.

Pam Firth, Isabel Hospice, Head of Family Support and
Deputy Director Hospice Services

I enjoyed reading this book. It is a very refreshing down to earth text that examines theory and research without becoming an academic tome. It is comprehensive, focused on practice and includes some very interesting reflective exercises that allow you to engage with the text by comparing and contrasting your experiences with the author's ideas. The book contains important insights for developing the essential skills required to provide effective bereavement care. It covers a wide range of issues from bereavement support to the importance of dreams. Brenda points out that death is one of the most difficult experiences we encounter. After reading this book, I believe practitioners from many areas of health and social care will improve their knowledge and self confidence and be able to make a difference to the experience of dying for the individual and the grieving family.

Dr John Costello, Head of Primary Care, University of Manchester

The term 'grief counseling' has been bandied about for several decades. Brenda Mallon gives the term definition in a way no one has done before. Her book provides a very readable introduction on helping bereaved people. The author recognizes that help comes from friends, lay counselors, leaders of self-help groups, and para-professionals as well as from mental health professionals. She has written in a way that will be useful to all of them. Well-chosen quotations, some from contemporary bereaved people and some from literature, illustrate almost every point. Each chapter ends with excellent exercises readers can do alone or as part of class to make the chapter's material their own. If you are new to counseling the bereaved, this book is the best introduction I have seen. If you are an experienced grief counselor, this should be the next book you read.

Prof Dennis Klass, leading researcher on bereavement,
Webster University, USA

Dying, Death and Grief

Working with Adult Bereavement

Brenda Mallon

Los Angeles • London • New Delhi • Singapore

Holy Family University
Newtown Campus - LRC

First published 2008

Apart from any fair dealing for the purposes of research
or private study, or criticism or review, as permitted
under the Copyright, Designs and Patents Act, 1988,
this publication may be reproduced, stored or transmitted
in any form, or by any means, only with the prior
permission in writing of the publishers, or in the case of
reprographic reproduction, in accordance with the terms
of licences issued by the Copyright Licensing Agency.
Enquiries concerning reproduction outside those terms
should be sent to the publishers.

SAGE Publications Ltd
1 Oliver's Yard
55 City Road
London EC1Y 1SP

SAGE Publications Inc.
2455 Teller Road
Thousand Oaks, California 91320

SAGE Publications India Pvt Ltd
B 1/I 1 Mohan Cooperative Industrial Area
Mathura Road
New Delhi 110 044

SAGE Publications Asia-Pacific Pte Ltd
33 Pekin Street #02-01
Far East Square
Singapore 048763

Library of Congress Control Number: 2007942229

British Library Cataloguing in Publication data

A catalogue record for this book is available from the British Library

ISBN 978-1-4129-3414-5
ISBN 978-1-4129-3415-2 (pbk)

Typeset by C&M Digitals (P) Ltd, Chennai, India
Printed and bound in Great Britain by TJ International Ltd, Padstow, Cornwall
Printed on paper from sustainable resources

Mixed Sources
Product group from well-managed
forests and other controlled sources
www.fsc.org Cert no. SGS-COC-2482
© 1996 Forest Stewardship Council
FSC

To Angela Trinder and Stephen Brook, for their unfailing
generosity and support

Contents

Foreword

We live in an interesting time. Modern media such as television and the internet has brought death into our living rooms. We follow not only the tragedies of war and violence, but we read details of illness and death in the newspapers. We become aware of how people from many parts of the world deal with these losses and with their accompanying grief. One way of coping in the western world has been to label these experiences in ways that removes some of the immediacy of the associated pain, at least for the observer. We talk of the 'symptoms' of grief. A symptom is usually associated with an illness thus implying that something is wrong with the individual who is suffering in this way. This can evolve into giving a mourner a diagnosis of having a psychiatric illness. What follows is the suggestion that these people need treatment and care, so that they will get over their pain and move on. This language gives the impression that people can be cured of their grief. Some of us have talked about this as the medicalization of grief. We have arrived at a point where concerned family and friends tell mourners who are upset that they need treatment, that they need the skills of a professional to cure them. In so doing they move the responsibility for care and concern about the grief they see to a professional and become very self conscious about their not knowing enough to help.

In this atmosphere, Brenda Mallon, has written a book that gives a contrasting view of grief. She writes that grief is not an illness from which one recovers with the proper treatment. Rather she provides the reader with information, and guidelines so that those who want to help the bereaved can see how to provide support, and friendship and be there for those they know who are grieving. Much of what she says is directed to the professional counselor. However, much of it is also of great value to friends and family who want to help. She doesn't use jargon, she doesn't judge, she recognizes that there is no one way to mourn, and that in the long run, with appropriate support, the bereaved find their own direction. A creativity emerges as the bereaved cope with their pain. She clearly reviews what we know, from current research, about the pain and suffering that can be associated with grief. She highlights the fact that this is not a condition for which there is a cure. People are changed by the loss; they find a new sense of self, and a new way of living in the world. She reminds us that the deceased stay with us, and in some way are always a part of who we are.

As she writes to prepare professional counselors for this work, she points to the importance of dealing with our own experiences with grief. This is not a situation where the counselor can look out at those they are trying to help as the 'other'. Dealing with death is something all of us must do. The line between the personal and the professional becomes very thin for those of us who are working and doing research in this part of the human experience. It becomes important to recognize our own humanity and vulnerability, to review our own experience to see how it informs our practice.

Mallon emphasizes the need for relationships at a most difficult period in human experience – that is, when someone we care about dies, such as a parent, a spouse, a child or a friend. She points to the value of meeting others who have had a similar experience. This makes it possible to find a common language and to learn from the experience of others. It helps the mourner to not feel unique or alone with their pain and provides them with various options for how to cope. In sharing an experience a mourner gets another perspective on their experience and can see that what they are going through is part of being human; providing them with new options they may not have seen before. We need to keep in mind that the helper in this process is also helped.

At the end of each chapter Mallon has recommended exercises. These range from questionnaires that document what the bereaved are experiencing to suggestions for art work and other activities that help the bereaved understand what they are experiencing and finding directions for ways through the grief. These exercises put control in the hands of the bereaved, empowering them to act on their own behalf. In some ways these exercises complete this book. They provide another level of understanding and an opportunity for bereaved to share very personal experiences that can be very difficult for any author to otherwise capture. This book is a step in our effort to remind the reader that grief is part of the human experience that we all have to deal with; and that the real experts are the mourners themselves.

Phyllis R. Silverman, PhD, 2008
Women's Studies Research Centre, Harvard, USA

Acknowledgements

I would like to thank so many people for helping me with *Dying, Death and Grief*. The patrons of The Grief Centre, Manchester Area Bereavement Forum provided inspiration in their conference presentations and personal discussions, so thanks to Professors Phyllis Rolfe Silverman and Steven Wright, the late Jack Morgan and Jim Kykendall. Many others including David Trickey, John Holland and Jeanie Civil added to this book by their empathic insights and wisdom.

My fellow volunteers at The Grief Centre, Manchester, Angela, Steve, Diane, Rachel, Mandy and Terza who always offer unstinting support and good humour.

My debt to my clients who have shared their grief cannot be overstated. Their courage, honesty and willingness to share some of the hardest experiences that can ever be experienced taught me so much. It has been a privilege to journey with them.

I want to thank Alison Poyner for commissioning *Dying, Death and Grief* to applaud the editorial team, Claire Reeve, Alice Oven and Rachel Burrows who worked so hard to polish the manuscript.

Finally, without the love and support of my family in both my bereavement counselling and writing, this book would not have been possible. So, thanks to Styx, Crystal and Danny.

Brenda Mallon
Manchester, February 2008

Introduction

Grief is nothing we expect it to be.
It comes in waves, sudden apprehensions that weaken the knees and blind the eyes.

(Joan Didion 2005a)

Dying, Death and Grief brings together new research that integrates socio-logical and anthropological theories as well as psychological ones. It also addresses areas frequently overlooked in bereavement counselling, includ-ing the spiritual and cultural dimensions of grief (Ribbens 2005). In addi-tion it demonstrates how as counsellors and supporters of those who have experienced loss, we can use creativity and dreamwork to extend our reper-toire of helping techniques.

Death, pain and disability are unwelcome intruders in our lives yet they arrive unannounced and have to be accommodated. Grieving is a normal response to loss and in the process of grieving, lives are transformed. For some this period of transformation is overwhelming and they require help and support to manage their feelings and this is where bereavement sup-port can be truly beneficial. It is often more flexible than formal coun-selling: it may take place in the person's home, it may involve practical advice and can take place face to face or by telephone and it does not need a counselling contract. It does not require the same in-depth training as formal counselling though training is an important aspect for volunteers and befrienders who work with the dying and bereaved. Support can come from a variety of sources, family, friends, chaplains and spiritual advisers, self-help groups such as the Compassionate Friends, volunteers and profes-sionals (Alexander 2002). Professionals and self-help organisations can work together successfully to meet the range of needs of the bereaved (Giljohann et al. 2000; Harris 2006; Klass 2000).

Whilst formal counselling is about support it is more specific in that it has professional regulation and counsellors will have undergone lengthy training. They have a theoretical basis for their work and are able to work in depth on complex emotional issues. Many people will consider coun-selling carefully before engaging in it because for some people, counselling is linked to mental health difficulties and the associated stigma.

Those who opt to come for bereavement counselling do not want to be slotted into a straitjacket of early grief models, which are discussed in the first chapter, which emphasise the stages of grief and its resolution. They don't want to feel guilty if they are not grieving in the 'correct' way or if they are not going through the process in the right order. One example of this is described by Sally Taylor, who reported that clients felt that their counsellors avoided some areas such as the sense of the presence of the deceased, sexuality, belief in an afterlife and spirituality. Yet, she says, research has shown that sense of presence of the deceased is the experience of 50 per cent of bereaved people, both in the short term and the long term (Taylor 2005). This is a view supported by the empirical work of Bennett and Bennett (2000). We will explore these areas as ways of enhancing confidence when working with bereaved people.

In a sense what we have is a continuum from those who need basic support or information to those who need more in-depth work where there are issues of complex grief, chronic grief or trauma following violent death (Lindemann 1944). I hope this book will answer the needs of any helper on this continuum. You can choose to work at the depth that is most appropriate for you and your organisation.

It is useful to keep in mind the fact that not all people need or want bereavement counselling. Some clients may find their way to you because other people, such as their GP, partner or employer, think they need it. It's important to clarify their reasons for accessing bereavement counselling at the earliest opportunity since their motivation will affect the effectiveness of the counselling (Prigerson 2004). Most people manage with the help of family and friends but a significant number do require additional support.

The opportunity to have a period of bereavement counselling can bring a great deal of relief to the bereaved, provided the timing, motivation and therapeutic rapport are present. This in turn has a knock-on effect in other relationships, in better physical and mental health and reduced likelihood of the use of drugs and alcohol to mask the pain of bereavement.

As we offer this support we need to recognise our own needs and limitations so that we do not become overwhelmed (Evans 2003). So, in the process of cherishing others make sure you cherish yourself. Take care of yourself. Your safety, and the safety of those you work with, is of paramount importance. It is essential to access supervision and to ensure you have support between supervision sessions. Supervision will enable you to keep your boundaries in place.

At the end of each chapter you will find reflective exercises. These personal awareness exercises are to enable you to learn more about yourself and your feelings and beliefs about dying, death and grief (Gordon 2004). These notes are for yourself, though you may choose to share them with others. Wherever possible have someone available that you can talk to if an exercise causes you distress or puts you in touch with feelings that were unexpected and disturbing. If you are using this book as part of a training course then hopefully the course leader will provide opportunities to share thoughts and feelings in a supportive and compassionate way. It is important to address such feelings here and now rather than when they emerge when working with someone who has been bereaved.

Set aside some quiet, private time so you can complete each exercise and have time to reflect. Allow yourself two hours for each exercise. You may complete some more quickly than others but do build in some reflective time. Give yourself several days between exercises so you have time to consider the feelings and thoughts that emerge over time.

Finally, it is a privilege to work with those who are dying or have been bereaved. We may find our lives are transformed in the process just as the lives of those we help are transformed. Included are stories of people I have worked with though names and identifying details are changed to provide anonymity. Their wisdom, courage and resilience in the face of tragic bereavement has taught me a great deal and this book is an opportunity to share that knowledge. I hope *Dying, Death and Grief* will be a positive guide as you travel the path of loss.

Brenda Mallon

October 2007

Throughout the text I have used he and she interchangeably to indicate the gender of the person I am referring to. Also, I have changed names and minor details to ensure client confidentiality.

1

Attachment and Loss, Death and Dying. Theoretical Foundations for Bereavement Counselling

Grief is the price we pay for love.
Without attachment there would be no sense of loss.[1]

This chapter explores the different theories that underpin bereavement counselling. Views on the most effective ways to support those who are bereaved have changed over many years (Parkes 2002). In looking at the variety of approaches to grief work you will discover many overlaps and see how growth from one view to another has taken place. It will show how today's thanatologists, those who study death and the practices associated with it, think and practice. They bring sociological, anthropological and cultural perspectives to their work (Boerner and Heckhausen 2003). However, throughout this exploration we need to hold on to the idea that grief takes as many forms as there are grieving people (Alexander 2002; Benoliel 1999).

---

1 I first used this quotation in my book *Managing Loss, Separation and Bereavement: Best Policy and Practice* (July 2001) though its origins were unclear to me. Since then it has been attributed to Queen Elizabeth II who sent it in a message of condolence to the American people following the attack on the Twin Towers on 9/11 2001. The line is carved in stone at St Thomas's Cathedral, New York and on a wooden pergola in the memorial garden in Grosvenor Square, London.

The first bonds: why love gives us hope

Why is attachment relevant to bereavement counselling?

It is important to understand attachment since it is essential for healthy emotional growth and for building resilience (Huertas 2005). Numerous theories of attachment provide a foundation for bereavement counselling (Purnell 1996). Without attachment to a significant other person, usually the parent, a child's emotional growth will be impaired and he may experience severe difficulty in relating to others in a positive way (Bowlby 1980; Ainsworth et al 1978). When a baby cries he is looked after and so he learns to trust others in his world. From this foundation of trust grows his ability to relate to others and to empathise. Later, he will make other attachments to siblings, friends, a partner and, possibly, his own children. When a primary attachment, as these are termed, is ended through separation or death, then grieving takes place. Grief is the price we pay for love, or attachment. This is pivotal in the research by Bowlby which we will examine later in this chapter.

In her book *Why Love Matters*, Sue Gerhardt demonstrates how early experiences within the womb and during the first two years of life influence the child physically and emotionally. She says, 'This is when the "social brain" is shaped and when an individual's emotional style and emotional resources are established' (2004: 3). This part of the brain learns how to manage feelings and how to react to other people, as well as how to react to stress, which in turn affects the immune system. This mind–body link is important when we recognise that a bereaved person will react physically, emotionally and cognitively to death: 'It is as babies that we first feel and learn what to do with our feelings, when we start to organise our experience in a way that will affect our later behaviour and thinking capacities' (2004: 10). A person who has had early stress, trauma and poor attachment may find grieving more difficult than someone who had secure early attachment. Those who have been bereaved as a child may find that their grief is reactivated when they experience someone's death in adulthood. Research by Margaret Stroebe demonstrates that insecure attachment is linked to complicated grief in the adult bereaved population (Wijngaards-de-Melj et al. 2007).

Reactive attachment disorder (RAD) is caused by the disruption of the normal cycle of loving care that a baby receives from her parents. Instead of care she may be neglected, abused or have inconsistent care which may impair the ability to make bonds with others (Bowlby 1980; Frayley and Shaver 1999). In later life the child may be unable to trust others or to allow others to have control. Accessing bereavement counselling can be problematic for someone with RAD since building therapeutic rapport may be difficult.

What you need to know about attachment – the basics

The first thorough study of grief and loss was by the father of psychoanalysis, Sigmund Freud. His early paper 'Mourning and Melancholia' published in 1917, is regarded as a classic text on bereavement. He argued that the psychological purpose of grief is to withdraw emotional energy from the deceased (cathexis) and then to become detached from the loved one (decathexis). He believed the bereaved person has to work through his grief by reviewing thoughts and memories of the deceased (hypercathexis). By this process, painful as it is, the bereaved can achieve detachment from the loved one and the bereaved's bonds with the deceased become looser. This 'attachment' became a major factor in understanding grief for many later theorists. However, this theoretical position is not echoed in a letter Freud sent to his friend Ludwig Binswanger in 1929.

Binswanger's son had died and Freud wrote: 'Although we know after such a loss the acute state of mourning will subside, we also know we shall remain inconsolable and will never find a substitute. No matter what may fill the gap, even if it be filled completely, it nevertheless remains something else. And, actually this is how it should be, it is the only way of perpetuating that love which we do not want to relinquish' (Freud 1960: 386). His words indicate the need for continuing connection with the loved one which is central to the theoretical position of Attig (2000), Silverman, Klass and others who write of the importance of continuing bonds (Klass et al. 1996).

Freud's concept of grief as a job of work which we neglect at our peril is very useful when we consider grief to be part of a reconstruction process which Colin Murray Parkes (1971, 1996) calls 'psychosocial transition'. Parkes (1988) introduced the concept of the 'assumptive world' which is changed in bereavement. All that we assumed was securely in place, our expectations about the world, our relationships and our place in it are thrown into disarray when death appears: the familiar world has become unfamiliar. Each day most of assume we will come back home. We assume we will see our friend at the usual time. We assume we will shop on Thursday after work. Then something awful happens, like a sudden critical illness, and our assumptive world is undermined.

Where the event is a traumatic bereavement then the assumptive world may be utterly shattered (Trickey 2005). Where the loss has been traumatic the rebuilding of the bereaved's world may be more difficult because trauma impedes grief. Making sense of the event, talking about it, remembering the deceased and thinking about it may cause hyper-arousal, which the bereaved seeks to avoid. Thus, bereavement counselling or bereavement support may be much more problematic and in-depth psychological or psychiatric intervention may be needed. Parkes says that in mourning we make readjustments to our assumptive world and this constitutes a psychological shift and psychosocial change. People may need help to rebuild their assumptive world following bereavement because loss has shaken the foundations of their world (Neimeyer 2005).

For the bereaved their sense of identity may have to be redefined. Who am I now that I am no longer a father? Where do I fit in now that I am no longer a part of a couple? (Caserta and Lund 1992) Some people will retreat from social interaction perhaps because of an unconscious fear of further losses, feeling it is better not to invest emotionally in case others are taken away. Others re-evaluate their social relationships and take greater care in maintaining those relationships; may pay more attention by prioritising relationships above work, for example. The experience may lead to greater maturity and a deeper sense of understanding of the emotional life of others.

Psychoanalyst John Bowlby established attachment theory in the 1960s. In his research with babies and young children and their mothers he studied the impact of separation and the situations that cause us to feel fear and anxiety. He concluded that fear is initially brought about by elemental situations: that is, darkness, sudden movement or separation. Though these situations may be harmless in themselves, they indicate an increased risk of danger. Bowlby examined the way young children respond to the temporary or permanent loss of a mother figure and noted the expressions of sadness, anxiety, protest, grief and mourning that accompany such loss. From his observations he developed a new paradigm of understanding attachment and the impact of the breaking attachment bonds (Bowlby 1980).

With psychologist Mary Ainsworth, Bowlby recognized that in order to understand a person's behaviour you had to understand their environment. The child and parent, the patient and doctor and the bereaved and bereavement counsellor are in a mutual field of activity, a system in which each influences the other (Bowlby 1975; Wiener 1989). This systemic approach takes into account the fact that we are influenced by other people, the food we eat and the air we breathe. Bowlby saw grief as an adaptive response which included both the present loss as well as past losses. He said it was affected by environmental factors in the bereaved person's life as well as by the psychological make-up of the bereaved person.

Bowlby and Parkes (1970) presented four main stages in the grief process:

1 Numbness, shock and denial with a sense of unreality;
2 Yearning and protest. It involves waves of grief, sobbing, sighing, anxiety, tension, loss of appetite, irritability and lack of concentration. The bereaved may sense the presence of the dead person, may have a sense of guilt that they did not do enough to keep the deceased alive and may blame others for the death;
3 Despair, disorganisation, hopelessness, low mood;
4 Re-organisation, involving letting go of the attachment and investing in the future.

At the time the theory did not make reference to wider cultural differences which are highly relevant in the grieving process. In Japan, for example, the bereaved are encouraged to maintain emotional bonds with the deceased, and letting go of the attachment, stage 4 above, would be counter to their cultural mores (Deeken 2004; Yamamoto 1970). In other cultures yearning for the dead person would be regarded with disapproval since the dead person is on his designated karmic journey (Laungani 1997). However, Parkes, Laungani and Young (1997) redressed the balance in *Death and Bereavement across Cultures* which covers variations in grief responses in different cultures in great depth and is an excellent addition to the body of knowledge in bereavement care in the twenty-first century.

In the 1960s Elisabeth Kubler-Ross, a Swiss-born physician and psychiatrist, pioneered death studies. Her seminal book *On Death and Dying* (1970) was based on her work with dying patients. She adopted Parkes' stages of grief to describe the five stages of dying experienced by those who were diagnosed with terminal illness:

1   Denial – the patient does not believe he has a terminal illness.
2   Anger – Why me? Anger towards family or doctors because they have not done enough.
3   Bargaining – The patient may bargain with God or some unseen force, to give him extra time.
4   Depression – The patient realises he is about to die and feels very low.
5   Acceptance – Given the opportunity to grieve, the patient may accept his fate, which may lead to a period of quiet reflection, silence and contemplation.

Kubler-Ross emphasised that these stages are not linear and some may be missed out altogether. Some people may never reach the point of acceptance and may die still filled with anger or other strong emotion. For others, denial fortifies them: when they have to live for a long time with a terminal illness, their hope sustains them. However, the views of Kubler-Ross have been challenged because a number of researchers have not found evidence to support them and dying people show a range of conflicting reactions (Spiegel and Yalom 1978; Stroebe and Schut 1999).

Rachel Naomi Remen has worked with people with life-threatening illness for many years. She believes that the Kubler-Ross stages are useful but she disagrees that the final stage is acceptance. She says:

> I have counselled people with life-threatening illness who have lost valuable parts of their bodies, relationships and capacities. And in my experience of watching people heal from loss, the final step is gratitude. And wisdom. That's the final step of healing from loss. It doesn't make cognitive sense, but it makes deep emotional and spiritual sense.

(Redwood 2002: 6)

Reactions to dying are very much influenced by cultural views and religious beliefs. The response of someone who believes in reincarnation will be quite different from someone who believes in heaven and hell and who fears eternal damnation. Negative reactions to death and dying are not universal and personal philosophies will influence individual reactions.

J. William Worden, an Associate Professor of Psychology at Harvard University and grief specialist, introduced the concept of 'grief work' in the 1980s. Continuing Freud's concept of grief as a job of work he described four 'tasks' of mourning that the bereaved person must accomplish (Worden 1991):

1 The individual needs to accept the reality of the loss and that reunion is not possible.
2 The individual has to experience the pain of grief. The extreme hurt and sadness felt may also physically affect the bereaved.
3 The individual needs to adjust to the environment where the deceased is missing. The consequences of the death may be enormous emotionally and financially, and the bereaved may be forced to adopt a completely new lifestyle. Some, though, will be stuck in an old pattern of existence, especially with the death of a spouse.
4 The individual needs to relocate the deceased and invest in a new life.

His theory points to the need to break bonds with the deceased person in order to invest in a new life. This view that the bereaved must disengage with the deceased was espoused by others (Dietrich and Shabad 1989; Volcan 1981). This last task is one that many people find the most difficult to complete (Stroebe et al. 1992). The deceased is not forgotten, nor are the memories, but the bereaved may still find enjoyment in life once more. The person who has been bereaved is not the person she was before and will never be the same again, as the following statement shows:

'I had first hand experience of healing which comes through confronting the pain. And I knew that however deep the grief, it has its own rhythm … I have been to the most dreaded place and come out altered but alive. I am re-engaging with life. I celebrate the life of my beautiful son.'

(Wendy Evans whose son aged 24 died in a house fire)

More recently, Worden's views have been challenged (Stroebe 1992–1993). Do people have to let go in order to make progress? Magaret Stroebe argues that there is little scientific research evidence to support this view and studies that have been done seem contradictory. Camille Wortman and Roxanne Silver (2001) found four differing patterns of grieving: normal, chronic, delayed and absent. If we consider Worden's last stage, 'relocate the deceased and invest in a new life', it is worth noting that many people are afraid of investing in a new way of living since this can feel like a betrayal of the dead person. Additionally, there may be fears about investing in a new relationship in case this, too, is taken from them.

The Dual Process Model of Grief and Loss was introduced in 1995 by Margaret Stroebe and Henk Schut and was the first to state that there were no defined stages of grief. They described two types of coping processes. 'loss-oriented coping' deals with the loss of the deceased person, and 'restitution-oriented coping' deals with specific problems and the development of new activities. People oscillate between these two as they go through grieving. Current thinking on grief encompasses both the letting go of bonds and the holding on to the attachment (Klass et al. 1996).

This Oscillation Model, going in and out of grief, remembering and forgetting, focusing on the past and paying attention to the present, seems to reflect the actual experience of the grieving process (Didion 2005b). The bereaved move between the emotions of grief work and the learning of new roles and adapting to a different life. In working with people who are bereaved we can help them let go and keep hold at the same time (Dutta 2006). As Dennis Klass says on working with parents whose child has died, 'The goal of grief then, is not severing the bond with the child, but integrating the child into the parent's life and social networks in a new way' (Klass 2000). In *Continuing Bonds: New Understandings of Grief*, which he edited with Silverman and Nickman (1996), he argues that bonds do not need to be broken in order to 'complete' the grieving process .

There has been a shift towards understanding that 'letting go' of the deceased – achieving 'closure', as it is sometimes termed – may be less helpful than recognising the importance of continuing symbolic bonds. Attig in *The Heart of Grief: Death and the Search for Lasting Love* says:

> Grieving persons who want their loved ones back need to look for some other way to love them while they are apart. Desperate longing prevents their finding that different way of loving. Letting go of having them with us in the flesh is painful and necessary. But it is not the same as completely letting go. We still hold the gifts they gave us, the values and meanings we found in their lives. We can still have them as we cherish their memories and treasure their legacies in our practical lives, souls and spirits.
>
> (2000: xii)

When writing about permanent loss as opposed to temporary separation, Bowlby (1980) recognised that a continued attachment to the deceased was the norm rather than the exception. Remembering events with the lost loved one may bring comfort and reduce feelings of isolation (Hedtke and Winslade 2004; Vickio 1998). Clearly, much depends on the nature of the relationship prior to death but where there was a positive relationship, recalling important times and sharing memories with others may facilitate the grieving process (Dunn et al. 2005). The wishes of the deceased loved one may guide the bereaved's actions, whilst visits to the cemetery may provide comfort and continued connection (Shuchter and Zisook 1993).

Robert Neimeyer, Professor of Psychology at the University of Memphis, argues that a new generation of theories in grief work is needed as we move beyond the assumption that mourning is a private and sequential process of emotional change (Neimeyer 2005). This view is supported by Rosenblatt, who talks of societies where the expression of grief is regulated; it is not a free form of expression. He argues that grief is in some way a public performance, which may not fit in with private thoughts and feelings (Rosenblatt 2001). The mask of grief may conceal hidden thoughts and feelings.

Neimeyer has been developing a new paradigm in grief theory in which meaning reconstruction is central to the process. This is described as a constructivist or narrative approach which fits in with the Stroebe and Schut dual process model. The social constructivist model is based on the view that the assumptive world is radically upset by any major loss. To function in the world we make many assumptions and have many core beliefs that give us a sense of security. They provide us with a set of expectations about the world, such as the belief that our home will be there when we return from a journey and that when we wake up in the morning our environment will be the same as it was when we went to sleep. Any disruption between the world we know and the world we are confronted by, at a death for example, brings about a sense of loss of meaning. We need to re-establish, reconstruct, meaning using psychological, social, cultural, emotional and cognitive resources (Bailey 1996; Berder 2004–5).

Neimeyer's research into the responses of people bereaved by violent death, for example survivors of suicide, homicide and accident, demonstrates that the inability to make sense of the loss is perhaps the primary factor that sets them apart from those whose losses are more anticipated in the context of serious illness in the loved one (Neimeyer 2005). Neimeyer says of his constructivist view of meaning reconstruction, 'The narrative themes that people draw on are as varied as their personal biographies, and as complex as the overlapping cultural belief systems that inform their attempts at meaning making' (p. 28).

Grief is not a passive process, nor a series of stages that happen to the bereaved: in recognising this we can help those who are bereaved to become empowered in their mourning (Parkes 1986). Grief work is an active process which is both personal and social. In grief counselling the bereaved may need to reconnect with the deceased and address 'unfinished business' or emotional ambiguity in the relationship as well as making adjustments to their new social status. People react differently to loss: some show great resilience and adaptability in the first months, others sink into chronic grief or depression, whilst others show considerable improvement in mood and outlook, particularly those who have looked after a chronically ill partner over a long period (Attig 1991). For some the death of someone close is a relief (Ellison and McGonigle 2003). A study by Bonnano, Wortman and Nesse (2004) confirms that there is no single trajectory which plots a linear path of grief.

The death of a loved one does not mean that the relationship has ended. The attachment described as 'continuing bonds' by Klass and his colleagues are maintained (Klass et al. 1996). They continue in memories of the person, dreams in which the bereaved feature and at significant points in the year such as anniversaries. The aim of bereavement counselling is not to extinguish these bonds. Fear of this may cause some bereaved people to avoid seeking support earlier because 'I thought you'd make me forget about him and I can never do that.'

The need to understand loss

The dead help us to write their stories – ours as well. In a sense, every story has a ghost writer.

(Becker and Knudson, 2003: 714)

Humans are meaning-making animals, and when confronted with the death of someone we care about we need to understand what happened and why, and build a narrative around loss (McLeod 1997; Walter 1999). As social animals we try to explain what happened, the sequence of events, how we felt and how we are different or the same (Gilbert 2002). Others also have a part in telling the story of the dead: coroners and forensic scientists give information and more is stored in obituaries (Walter 2006). Evidence indicates that where we can find meaning in the experience of loss we are more likely to experience positive adaptation (Hansen 2004; Walter 1996b; Wortman et al. 1993). Where the bereaved struggle to make meaning of the loss, they may become susceptible to chronic, or complicated forms of grief (Roos 2002). People reorganise their life stories following significant loss and can find meaning in future stories that are waiting to be scripted (Walter 1996a). Nadeau's work on family stories which seek to make sense of death and its impact have also added to our understanding of this aspect of grief work (Nadeu 1998).

The social dimension of grief

Grieving is a social as well as an individual process. Families and others in social groups may facilitate or hinder the grieving process, because the support of others has a significant impact on the resolution of mourning (Maddison and Walker 1967). David Kissane and Sydney Bloch (2003) use Family Focused Grief Therapy to promote mutual support and problem-solving in bereaved families. Their research shows that relationships with the family are crucial in the grieving process and interventions that strengthen family relationships and interpersonal communication have much to offer the bereaved.

Marc Cleiren (1999) likens life to a building with cornerstones that keep it stable. For some a cornerstone will be marriage, for others 'career', being a parent and so on. In bereavement, when the cornerstone crumbles we are forced to look at where we can gain stability in order to keep going. 'Systematic studies constantly show that attachment, coping style and personality characteristics are highly related to coping with loss' (Cleiren 1999: 110); these include a flexible problem-focused and an emotional-focused coping style which are responsive to the demands of the unique situation in which the bereaved finds himself (Parkes 1986).

Research from a family systems perspective shows that the ways in which a family sticks together and communicate predict the course of grieving

(Traylor et al. 2003). Where a member of a family dies, the roles of all are affected, the system is altered.

Social support has been identified as a crucial factor in managing antici-patory grief positively as well as indicating greater successful adaptation to loss post-bereavement (Berkman and Syme 1979; Irwin et al. 1987; Spiegel 1993). Work by House and his colleagues (House et al. 1988) shows strong evidence that social support reduces the risk of the bereaved experiencing health problems and of dying following bereavement. In working with the bereaved it is helpful to ascetain the way in which they see their social net-work (Rubin 1984). If they can identify it, can they access it?

A new model of grief

British sociologist Tony Walter approaches the experience of grief in a post-modern way. Moving away from 'grand theories' he says that in our pre-sent world it is the individualisation of loss that is significant; the journey through bereavement is more to do with personality, habits of coping with stress than a 'one size fits all' overarching 'grief process'. Those who live on want to talk about the deceased and to talk with others who knew the dead person. In this way, Walter (1996a) says, the bereaved construct a story that places the dead person within their lives and the story they create is capa-ble of enduring through time. Using this model, the purpose of grief is therefore the construction of a durable biography that enables the living to integrate the memory of the dead into their ongoing lives; the process by which this is achieved is principally conversation with others who knew the deceased. In bereavement counselling it may be constructed by the bereaved telling the counsellor about the life and death of the deceased and the relationship they had. As the relationship with the deceased can-not exist in the same way as it did before death, in the process of transfor-mation the bereaved build a relationship that can endure beyond death (Attig 2000; Bowlby 1980; Klass 2001; Rando 1993; Rubin 1999).

Walter notes that it can sometimes be useful to repress painful emotions. In his article 'A new model of grief'(1996b) he points out that bereavement is part of the never-ending and reflexive conversation with self and others through which we try to make sense of our existence. In a sense we are telling our stories or trying to make a narrative that is bio-graphical. His 'Reintegrative, sociological model of grief' (Walter 1999) is different from the 'get over it' model which seeks for 'closure'. The terms 'closure' and 'resolution of grief' are not particularly helpful if we think the bereaved have to forget the past and start again – the past is always with us (Parkes 2007). The work for the bereaved person is to weave the loss into their altered life, both personal and social (Ashby 2004). After a major loss, there is no usual or normal world to go back to because everything has changed.

Walter's (1996a) model recognises the importance of social support and connection with others in bereavement. It emphasises the significance of cultural differences in mourning and the need for counsellors to be both aware and respectful of cultural diversity. Attitudes to death vary widely across cultures. As Tony Walter points out, 'One Hindu describes his practice "The belief is that you should die on the floor (to be closer to Mother Earth). Here a lot of people die in hospitals and a lot of us families are very shy to ask for what we want. We feel out of place ..." Dying on the floor, with a dozen or more family members praying and chanting is certainly not the way of a British hospital and may disturb other patients as much as staff' (Walter 2003: 219). Yet, by not making the opportunity for cultural traditions and religious practices to be followed, we may make the process of dying and subsequent bereavement much more problematic.

The relationship with the deceased continues in the bonds we have with them, and Walter believes these can enhance and influence the life of the bereaved. He cites the following roles:

- The deceased is a role model for the bereaved.
- The deceased gives advice or guidance.
- The deceased provides basic values in life that are emulated.
- The deceased is a significant part of the life or biography of the bereaved.

The purpose of grief involves the construction of a biography 'that enables the living to integrate the memory of the dead in their ongoing lives' (Walter 1996b: 7).

Bereavement support and counselling can help the bereaved to reconstruct their personal story and their family system, because we do not live with or face grief in a vacuum. Irish writer John McGahern's *Memoir* movingly describes his close relationship with his mother who died when he was nine years old. His time with her was precious and his writing reveals the continuing bond he still felt with her:

> When I reflect on those rare moments when I stumble without warning into that extraordinary sense of security, that deep peace, I know that, consciously or unconsciously, she has been with me all my life.
>
> (2005: 272)

Patrice Cox says, 'Our life stories, and those of our families and communities, are filled with weaving and reweaving of webs of connection, patterns of caring within which we find and make meaning. Bereavement strikes a blow to those webs, to our personal, family and community integrity. The weaves of our daily life patterns are in tatters' (2005: 1). She described grief as a process of relearning our worlds in general and in particular relearning the relationship to the deceased (Boerner and Hechkhausen 2003).

Phyllis Silverman, an eminent American thanatologist, adds to our understanding of the grief process in her ongoing research (Silverman 2001).

She argues that our values, attitudes and beliefs about death and bereavement are not fixed in stone, but are responsive to and modified by dynamic historic, economic and social forces. Our attitudes to death are socially constructed so what we expect of mourners differs across cultures. Loss also involves taking on new, probably unwelcome roles – 'widow', 'orphan' – and ways of life previously unknown.

In the final analysis, it is our clients and patients who know what is helpful to them. Bereavement counsellors and others may do more harm than good by sticking to a rigid theory which dictates what is the right or wrong way to grieve for the loss of someone the person has loved and still loves. Also, the fact of death of a significant person involves not only the loss of that person but the loss of 'self', the self that is so inextricably linked to the dead person (Howarth 2000).

There are no easy formulas for dealing with grief and bereavement. Each person has to live with it, live through it and grow through it. There are no fixed times for its duration, despite theories of time-bound grief models, nor are there certainties about when or if understanding or acceptance will occur. Responding with sensitivity and care, and holding the emotions of the bereaved as they travel through their grief, are essential healing aspects of our work. Though our work is underpinned by theory it is the quality of the relationship we build that matters most. As Yalom says, 'Therapy should not be theory-driven but relationship-driven' (Yalom 2000: 10).

Reflective exercises

Exercise 1 – Working with the bereaved

- Think about a person you have worked with in the past.
- Which of the models discussed in this chapter reflect their grieving process?
- In what ways did their social group – family and friends – support them?
- Can you identify any factors that inhibited the grieving process?
- Having read this chapter, what changes might you make to the way in which you work with the bereaved?

Exercise 2 – Words associated with death and dying

Write down any words you associate with death and dying.

How do these words reflect societal or cultural aspects of your world?

How many are euphemisms that mask the finality of death?

Some euphemisms for you to consider:

Lost
Gone to sleep
Asleep in the arms of Jesus
Passed over
Passed on
Passed away
Gone to a better place
Kicked the bucket
Pushing up daisies

Clear communication is essential when talking about death, particularly with children, vulnerable adults and others who may take the euphemism literally.

Exercise 3 – Early experiences

Complete the following statements. Not all the statements may be relevant for you, but complete any that are.

The first experience of death was when .... died.
I was ....years of age.
At that time I felt................................
I was puzzled by...................................
I was frightened by ....
When I think about that death now I remember ....
The funeral was ....
I was curious about the funeral because..........................
The first significant death of someone my own age was ....
This person died .... years ago. I felt ....
The most traumatic death I have experienced was..................
At .... I had an experience that brought me close to death. I felt .... and I thought............................
These events have changed the way I live because now I ....
In reflecting on these events I realise I can build on them in my work supporting bereaved people because ....

2

When Death Happens

Life changes fast
Life changes in an instant
You sit down for dinner and life as you know it ends.

(Joan Didion 2005a)

Death is one of the most difficult human experiences that face us. In this chapter we will explore common early responses to bereavement, anticipatory grief and gender differences in response to bereavement. The ability to manage the experience of death depends on the individual, the nature of the support available to them and the circumstances of the death (Spall and Callis 1997). Decades of research examining the impact of loss confirms the commonsense knowledge that loss changes people (Lehman et al. 1989; Rubin and Malkinson 2001; Shalev 1999). There are changes in their self-view and their world view (Raphael and Martinek 1997). Alongside this is a greater sense of vulnerability to external control (Janoff-Bulman 1992). People need to mourn these losses too. In each case there is a need to recreate a coherent network which includes safety, meaning and continuity in the face of the life changes that bereavement brings (Herman 1992; Neimeyer 2001).

All too often there is little support available to people affected by the death of someone they care about. After the death certificate has been issued, after the funeral tea is finished and the door is closed, the bereaved are expected to 'get on with it'. But what do they 'get on' with? What if life has no meaning because their partner has died? What if work seems pointless when a son has committed suicide?

The stark reality for many is that there is no one to talk to about feelings of despair which, if unresolved, may lead to mental ill health (Parkes 2002). In working with a bereaved person we help them to understand what grieving is and to recognise that their immediate reactions are 'normal' (Attig 1991; Gerner 1991). We need to help them clarify the meaning of their feelings. A question many recently bereaved people ask is 'Am I going mad?' Here are a few examples:

- One woman rang a bereavement charity helpline in a highly distressed state saying her husband had committed suicide by jumping from a cliff top which she could see from her kitchen window. She wanted to know if it was normal to keep on crying, because her friend said she would stop feeling sad after two weeks. She wanted reassurance that she was not 'going mad'.
- A young man came for counselling because he didn't know how to cope with the grief of his two children after the death of his young wife. What could he say? Would his children be normal when they grew up? And was it normal for him still to feel sexually aroused when he thought of her?
- A widow needed help to accept that she was not 'going insane' because she still felt her husband's presence and heard his voice though it was a year since his death.

Talking of the normality of such reactions can be very helpful to the bereaved (Mander 2005). The Tübingen Longitudinal Study of Bereavement found that, two years after bereavement, one third of the bereaved still sensed the presence of their spouse (Parkes and Weiss 1983). The sense of presence may come in many ways: an aroma, objects being moved, seeing the deceased, electrical appliances going on or off independent of any human control (Taylor 2005). When the bereaved knows it happens to other people it can give a welcome feeling of reassurance.

Pauline Blackburn's son Zennen was shot dead in Manchester. She recalls the sense of presence: 'We used to smell his aftershave … On one occasion – he used to have a shop in Oldham, the girl across the road used to work in it, and I'd taken her to work one night. We were driving down the road and this smell came over me so much that I couldn't breathe. I had to stop the car and wind down the windows – and the same happened to her.' She goes on to say, 'So that bond between you – it's got to carry on, hasn't it? If there's an afterlife, it can't stop, can it?' (Jenkins and Merry 2005: 21).

Isolation following bereavement

Tears fall in my heart as rain falls on the city.

(Paul Verlaine, *Romances sans paroles*, 1874)

Simon Stephens set up the Compassionate Friends after many years of witnessing the way in which those who were bereaved at the death of a child were socially ostracised by their community. In *Death Comes Home* (1972) he wrote of a man and woman whose son died unexpectedly after a routine appendectomy:

Margaret and Peter had been bereaved. In the eyes of the community in which they lived they had come into contact with something that was contagious – death.

Contagious because it had the strength to break the conspiracy of denial and to confront people with the awful facts of their mortality. To avoid such an encounter, and all the repercussions that would follow, there was a need for the carriers of infection to be isolated.

(1972: 40)

The difficulty that friends and neighbours had in speaking of death reflects the taboo that surrounds death, which is still apparent today, even though Stephens was writing in 1972. Others have also noted the significance of social isolation and its impact on relationships following bereavement (Helmrath and Steinitz 1978; Nadeau 1998; Riches and Dawson 2000). There is often a dreadful emptiness after a loved one's death. As Shakespeare says in *King John*, 'grief puts on the habit of my absent child, walks up and down with me' (III.iv). Grief accompanies the bereaved as their silent companion and observers may have little awareness of this shadow that darkens their world.

Early responses to death

And if there is one other thing that I have learnt from my father's death, it's that, no matter how clever, sophisticated, sensitive, grown-up and prepared you are, you cannot second guess the mourning process. It is a process without reason … Grief has its own terms and they are never the same as yours. That's the point of it.

(Coleman 2007: 2)

As we saw in Chapter 1, there are no fixed stages for the grieving process, nor is there a linear path through the stages or phases of grieving. Each of us is unique and grieves in our own way. However, there are certain responses that are commonly found. I will include them here as a reminder of what you might find when working with the bereaved but remember this is not a checklist and the reactions will not be experienced by every bereaved person. The time-bound model of stages of grief was re-evaluated by Colin Murray Parkes, an eminent British thanatologist: 'I am inclined to agree that the phases have been misused but I think they served their purpose in providing us with the idea of grief as a process of change through which we need to pass on the way to a new view of the world' (Parkes 2002: 380).

Three main phases of mourning

Phase 1 – Early Grief – the Protest Stage
Phase 2 – Acute Grief – the Disorganisation Phase
Phase 3 – Subsiding Grief – the Reorganisation or Adjustment Phase

Phase 1 – Early Grief – the Protest Stage

Feelings of shock, numbness, alarm, disbelief and denial are common at first. The numbness, the lack of feeling, probably acts initially to prevent the bereaved from being overwhelmed. Numbness allows the bereaved to feel the loss slowly. The 'protection' of the shock may help the bereaved to get through the practical aspects of life following a death. Hysteria, uncontrolled emotional excitement or euphoria – an irrational feeling of happiness – may arise. Emotionally flat behaviour with sudden outbursts of anger or tears may dominate and insomnia and heightened fear of separation are common, as are disturbing dreams. 'Knowing' a loved one has died may sit side by side with 'disbelief' that it has happened.

> 'Denial is seeing your husband on the street, seeing him with that familiar stride. Your joy is overwhelming, it wasn't true after all. Some nights you walk into the house and smell his aftershave. Part of my denial was lighting the lamp on his side of the bed so it would be light when he came up to sleep. Then it hits you and you know he'll never come home again. Not ever.'
>
> (Hannah)

Physically the bereaved person may experience an increased heart rate, deep sighing, muscular tension, sweating, dryness of the mouth, and bowel and bladder changes. These reactions may last for a few moments or come in waves, and leave the grieving person feeling exhausted. Asthma and eczema may appear or become aggravated. Bereavement may create physiological stressors which impact on the immune system and lower the efficiency of the T-cell function (Bartrop 1977; Stroebe et al. 1992). A survey carried out with Family Practice physicians found the majority believed that the death of a loved one brought significant health risks to their patients (Antoni et al. 1990; Lemkau et al. 2000).

> 'Organising the funeral was like organising a party with a knife in your back. I was shocked by the physical nature of my grief – which often manifested itself in physical paroxysms, ironically similar to childbirth.'
>
> (Wendy Evans, whose 24-year-old son died in a house fire)

Cognitive functioning and thinking may be affected, slowed down or confused, or the bereaved's mind may race with all sorts of questions. Suicidal thoughts sometimes come: the bereaved wants to join the deceased. A mother told me, 'I wanted to kill myself when Tom died. I couldn't bear the idea of my six-year-old being alone with no one to look after him.'

Charles Darwin (1872) noted that the facial expressions of grief are like those of an infant who has been abandoned by its mother. The posture of the bereaved calls out for care-giving. This form of care-eliciting behaviour is seen by Henderson (1974) as a form of attachment. Darwin also noted that 'he who remains passive when overwhelmed with grief loses his best chance of recovering elasticity of mind' (1872; Bowlby 1980: 345).

Phase 2 – Acute Grief – the Disorganisation
Phase

As the reality of the loss sinks in, the process of grieving continues. During this time reactions include anger, which may be displaced on to partner, family, or medical staff if the person was treated in hospital prior to death. There are also blame, irritability, continued denial or disbelief and an all-pervading sadness. There may be a sense of despair, which is draining and affects relationships, or there may be feelings of relief.

Guilt may be expressed in 'if only' statements or 'I should have'. The bereaved may blame themselves for words that were spoken or unspoken or actions taken or not taken. Yearning may continue as the loved one's presence is longed for and the bereaved may have a sense of the presence of the deceased (Bennett and Bennett 2000; Walter 2006). Thoughts of the deceased may preoccupy the bereaved, and the deceased may appear in dreams and nightmares (Barrett 1996; Mallon 2000a: Orbach 1999).

The bereaved may regress in terms of skills and ability to complete tasks. He may become unpredictable, with mood swings, rejecting and demanding at the same time; the outer chaos he creates around him mirrors his inner storm. Some people escape into fantasies and daydreaming, whilst others engage in frenetic activity which leaves no time to think about loss. This hyperactivity keeps the bereaved's mind off his hurt, as does being with others; being alone may be too distressing.

Some people continue to 'search' for the person who has gone and hope for their return even though they have seen the dead body, attended the funeral and even had a memorial service, as Joan Didion describes in her compelling book, *The Year of Magical Thinking* (2005a). Impatience with a person who is preoccupied with searching can delay rather than facilitate grieving. There may be a preoccupation with the deceased's image and feelings of fear that they will not be able to remember what their loved one looked like. They may believe that they caught sight of the person in the street. The bereaved is compelled to go through his own process of hoping and searching. There is some resolution of the grieving process once he accepts the reality of the death.

Phase 3 – Subsiding Grief – the Reorganisation
or Adjustment Phase

Like mourning, the reinvestment of emotional energy in the present and future is part of the process, not a single act. The person moves through feelings of wanting to 'hold on' to the deceased and needing to 'let go'. The continuing bonds to the deceased, described by Dunn, Oyebode and Howard (2005) may be found in activities such as searching, dreaming, hallucinating, keeping possessions, conversing, sensing the presence of the deceased, incorporating aspects of the person such as behaving as they did and acting in a way the deceased would have approved of.

Recovery from grief is natural, and by helping people to understand that accepting the loss is not a betrayal we can assist in their recovery. The continuing bonds do not generally inhibit the grieving process and they can bring both comfort and distress. The bereaved may also have sexual or intimate fantasies which may provoke strong feelings of sadness, anger or a feeling of being overwhelmed because they may never experience that intimacy again (Dunn et al. 2005; Wallbank 1992). The following comment from a client illustrates this:

'My dreams of my wife are sometimes healing but it's painful when they raise again feelings of being utterly bereft because she has gone and cannot be touched or kissed and that her warmth that I long for, has gone for ever.'

Following bereavement, there may be physical impairment. The bereaved person may develop an increased susceptibility to colds, sore throats, stomach upsets, fatigue and be more prone to minor ailments. Parkes' work with Benjamin and Fitzgerald (1969) showed clear evidence of increased mortality among widowers during the first year of their bereavement. Unconsciously the person may find that asking for help for physical ailments is easier than asking for help to ease his emotional pain.

Intense physical reactions to death may lead to death because of a 'broken heart'. Murray Parkes reflects on Montaigne, who described the reaction of King John of Hungaria to the death of his son: 'He only, without framing word or closing his eyes, but earnestly viewing the dead body of his son, stood still upright, till the vehemence of his sad sorrow, having suppressed and choked his vital spirits, fell'd him stark dead to the ground' (1603: 3–4).

In adjusting to their loss the bereaved may develop more balanced memories of the deceased, not seeing them only as a 'plaster saint' without any negative attributes. There may be pleasure too in recalling happy times. There is also more control over remembering the past, with fewer intrusive memories or flashbacks. Return to previous levels of ability and functioning is achieved, though the bereavement may lead to a change in values and priorities in life, and a different sense of purpose. However, we need to bear in mind that the return to previous equilibrium for the bereaved does not mean the bond to the deceased is severed. Dennis Klass (Klass et al. 1996) found that two-thirds of bereaved people want to maintain a continuing bond with the deceased and do so without marked detriment to themselves.

There may be an upsurge of grief some months or years after the death, particularly at the anniversary of the death and on birthdays (Pollock 1971). Beverley Raphael (1984) says there may be an increase in distress nine months after a bereavement. 'This may be linked to deep inner fantasies that something left behind, some bit of the dead person, will be reborn again then' (1984: 58). When this does not happen, distress returns. 'Magical thinking' often exists below the adult 'knowledge' that the death has happened and is permanent. As Freud (1917) said in 'Mourning and Melancholia', an object that has been loved is not readily relinquished.

Anticipatory grief

What hurts most is losing the future. The future will get on just fine without me ... It's just that I'll miss it so.

(Ruth Picardie 1998: 58–9)

Schoenberg et al. (1974) were the first to write comprehensively about the concept of anticipatory grief. The term is used to describe 'the premature emotional experiences of people who face impending death and can include both the dying person and family members' (Costello and Trinder-Brook 2000: 32). The threat of loss often leads to anxiety and anger while actual loss is more likely to lead to anger and sadness (Raphael 1984: 68). When first presented with a diagnosis of a life-limiting illness, Spiegel (1993: 14) describes a sequence of three initial responses: disbelief, dysphoria and adaptation. The disbelief gives way to dysphoria, feelings of being unwell and unhappy, often accompanied by sadness and depression (Oliviere et al. 1998). Gradually, there comes an accommodation to the reality of the illness though this may take some time. It may be aided where those anticipating death have someone with whom they talk through their feelings and explore the impact of the diagnosis on their present and future life (Hinton 1967). However, if accommodation does not take place, emotional states such as anger, depression or denial may be dominant (Nuland 1994). Research into anticipatory grief has found no clear evidence that it leads to an easier post-death grieving process.

Anticipatory grief may involve what Spiegel terms 'detoxifying dying' (Spiegel 1993: 113). The person facing death may develop a life project, revise relationships with families and friends and clarify communication with others. The dying person may also make efforts to complete 'unfinished business'. This may also happen for those who will become the bereaved. It involves discussing feelings about death: Spiegel found, in working with groups of people with advanced cancer, that it was not death itself that was mainly discussed. They wanted to talk about the process of dying, losing control, being in pain, being dependent on others, being unable to make decisions about medical care and the leaving of loved ones. Confronting death may also bring with it a sense of a connection with something greater and enriching (Cassidy 1988; Orbach 1999; von Franz 1986). Once we acknowledge that time is not infinite we may appreciate the true value of what time we have.

'At this grief, my heart was utterly darkened ... I was miserable and without joy.

(St Augustine in Chadwick 1991: 57)

Anticipatory grief and palliative care

Palliative care is defined in the NICE guidelines as 'the holistic care of patients with advanced, progressive illness. Management of pain and other symptoms and provision of psychological, social and spiritual support is paramount. The goal of palliative care is achievement of the best quality of life for patients and their families' (2007: 20). The word 'palliative' comes from the Latin *pallium,* a cloak. 'Palliation therefore means a covering; not treatment of the underlying cause but an amelioration of its effects' (Clare 2000: 8).

Sensitive listening, communication of significant news, exploring the unknown territory that the patient, family and carers journey in and the discussion of end-of-life concerns all play a part in counselling and supportive listening in palliative care (Hinton 1967; Walker et al. 1996). In palliative care, nothing the patient talks about is insignificant so it is vital to listen attentively. The transition from active treatment to 'survivorship' is one of the most demanding phases for patients in palliative care.

Dame Cicely Saunders, who founded the hospice movement in the United Kingdom, sums up the philosophy of caring for the dying. She says of a dying person: 'You matter because you are you, and you matter until the last moment of your life. We will do all that we can to help you not only to die peacefully, but to live until you die' (Clare 2000: 9). In this period all the concerns that are encompassed in anticipatory grief of the dying and their families can be addressed (Kellaway 2005).

The NICE guidelines emphasise the need for palliative care services to be ethnically and culturally sensitive, to take account of language differences, disabilities and communication difficulties in order to empower patients and their families. The users of palliative care services need to be involved in their treatment and care plans. Marilyn Relf (2000) in her evaluation of the effectiveness of voluntary bereavement care in a palliative care bereavement service found that effective bereavement support significantly reduces the use of health services. Also, that efficacy was related to 'the quality of the relationship and was influenced by factors including cultural norms, mourning styles, volunteer skill and service coordination' (Edwards 2002: 17).

Psychological distress on diagnosis and subsequent treatment is not unexpected given the traumatic nature of the experience and the treatment. The diagnosis of a life-limiting illness frequently brings about a re-evaluation of beliefs, spiritual, religious or philosophical (Calhoun et al. 2000; Walsh et al. 2002). It may also bring the person a sense of disconnection from herself as the person she used to be and from other people (Carroll 2001). In counselling and in offering support it is important to be sensitive to these needs and to be able to provide access to spiritual caregivers who can be available to the patient (Koenig and Gates-Williams 1995; Leichtentritt and Retting 2002).

In her book *Salvation Creek*, Susan Duncan describes her reaction to the impending death of her friend:

> I want to run away from all this. I don't want to go through it all again, the sense of helplessness, the drawn-out wait for death, the grief that grinds through every day even while a loved one is still alive. Grief that leaves you without the strength to feel, for a little while after they die, anything but relief. And when the relief fades the final reality of death seeps in, you're left with huge waves of pure, lonely grief and it's all you can do to keep standing.
>
> (2006: 336)

She dreads revisiting the grief she felt when her brother and husband died within three days of each other.

The quality of death affects the quality of the grieving process. Where a death is anticipated, the quality of end-of-life care is of crucial importance. Within institutional settings such as care homes and hospitals, patients may feel depersonalised. They may feel that their needs come after those of the medical staff or hospital routines. Patients with advanced Alzheimer's Disease may be viewed as biologically alive but socially dead. The world of the living and the world of the dead have a liminal territory which is a painful place to inhabit for both patients and their loved ones. The rise of palliative care and the hospice movement have provided much-needed emotional, spiritual and psychosocial interventions at this point.

Where symptom control is not managed well, other patients may witness a distressing death which fills them with fear that their own death will be as painful. As the wife of a man who died in a six-bed ward said, 'Everyone on that ward shared my husband's death' (Carlisle 2005: 1).

Anticipatory grief impacts on the physical as well as the spiritual lives of those involved. Chodoff, Friedman and Hamburg (1964) found differences in corticosteroid excretion in those experiencing anticipatory grief. Others have noted the impact of bereavement and the increased risks to physical health (Engel 1961; Hofer et al. 1977; Newman 2002; Raphael 1980). Parkes (1972) offered the idea that grief can be likened to physical injury, in that a physical injury may heal quickly or develop complications or it may fail to heal or reopen unexpectedly or there may be a hidden impact at a later date. In much the same way, bereavement has many trajectories and implications which are not immediately apparent. Cottington et al. (1980) found that women between the ages of 25 and 65 who suffered sudden cardiac arrest were six times as likely as the control population to have experienced the death of a significant person in the six months prior to their own death.

Dying and living

It is precisely because we die that living is so wonderful a gift – whether for a minute or a full lifetime, sick or well, crazed or serene, in pain or in delight, no matter, still wonderful.

(Malcolm Muggeridge 2007)

As mentioned earlier, each person's response to dying is influenced by their beliefs, their social support network, the quality of their life and many intensely personal factors (Imara 1975). Dina Rabinovich died of cancer aged 45. She recorded her treatment and thoughts as she journeyed towards her death. They included the 'indignities, absurdities and daily brutalities of the illness' that affect many dying people. In an interview a few months before her death she spoke frankly: 'I feel sad and sometimes very scared. I feel intensely jealous of other women who I see walking their children to school. I look out on a beautiful sunny day and think: "I'm not ready"' (Katz 2007: 39). Such personal, moving accounts of dying are very useful for those who work in bereavement care. They allow us to gain insight into the whole range of responses that come when a person is facing death. We learn that there is no single response; rather, a wide gamut of emotions prevail – fear, anxiety, sadness, loneliness, powerlessness, jealousy, relief and many others.

Malcom Muggeridge, the distinguished British journalist and broadcaster, said that he often experienced ridicule because he spoke about dying. His own thoughts about dying were crystallised in 'an unlikely suicide attempt' (Muggeridge 2007: 22). In the event, he decided not to go through with his bid to die by drowning as he swam out to sea, and instead he returned to the shore. 'As I struggled back … I felt great joy at returning … Thenceforth I have never doubted that every life must be lived out to the end, just as King Lear must be played to the end: that to interrupt or terminate the performance is to rob it of its point.' Muggeridge's view on dying and death coloured each day of his life. He explained, 'It is difficult today, without feeling a humbug or a fool, to explain that death is neither a misery to be evaded, a fate to be dreaded, nor an outrage to be endured but a joy to be welcomed That each moment of life, whatever the circumstances, is made more precious because it passes' (2007: 22).

The words of Muggeridge reveal an abundant joy in living, whatever the quality of life. For him, celebration of life and of living each moment was the essence of existence. Perhaps he was influenced in some way by Bakunin's sister, whom he was with as she died. On her deathbed she said, 'It's lovely to die; to stretch oneself out' (Muggeridge 2007: 22). He repeated these words to himself again and again. Some might find the words incomprehensible or upsetting; however, they demonstrate the fact that each person's dying and death is a unique experience.

Most people do not leave life in a way they would have chosen. A drawn-out, painful illness prior to death may isolate the individual and her family.

Medical intervention may be painful and demeaning. The loss of independence may be a cruel blow for many individuals. As Nuland states, 'In previous centuries, men believed in the concept of *ars moriendi*, the art of dying' (1994: 265). In today's fast-moving world, with highly technical interventions to preserve life, death may be seen as something that happens to others, not ourselves.

Thomas Bell was diagnosed with a terminal illness. He charted his response to his situation in a book *In the Midst of Life* (1961):

> Now and then the whole thing becomes unreal. Out of the middle of the night's darkness, or bringing me to a sudden, chilling halt during the day, the thought comes: This can't be happening to me. Not to me. *Me* with a malignant tumor? *Me* with only a few months to live? Nonsense. And I stare up at the darkness, or out at the sunlit street, and try to encompass it, to feel it. But it stays unreal.
>
> Perhaps the difficulty is my half-conscious presumption that such things happen, should happen, only to other people … People who are strangers, who really don't mind, who … are born solely to fill such quotas. Whereas I am me. Not a stranger. Not other people. Me!

The shock of learning that you are dying is real and visceral. Accepting the reality of that truth may take a great deal of time. The patience and care of loved ones and caregivers in that period is vital; as Nuland says, 'Death belongs to the dying and those who love them' (1994: 265).

Gender differences in grieving

Gender is one of the most significant factors which influence the individual expression of grief (Attig 1996; Filak and Abel 2004). The expression of grief in men and women differs, though of course there are many common emotions (McGoldrick 2004; Thomas 1996; Versalle and McDowell 2004–2005). Most early research into how people grieve and the common patterns of grieving was carried out with female subjects, which may have influenced early notions of expected grief responses. When the daughter of a friend died, her mother cried a great deal and wanted to talk about Emma all the time. Emma's father didn't want to talk but went into practical mode and dealt with the death through problem-solving and practical activity. He made his daughter's coffin, he organised the funeral and the flowers for the church. He needed action, something to pour his heart and mind into. She needed company and connection (Corr 1992; Schwab 1996). Research by Dr Shelley Taylor (2003) indicates that there may a physiological basis for this.

Dr Taylor found that the 'fight or flight' response to stress was largely true for men but that women react differently. Women 'tend and befriend'. Early research into stress was male dominated since researchers did not want hormonal variation in female subjects to influence their results. Taylor argues that when women are stressed they move to nurture those around them (tend) or make social contacts with people with whom they feel they will be safe (befriend). She put this down to the hormone oxytocin, sometimes called the 'cuddle' hormone since it promotes maternal behaviour. The male hormone testosterone limits the effect of oxytocin, which is also present in men. These physiological differences are important when trying to understand the different ways in which men and women grieve (Kilmartin 2005). As Golden states in 'Why do men avoid support groups?', 'a greater understanding of the general tendency of men and women to choose different reponses due to our physiological differences can help us provide more effective and compassionate support to those healing from loss' (Golden 2005: 3).

> 'My husband thinks it better if we don't talk about Tim. He just wants to put it behind us, as if he had never lived but he was our son and I think about him every day. How can I not talk about my 15-year-old lad who I saw grow from a tiny baby to a fine young man? I've tried to talk to him: he just doesn't want to know.'
>
> (Angela)

'Incongruent grieving' is the term used by Peppers and Knapp (1980) to describe the ways in which heterosexual partners tend to grieve differently after the death of a child. They appear to conflict and not meet the expectations of each other (Littlewood et al. 1991). In my practice with bereaved couples, female clients often complain that their male partner is not really grieving, or doesn't care or is 'over it' because he chooses not to talk about the deceased. Male clients, on the other hand, say that their partner is over-emotional or not in control. Some men feel angry because they are told, 'You don't care, you never show any emotion.' Explaining that men in general tend to grieve in one way, whilst women in general tend to grieve in a different way can be a huge help to a bereaved couple, especially when they understand there is a physical basis for the difference.

There are also cultural factors which influence male and female expression of emotions (Filak and Abel 2004; Kilmartin 2005). There are still gender-appropriate responses for males in Western society, such as the view that men should be strong to hold the family together and not become overwhelmed by their mourning (Kilmartin 2004). Rando (1984) expressed the view that if individuals do not react to the grief in the 'proper way' then it might compromise other roles such as being the strong father or the head of the family. In order to remove gender titles from the styles of grieving, Martin and Doka (1996) introduced the term 'intuitive' for that style of grieving which is usually associated with feminine responses and 'instrumental' for that which is seen as typically masculine (Martin and Doka 2000).

Gender influences the way in which males and females adapt to widow-hood. Whilst some of this links to the level of distress, specifically that age-ing men are more emotionally distressed when their spouse dies, it also relates to strategies they use to adapt to living alone. Loss of the person who cared for them means that they have to find ways of caring for them-selves. For some the chaos left after bereavement makes adjustment very difficult (Davidson 2000).

This gender difference is also reported in men and women bereaved by homicide. According to Kenney, 'the traumatic grief experienced by women is characterized by intense sadness, obsessive thoughts about the victim, dwelling on the sense of loss, feeling unable to change patterns and an overwhelming fearfulness, particularly fear of the offender' (2002: 43). Men tended to express more anger and focus more on the need for action (Victim Support 2006).

Reflective exercises

Gender and grief

Consider a personal bereavement you have experienced.

- How was your personal cultural, religious, spiritual or social background reflected in the funeral and other events following the death?
- Did you find it easy to speak with family and friends about the death?
- Did you feel that family and friends were able to initiate conversation about your bereavement?
- Were there any gender influences in the way you were expected to grieve?
- What is your experience of a person of the opposite gender to you and their grief reactions? Was it different to the way in which you expressed your grief? If so, how did it affect you?

My life line

Draw a line on a piece of blank paper. At the beginning write 1 and at the end write your age now. Divide the line into five-year segments.

Think about key events in your life, and losses you have experienced. Below the line are negative feelings and above are positive. Chart your losses according to how positive or negative you felt the events were. The deepest below the line represents the most sad or distressing feelings, the highest above the line the most positive. Events may include the death of family or friends, death of a pet, moving house, sickness, hospitalisation and a sibling leaving home. Whatever felt like a loss to you can be included.

Take your time when recording the events, placing them in the appropriate age slot. When you have completed the diagram think about any positive outcomes of the painful experiences. Some positives are recorded below;

'I was really sad when my brother died when I was eight but on the positive side it meant my Mum and Dad weren't going to the hospital all the time. They had time for me again. I got my own room as well and didn't have to share any more.'

'When my Dad died I was upset but part of me was relieved because I could see the strain lifted from my Mum. She'd been caring for him for years and it felt like she'd got a life back.'

'My daughter's death had a profound impact on me but it gave me an impetus to think about my life and what I was going to do with it. I started to prioritise my own needs and hopes and do something about meeting them.'

'My Mum died when I was 13. I felt so bad I started cutting myself and became severely depressed. But over time I realised things can change suddenly and you have to take every opportunity to enjoy life so that's what I do now. It took a long time but my attitude to life is: make the best of every day.'

Reflect on any gains these loss experiences brought and how they have affected your outlook. Write them out on a separate sheet or, using a different coloured ink, add them to your diagram.

3

Core Skills in Working
with Those Who Grieve

... And the end of all our exploring
Will be to arrive where we started
And know the place for the first time.

(T.S. Eliot, 'Little Gidding', 1963: 222)

One of the greatest needs a person has in times of loss is the need for love, support and companionship. They need to be shielded from too many pressures and not be expected to change suddenly or to take on new roles too soon. Some will find that their friends and family help them through, yet others will find that those closest to them are too locked into their own grief to focus on anyone else. It is at this point that they may seek bereavement counselling. When they feel as if they are in storm-tossed waters, you may be the anchor in a sea of change.

In counselling there are essential skills which we need in order to develop a 'therapeutic rapport' with those we counsel (Jennings and Shovholt 1999). This means building a relationship which offers safety, emotional warmth, consistency, commitment and genuine care. It is backed up by a set of ethical guidelines whose first rule is beneficence: 'First do no harm'. Research has indicated that it is not the theoretical basis of the therapeutic work which matters most but the fact that the client has a positive relationship with the counsellor (Harris 2006). In this chapter we will explore core skills, the key competencies that underpin bereavement counselling and support positive therapeutic relationships.

As noted in the introduction, there is a continuum of support that can be offered to the bereaved ranging from bereavement support by volunteers, befrienders in church and other settings to other caring individuals in such places as hospices, and support groups such as the Compassionate Friends. It may be that those who have suffered similar losses are the best healers

(Humphrey and Zimpfer 1996). People who have experienced pain are often the best teachers for each other as they have known the experience of grief at first hand. As Relf points out, volunteers in support groups and mutual help groups do not carry the stigma that is attached to mental health services, counselling or therapy. Also, the fact that the volunteers are ordinary people reflects the concept that grief is a natural response to bereavement (Relf 1998). Members of groups find support in these meetings based on mutual understanding (McKissock et al. 1994).

Support groups give the opportunity to talk about the experience of loss, the chance to share with others who have had or who still are experiencing similar events and the setting to express emotions which are suppressed in other settings. Support groups can improve the quality of life, as participants report decreased depression and anxiety, better coping skills and gain greater information which reduces fear (McKissock et al. 1994; Spiegel and Glafkides 1983; Spiegel and Yalom, 1978; Yalom and Greaves 1977).

Other support may be offered in bereavement counselling, which is carried out by a trained counsellor working to a code of professional ethics and guidelines with a theoretical basis for their interventions and with support from a supervisor. In cases where there is complicated grief, traumatic loss and where more in-depth skills are judged necessary, then it is appropriate that the bereaved person see a bereavement counsellor. However, most bereavement support workers, palliative care workers and befrienders will use the core skills described in this chapter as the basis of their work (NHS 2007; Osterfield 2002; Relf 1998).

Essentially, the most important issue is not about the model of grief but about the person who is mourning their loss and the rapport between the person offering support and the bereaved (Cruse 2005; Harris 2006). Help is about supporting the bereaved in ways with which they feel comfortable, not in ways we think appropriate. It is also about expanding their options by opening new doors for them (Berzoff and Silverman 2004). The models of grief mentioned earlier (in Chapter 1) are helpful but there is no one formula and everyone grieves in their own way. The nature of the loss and the relationships involved influence the grieving process: a spouse whose husband of forty years has died of a long drawn-out illness will grieve differently to a father whose pre-school child has died suddenly. These are important factors which we keep in mind as we listen to the bereaved. Also, we are constantly aware that the basic rule of counselling is 'First do no harm'.

The timing of bereavement counselling is important: if it is too soon after the death, the person may not be ready to face the reality of what has happened (Schut 2005). Engagement and the relationship with the client are as important as the words that are used in the counselling session. Mind, body and brain are all part of the whole person and we need to engage all in the process. The bereaved can be helped by cognitive understanding of what is happening as well as an awareness of their emotions and what is happening in their body.

Literature such as printed booklets which are designed to help a bereaved person after death must not refer to stages of grieving. The bereaved may think that they have to grieve in that way otherwise they are abnormal or that because their experience does not fit with what is written on the page they are doing something wrong. Counsellors working with those who are bereaved need to facilitate the telling of the full story, including not only the story about the death but about how it has impacted on other areas of their life, including ongoing relationships, beliefs and cultural issues (Tschudin 1997). The ripple effect of death may well bring other circumstantial losses (Lendrum and Syme 1992).

The significance of sexuality in grieving is an area often overlooked in counselling training yet for many it is central to the experience of living. In addition, following bereavement, a partner may become anxious about sexual desires which are not automatically switched off because death has taken their loved one away. In my experience, there is often a feeling of shame or guilt about missing the physical side of their relationship and still having sexual urges. It is an area that many are reluctant to talk about though we know that continuing bonds with the deceased may involve sexual or intimate fantasies. Dunn and his colleagues (2005) found that some adults whose partner had died found the sexual ruminations a comfort while others found them distressing. This reaffirms the unique nature of each experience of bereavement. As counsellors, we need to be able to explore these delicate topics with sensitivity and compassion. Spirituality is also highly significant in grief work and it is explored in depth in Chapter 7.

Intellectual disability

People with intellectual disabilities are defined as having a reduced ability to understand new or complex information and, because of impaired intelligence, a reduced capacity to learn new skills. They often have a reduced ability to cope independently. However, none of this means that they do not grieve. As Bonnell-Pascual et al. (1999) point out, the response to bereavement by adults with learning disabilities is similar in type, though not in expression, to that of the general population. The low expectations of those who care for the bereaved person with intellectual abilities, their inability to communicate effectively and uncertainty about what has been understood may cause the bereaved to be isolated in their grief (Hollin and Esterhuyzen 1997).

Many people with learning or intellecual difficulties are marginalised when it comes to dying, death and grief (Read 2006). Often they are not told of the death and are not allowed to participate in the rituals associated with death. This exclusion may cause complicated grief reactions. Those with learning and other disabilities rely on others for support. If their loss is unrecognised then, effectively, their grief is disenfranchised; however, bereavement support groups for people with learning disabilities can help in adjustment to life after loss (Persaud and Persaud 2003). We will explore the concept of disenfranchised grief in Chapter 5.

Research by Bonnell-Pascual et al. (1999) found that people with learning disabilities adapted to the loss more easily when basic emotional needs were met by their carers. Should the bereaved person require support or counselling, then creative ways can be explored to express grief if talking is inappropriate because verbal skills are not adequate. Artwork, family trees, memory boxes, life story work, photographs and reminiscence work can all help in the process.

The counselling setting

The counselling setting needs to be private, comfortable, warm and calming. Where you put the furniture makes a difference to how your client feels so the way you set up your room is important. The client needs to be able to see you but also to look away when they wish to. In *Coming into Mind* (2006), Margaret Wilkinson explains how this is linked to research into neuroscience and attachment. She describes the significance of the baby being able to look into her mother's face, to look away and the early development of shame. This relates to what is happening in the new counselling encounter. It is still associative and relational: those early experiences have been laid down and carried forward. As she says, 'Neuroscience helps us to see the significance of the baby's early relationships, and therefore that what goes on in the consulting room will be a very important re-experiencing of the relationship. And as well as the re-experiencing, there will be a new relationship, not just a replaying of the old' (Pointon 2006: 34).

Of course not all support takes place in a dedicated space. It may happen in a hospital corridor, at a hospice bedside, in the home of the bereaved or in a group setting. Essentially we need to use whatever space we work in as a place of safety and respect in order to enable the bereaved to address the issues they need to talk about.

Core counselling skills

Active listening

When you use this core counselling skill you are attentive and aware of both verbal and non-verbal communication. Albert Mehrabian (1981) emphasises the importance of non-verbal communication in face to face communication. His research found that words constituted only 7 per cent of communication, while tone constituted 38 per cent and non-verbal cues 55 per cent. Active listening means paying complete attention to the client and avoiding diversions, as listed below, which draw attention away from the process. By listening and being comfortable with silence, we enable the bereaved to tell the story she needs to tell at her own pace and in her own way. By listening we enable the client to find the words to express her deepest feelings and thoughts. And we listen to the music behind the words, not just the words but how she says them, her intonation and her body language. Also, we listen to the gaps between the words, sometimes, as in musical terms, 'the spaces between the notes are more important than the notes' (Spiegel 1993: 187).

In active listening there is acceptance and understanding and the space to explore whatever comes up. It gives you time to be with the client, not 'doing' something to fix the problem, which often can never be fixed, but sharing the space while they explore their situation.

'What is wanted is a *compassionate listener* who will let you talk about your loss from every angle. This is something I miss among my relatives and friends. However sympathetic they may be, their main aim is to distract and cheer me. How can you be expected to cut off from your thoughts and conversation someone who has formed fifty per cent of your thoughts almost from the day of conception.'

(Bereaved mother in Stephens 1972: 66)

Diversions from Active Listening

There are number of activities which can distract or divert the client and which we need to take into account when providing the optimal conditions for counselling to succeed.

External:	noisy surroundings, doors slamming, overheard conversations, telephones. Intrusive pictures or photographs, very personal belongings of the counsellor.
Counsellor's behaviour:	fidgeting, clock-watching, slouching or negative body language, lack of eye contact or too daunting eye contact, tone of voice.
Counsellor's beliefs:	personal beliefs and attitudes may get in the way of listening; you may be diverted into thinking about yourself and how your views are at odds with the client.
Counsellor's feelings:	your own emotions may interfere or be churned up by what your client says; and your feelings about your relationship with the client can divert your attention.

Active Listening Guidelines

Keep an open mind.
Listen to *how* things are said.

Observe non-verbal communication.
Ensure that your verbal contributions are clear and relevant.
Ask for clarification if you haven't understood.
Be honest when feeding back feelings.
Be prepared to work hard at listening especially when the bereaved person is exploring painful areas which may be upsetting for you too.

Empathy

Empathy is vital in bereavement counselling. It is the ability to understand and share the feelings of others. It involves compassion, concern, understanding and the ability to share the perceived emotions, thoughts and feelings of another person. Empathy is concerned with developing insight into the bereaved person's private world and communicating that understanding (Mallon 1987). As Egan says, 'In interpersonal communication, empathy is a tool of civility. Making an effort to get in touch with another person's frame of reference sends a message of respect. Therefore, empathy plays an important part in building a working alliance with clients' (1994: 117).

Empathy involves trying to see the world through the eyes of the person you are counselling. When they look at the world what do they see? The world looks very different to an isolated young person who has just left care and is living in a bed and breakfast hostel than it does to someone who lives in a detached house in a leafy area with secure family relationships and good health. The world changes rapidly when your 24-year-old fiancé kisses you goodbye in the morning and you get a phone call at three o'clock in the afternoon to tell you to come to the hospital because he has fallen off a crane and is in intensive care. Part of the empathy we need is in recognising how the person's life is radically altered and how we help them rebuild security. As counsellors we cannot make life meaningful for someone else but we can create a safe space in which they can find meaning themselves.

Annie Hargrave, a counsellor specialising in working with people in the overseas emergency aid and development business, wrote of her experience when her son died of cancer. In her article she describes how difficult it was to be empathic for some time after her son's death:

For a long time I couldn't accommodate anything beyond my immediate distress. I listened to the news. I heard about people's woes. I kept it up. But it was all cognitive. I couldn't take it in. My capacity for empathy had been crushed.

(2003: 29)

Gradually she regained her ability to feel the joy and pain of others but until she did so she knew she was not fit to work as a counsellor.

Unconditional positive regard

People who are grieving need to feel that the counsellor cares for them, warts and all. In unconditional positive regard you need to put aside your prejudices and preferences, and avoid being judgmental. You also need to be sensitive to cultural and religious differences and respect the value system of the individual. Show by your balanced, compassionate attitude that you can accept their feelings whatever they are. When you do this, the client is given permission, tacitly, to explore her concerns without fearing your disapproval. A high degree of unconditional positive regard is associated with greater successful outcomes in counselling (Kirschenbaum and Hendersin 1992: 117).

Unconditional positive regard means that there are no conditions of acceptance (Standal 1954). No 'I'll like you if you behave in such and such a way'. Carl Rogers, the psychologist who founded Client-Centred Counselling says, 'It involves as much feeling of acceptance for the client's expression of negative, "bad", painful, fearful, defensive, abnormal feelings as for his expression of "good", positive, mature, confident, social feelings, as much acceptance of ways in which he is inconsistent as in ways he is consistent' (Kirschenbaum and Hendersin 1992: 225).

Geoffrey Gorer (1965) noted that death had become the new 'pornography': it had replaced sex as society's taboo. Some people still feel that to talk about death, dying, grieving or any other related matters is out of bounds. In the counselling setting it is imperative that you enable the person to talk about whatever aspect they wish to without fear of being judged by you. One client was very hesitant about her response to her partner's sudden death:

'I had no idea it would happen. We'd made love before we went to sleep. Everything was fine, then I woke up, it was four o'clock, and I knew something was wrong. I just knew it. I turned on the bedside lamp and looked at him. He looked like he was sleeping but he wasn't breathing. He just looked as beautiful as ever but pale. I was shocked, I knew he was dead but I didn't want anyone to know. I didn't call my sister or the ambulance or anything. I knew it was the last time I would ever be with him, the last time I would ever lie with him. I wanted to smell him, to touch him, to stroke him – just this last time. I put my arms round him and I stayed with him until it was morning and the light came into the room. I had to have that time with him. I had to say Goodbye in my way.'

She hadn't told anyone about this because she was afraid people would be shocked and that the coroner's office – there had to be an inquest because it was a sudden death – would castigate her. The non-judgmental acceptance of her actions by me, as the bereavement counsellor, brought visible relief.

In using core counselling skills we have to recognise that there are diverse values, attitudes, beliefs, feelings and cultural perspectives. Though people may have different views to our own this does not make them deficit (Rosenblatt 1993). Whatever you feel is the correct response or behaviour, you need to try to see how it is for the person who has come for your support. You may feel that you need to challenge rather than accept a client's perception or view and it can be therapeutic to do so; however, ensure you do it in an appropriate, sensitive and enabling way, not in a judgmental way.

As the counsellor or befriender, you may find yourself the object of hostility as well as a source of support at the same time. Penson highlights this: 'Neither is bereavement support all sweetness and light. Relatives may hate the person who has died (and feel very guilty about this). There may be complex family problems. Worse still, the bereaved person may not always appear grateful for the time and effort given by the helper; they may even, occasionally, hate the helper too!' (1990: 24). The bereaved person may see your help as something that will make him leave the past behind though part of him may not be ready to do so. Working through this conflict is an essential part of the healing process.

Some people react with heightened sensitivity following loss. They imagine injury in harmless remarks or feel undermined by any form of criticism, so sensitivity is essential. Grieving will not be hurried and the greater the loss, the more difficult it may be. As people who wish to play a part in the healing process, we have to accept that while we can validate the person's feelings we cannot stop his pain.

Reflection

As a bereavement counsellor, you act as a mirror in which the client can see herself and her situation more clearly. Practically, what you do is listen to the client and then reflect back to her what you have heard. You may use the same words or slightly different ones to express the same feeling. For example:

Therese: When they came out of the emergency room and they said my son had died, I screamed and told them they were liars. John couldn't be dead! I tried to hit the doctor who said it. I was so angry.

Counsellor: You were so shocked and angry that you couldn't take in the awful news that John had died.

Try these out for yourself:

Harry: My wife had breast cancer for years and so I got into a take-it-for-granted kind of attitude. I didn't think she would die from it then one day she said we need to talk about what you'll do with the kids when I'm gone. I was numb. I never believed it could happen to me.

Counsellor:

Leanne:　　My Dad was a good man most of the time but when I was little he bullied me and my sister. And he was still a bully till the day he died. I loved him but, I don't know, I've got mixed feelings. When he died I thought I'd be really sad but I wasn't.

Counsellor:

Non-possessive support

A person who has experienced loss may go through a period of dependency. This need not be problematic. Counsellors should ensure that they do not encourage the person to become solely dependent on them. Possessiveness discourages personal autonomy and will not help the person in the longer term. Helping the person develop independence and self-confidence is a key factor in overcoming loss of any kind. If the person feels positive about himself he can usually seek help from others when he is distressed or when customary support stops. Fear and self-blame may cause his self-belief to be undermined so he will need affirmation to build resilience.

Confidentiality

If you are working for an organisation such as a hospice or voluntary organisation, you should have a set of guidelines that cover issues of confidentiality, data protection and so on. Make sure you read these and adhere to them. The British Association of Counselling and Psychotherapy has an ethical code of practice which includes confidentiality. In working with clients, explain what you can or cannot keep confidential and do not promise to keep information confidential, such as in child protection issues, when you know you will have to pass that information on to someone else (Jenkins 2002).

Factors that influence the grieving and counselling process

Essential to the counselling process is a genuine relationship between client and counsellor. For this to happen, the counsellor has to be deeply aware of herself and her feelings. It is the opposite of putting on a façade or front or hiding behind a role. During the counselling session, the counsellor needs to be fully present and congruent. As Carl Rogers said,

When as a parent or a therapist or a teacher … I fail to listen to what is going on in me, fail because of my own defensiveness to sense my own feelings, then … failure seems to result. It has made it seem to me that the most basic learning for anyone who hoped to establish any kind of relationship is that it is safe to be transparently real.

(1974: 51)

In being genuine with the client, the counsellor provides a model of openness and acceptance. This can be of great help to someone who has not been able to express their true sense of self because of family or other pressures.

There are many factors that influence our attitudes, beliefs and circumstances. In working with the bereaved it may be helpful to explore the questions and comments listed below. These are for you to consider in relation to your client and are not meant to be a list to work through.

> What factors in the nature or circumstances of the bereaved person influence the grieving process?
> What is their psychological make-up?
> Is their mental health robust or poor?
> What was their emotional life like prior to bereavement?
> How have they managed previous loss?
> Do they have other stressful situations in their life?
> How much social support do they have? From whom: family, friends, faith group?
> Do they have a trusted person with whom they can talk and on whom they can rely?
> How is their physical health?
> What do they want and need from you?

It is also useful to find out the nature of the norms of the person you are working with (Leichtentritt & Rettig 2002). These may be dictated by cultural expectations or family customs (Caring Connections 2006) You may explore the following questions:

> What are the cultural rituals for coping with dying?
> What are the customary rituals for the deceased person's body and burial?
> How are the dead honoured in their culture, at the burial and thereafter?
> What are your family beliefs about what happens after death?
> Are there any defined family roles that are adopted after a death?
> What do their family think is the acceptable way to express grief?
> Are there certain types of death that are unacceptable, for example suicide?
> Are there certain types of death that are more difficult to manage, such as the death of a child?
> Are some deaths more acceptable, such as death in old age, and if so, would mourning and grieving be different?

Ending the session

It is important to end the session in such a way that the person feels as composed as possible when they leave the room. This means helping them to realise the session will end shortly: to do this you can summarise what has happened, reinforce any positive actions they said they wanted to pursue and make arrangements for further meetings. This will increase their sense of confidence in you and help to build their resilience. Affirm your belief in their ability to explore the issues and to express their feelings and the narrative of their bereavement.

Table 3.1 Core support skills

	Types	Purpose	Examples
1	Warmth, support	To help the person to feel at ease	I'd like to help...Are you able to tell me what happened ?
2	Clarification	To bring out complete information	Can you tell me more about...?
3	Restatement	To check our meaning is the same as the person's To show understanding	From what you are saying I understand that... So, you've decided to...
4	Encouragement	To encourage the person	I realise this is difficult for you. You're doing really well...
5	Reflectiveness	To act as a mirror – to see what is being communicated To help the person evaluate their feelings To show you understand the feeling behind the words	You feel that... It was very hard for you to accept... You felt angry and upset when they...
6	Summarising	To bring together the areas discussed so far To provide a starting point for future work	The main points we talked about today were... As I see it, you want to... next time we meet.

The effectiveness of counselling

There has been much discussion about the effectiveness of bereavement counselling. 'Most bereavement caregivers accept as a truism that their interventions are helpful' (Jordan and Neimeyer 2003: 765); however, there are a number of factors which may not be helpful, as we will discover. Personal experience in working with clients and relevant research indicate bereavement counselling can make significant contribution to the recovery process when appropriately targeted (Parkes 2000). In a study of the effectiveness of counselling with couples following a perinatal bereavement from congenital disease, Lilford et al. (1994) found that women who attended for counselling had a much better outcome than those who withdrew. Circumstances in which intervention is not effective arise when the bereaved person is offered unsolicited help, where it is a routine referral and when it takes place shortly after the loss (Schut 2005).

The provision of support for widows during the critical period following the death of their partner results in fewer demands on the health service (Raphael 1977). This supports the idea that appropriate, well-timed bereavement counselling enhances the longer-term emotional and physical well-being of the bereaved and reduces the strain on health care provision.

Whilst sadness, anger, disbelief and anxiety are commonly felt following a death, inner natural drives will be working to help the bereaved to adapt to their new situation. In reality, there is no set sequence for the experience of bereavement. Emotional pain can flare up at any time, even when the person has a sense of reintegration and has reinvested in their present and future. As a counsellor you need to be able to work with intense emotions, the client's as well as your own, and with culturally diverse responses to death (Koenig and Gates-Williams 1995; Shapiro 1996). As we saw in the introduction (Taylor 2005), there are some areas that counsellors seem to steer away from, such as the sense of the presence of the deceased and belief in an afterlife. As counsellors we need to recognise that these are significant parts of the bereaved person's story, and it is the story they want to tell that is important rather than eliciting a story we, as counsellors, want to hear.

The importance of the story: narrative as therapy

When you tell a story, you mend things that are broken.

(Karen Blixen [Isak Dinesen] quoted in Busch 2001: 1)

A fundamental crisis in bereavement is not only the loss of the deceased but the loss of self (Howarth 2000). If a woman's baby dies at birth, she loses not only her identity as a mother but the anticipation of being a parent for a lifetime. The loss has to be placed in an ongoing narrative, not 'got over' like an illness. The grieving are altered and their future life narrative can only reflect and somehow absorb that experience (Richie 2000).

When grief, sadness and mourning strike, the bereaved enter a liminal, transitory state, a state between what was and what will be. The bereaved feel lost and bewildered. In counselling at this time the bereaved person is helped by reflection and exploration of what has been lost and how he feels about what may come. There is no sense of rushing this period: he has to make his own pace. He needs time to reflect on the territory he has found himself in and discover if there are any paths through this uncharted land (Yalom 1980).

After a death the bereaved person may fear that someone else is going to die, maybe another member of her circle – or herself. Bereavement brings us face to face with our own mortality, causing anxiety and fear. Great fear may be expressed about children or grandchildren, since the death of a child is out of the natural order. We think it is the old who should die after a fulfilled life, not those who are still at the beginning of their time.

Helen

Helen's grandson died after many months of treatment for an aggressive form of cancer. She could not accept his death, though she was present when he died. She would not attend the funeral nor would she visit the gravestone to mark the anniversary of his death. She felt she had let her son down because she could not stop this terrible event happening and she could not comprehend that her beloved grandson could die: not the child she looked after three days every week. For Helen, her grandson's death broke all rules of natural justice and her faith in life and living were betrayed. The void left behind was unbearable; it affected her physically and emotionally and caused her to question the meaning of her own existence.

Grandparents mourn the loss of their grandchild but also experience grief for the pain of their child who was parent to the dead child. There is often a sense of helplessness because they have failed to protect their own child from the pain of bereavement and feel their own grief too. As a grandparent, at this point, they are with their child at the most difficult time they are ever likely to experience. They may have other grandchildren who have been distressed by the loss too (Reed 2000).

It is helpful if the bereavement counsellor can elicit the story of the death and the relationship the bereaved had to the deceased. In the telling, extreme emotions are released and the bereaved can work through the meaning of the death and the impact on their life.

Some questions you might seek responses to:

- What was the nature of the relationship to the deceased?
- What were the circumstances of the death and the time leading up to it?
- How did Helen feel at the time of the death?
- What feelings are predominant – guilt, anger, relief, sadness?
- What has Helen lost in terms of the relationship – a companion, a dependable source of support?

In exploring present feelings, you could ask, ' What do you miss about...?' and 'What don't you miss?' You can ask what sustains the bereaved person so that she can name those parts of her life which provide stability while still recognising that it may be a year or many years before she recovers meaning and purpose in life.

The bereaved may develop self-harming behaviours and in counselling it is useful to ask in what ways they have changed since the death. The capacity or incapacity for self-care following bereavement may be linked to lack of care in childhood, where the baby did not learn to internalise self-care (Turp 2004). The self-harm may not be dramatic and obvious, such as cutting; but self-harm by omission, that is self-destructive behaviour, such as drinking excessively. This is part of the continuum of self-harm which goes from socially acceptable self-harming such as healthy dieting to extreme behaviour such as anorexia. What makes a difference is enabling people to access their resilience and self-confidence, particularly when depression has overwhelmed them.

Reflective exercises

My experience of loss

Before we work with others it is important that we have looked at our own experience of loss and our reactions to those losses. Consider the following list. How many of these losses have you experienced?

Circumstantial losses

Separation	Visual impairment
Divorce	Hearing impairment
Emigration	Loss of speech
Burglary	Disfigurement
Stillbirth	Amputation
Miscarriage	Mastectomy
Abortion	Infertility
Death	Death of a pet
Ageing	Natural disaster
Moving house	Accident
Imprisonment	Bankruptcy
Domestic violence	Loss of job
Being in public care	Assault
Adoption	Retirement
Rape	Bullying
Sexual abuse	Murder
Hospitalisation	Self-harm
Serious illness	Menopause
Birth of a child with lifelong disability	
Chronic serious illness in a child	
Diagnosis of disability	

Make a list of the ones that have happened to you and next to each one write down your response under these four headings:

Physical   Cognitive   Behavioural   Emotional

Sal wrote:

Domestic Violence: Physical: Felt sick, vomited, shaking, sweating, heart pounding.

Cognitive: I didn't believe it even though I could see the blood. I thought I'd imagined it. I couldn't think straight. My head felt in a whirl, going over it again and again.

Behavioural: I was like a zombie, I kept walking up and down the kitchen, telling myself it wasn't true, it couldn't happen to me.

Emotional: Crying, terrified, felt completely isolated, ashamed.

There is often overlap between these areas but the point is to explore your thoughts and feelings. When you do this you can respond more sensitively and empathically when you work with someone who has suffered a loss. Some adults may find that bereavement is the most painful experience of their lives and that it irredeemably changes them. Have any of your experiences irredeemably changed you?

Empathy

Draw a person you are working with at the moment or have worked with in the past. Think about the person's body language, facial expressions, posture, clothes and hair, etc. Use symbols if you want to – if you feel the person is a powder keg about to blow up then draw the powder keg too. Whatever you draw will be right.

Next, imagine you are the person and that you are introducing yourself to a counsellor. Try to really get into this person's skin, see the world through her eyes and from her point of view. Speak out loud and say what you want to come from the counselling sessions. You may tape yourself doing this exercise and replay it once you have finished.

Time for reflection

> How did it feel to be the person?
> Did you notice any physical sensations such as a racing heart or dry mouth?
> What insight did you get into what she might be thinking about her situation?
> How might this influence the way you work with her in future?

Finally, how did you feel about making the drawing? Some people feel stupid because they 'can't draw' and are afraid of being judged. If you felt out of your comfort zone, and even into your fear zone, you might reflect on the fact that many people feel just like that when they first come for counselling. They sometimes feel they haven't got the words to express their thoughts and feelings and worry that what they do say is stupid and worthless.

Thinking about my death

> What are your thoughts about your own death?
> Have you thought about your own funeral?
> Have you made a will?
> Have you experienced the death of someone close to you?
> If you have, what support helped you through the grieving process?
> What have you put in place for your clients should you suddenly become seriously ill or die?

'I don't have a fear about dying but only about what I'll leave behind and how they might be affected. My children are teenagers and I want to be here for them. I have discussed my death with them, they know what I want to happen and though they said, "Don't be silly, we don't need to talk about this stuff," I felt it was important'.

(Jenny, hospice volunteer)

4

When the Worst You Can Possibly Imagine Happens: Murder, Manslaughter and Suicide

Let me suggest that the bad things that happen in our lives do not have meaning when they happen to us. They do not happen for any good reason which would cause us to accept them willingly. But we can give them a meaning. We can redeem these tragedies from senselessness by imposing meaning on them. The question we should be asking is not, 'Why did this happen to me? What did I do to deserve this?' That is really an unanswerable, pointless question. A better question would be, 'now that this has happened to me, what am I going to do about it?'

(Rabbi Kushner 1982: 38)

The death of someone close comes as a tremendous shock but where the cause of death is sudden or where someone takes their own life then the shock intensifies (Cleiren et al. 1996). In this chapter we will explore the particular aspects that affect the counselling and supportive work needed when working with people who are bereaved by murder, manslaughter, suicide, and in disasters (Dixon 2001; Malone 2007).

Around the world, every year, thousands of people are bereaved by murder or manslaughter. As we move through the twenty-first century the world is changing and many people are living with multiple losses. These include refugees, asylum seekers, people with AIDS and those whose lives have been changed by chronic physical and mental illness. If we project this into the future, there are worrying possibilities: 'By World Health Organization projections, the leading causes of disease burden for the year 2020 are ischemic heart disease, unipolar depression and road accidents' (Benoliel 1999: 4). The need for counselling support looks set to rise and rise.

Grieving following murder, manslaughter, suicide and accidental death is usually even more complicated and problematic than in other forms of bereavement (Gibson 2006). The sudden and unexpected nature of the death make it harder to comprehend and if the bereaved witnessed the murder, accident or manslaughter, or found the body, for example in the case of suicide, the person may be plagued by horrifying images (Allen 1991; Harrison 1999a; Mezey et al. 2002). They may not want to bring the deceased to mind because frightening images get in the way of more comforting ones. 'Death images' preoccupy and disturb the bereaved because, even if they have not witnessed horrific injuries, press coverage and the legal system review the details. This makes it difficult to live in the usual way since such coverage preoccupies the mind of the deceased.

Decades of research examining the impact of loss has found that loss changes people (Lehman, et al. 1989; Rubin and Malkinson, 2001; Shalev 1999). There are changes both in self-view and in their world view (Raphael and Martinek 1997). Alongside this is a greater sense of vulnerability to external control. Traumatic events undermine our basic assumptions and belief that the world is a safe place (Papadopoulos 2001). They cause us to question what the world really is, since it no longer appears predictable, just or meaningful There is no meaning in arbitrary acts that change our world so drastically (Janoff-Bulman 1992).

People need to mourn traumatic loss. There is a need to recreate a coherent network which includes safety, meaning and continuity in the face of the life changes that bereavement brings. (Herman, 1992; Neimeyer, 2001; Papadopoulos 1997) After a traumatic death, families may become more anxious and protective towards those who remain. Sudden bereavement is a complicated, multifaceted process which has physical, emotional, psychological and sociological aspects (Cleiren and Diekstra 1995; Dyregov et al. 2003). Where the death has to be investigated by police, coroners and forensic specialists grief is intensified, as the bereaved may not be allowed to touch or hold the person who has died (Mowll 2007). In addition many parents whose child has been murdered find that the contradictory information or lack of information from the judiciary and criminal investigation teams causes greater distress (Black 2004; Dannemillar 2002).

The impact of traumatic loss

Grief is a way of healing our hurt psyche.

(Black 2005)

The word 'trauma' comes from the Greek word meaning 'to be wounded'. The psychiatric definition of trauma is 'an event outside normal human experience'. The experience is so far beyond the everyday in its shocking, violent and crushing violation that our 'psyches' are wounded and we feel as if we have been physically, emotionally and spiritually attacked by what we have seen, or heard directly or been informed about (Jacobs 1999). Traumatic grief relates to the experience of sudden loss of a significant and close attachment (McDermott and Moore 2004). Sanders (1993) argues that sudden death has a debilitating effect on the survivor probably because of the shock of the unexpected event.

A traumatic loss overwhelms the bereaved (Figley et al. 1997; O'Connor and Russell 2003). It is so intense that their world seems and is broken into a million fragmented pieces. Reg Keys' 20-year-old son, a soldier, was killed in Iraq. 'The day they came to tell me Tom had been killed was like being hit in the chest with a sack of cement. But my wife said, "This is not the worst. The worst will be when it sinks in." And she was right' (Pook 2006: 5).

Nina Bawden – author of *Dear Austen: A letter to my husband, who was killed in the train crash at Potter's Bar on 10 May 2002, to tell him what happened, both then and afterwards* (2006) – wrote of her grief and anger following his death. She said, 'A certain kind of grief does not improve with time' (Bawden 2006: 10). For some it feels that there is no conclusion to their grief, especially after manslaughter or murder or other devastating, unprepared-for loss (Wickie and Marwit 2000–2001). One father, ten years after his child was killed in Dunblane, where sixteen children and their teacher were murdered, said, 'You think you've got this far, you must be over the worst. But then things catch up with you, feelings I'd been deflecting over the years'(Dunblane 1996: 26).

A number of factors are typically found in traumatic loss (Attig 1996; Figley et al. 1997; Stroebe et al. 2001):

- Little or no time to prepare for the event;
- Little or no previous experience of such an event;
- Little or no guidance from others on what to do or how to respond;
- Little or no control over what ensues after the death, combined with a sense of utter helplessness that threatens to overwhelm;
- Feelings of being surrounded by disaster, destruction and despair;
- Feelings of being under threat of further life-endangering events either to the survivor or to others.

Some factors may confound the grief process, such as the reactions of others: for example, parents whose child has died suddenly or in traumatic circumstances may be upset by the way some hospital staff seem to care about organisational needs rather than their own (Awooner-Renner 1993; Jenkinson and Bodkin 1996).

All around the world people are suffering what Leviton (1991) describes as 'horrendous death' as a result of war, terrorism, racism, genocide or rape, as well as fear of violence and sudden death or destruction. Some of these groups will suffer multiple losses, for example asylum seekers and refugees and those who are caught up in public disasters such as the 9-11 attack on the Twin Towers in New York, the tsunami, of Boxing Day 2004 and the tragic murders on Virginia Tech campus in 2007 (Bedard 2006; Raphael 2005; Saari 2005). Where the disaster is man-made, the impact is even greater than in natural disaster as survivors try to comprehend the seemingly inhumane actions that have led to the desecration of human life (Attig 1996). It challenges our basic belief in a fair, just and predictable world (Janoff-Bulman 1992).

Murder and manslaughter

White Noise: The Underbelly of Homicidal Grief

Just one 9 mm bullet killed us both.

It is difficult to write
stop
moving
long enough to face
me, the
silence
that feasts off my chubby grief
stiff stale static
white noise that keeps singing
cause nobody got nothing to say.

Words flatline.

That bullet killed us both. It changed
everything around me and confiscated
the life I'd known – my home, my friends,
my love, my God.

I use to be someone really.

(K. Neycha Herford 2004)

Kimberley's 34-year-old partner was shot in the head by men who robbed him. This extract from Kimberley's poem reveals the intensity of the burden of survival in which every day there is the attempt to make sense of what has happened. It takes courage 'to carve out for ourselves the space we each believe we need to assimilate and integrate our different losses into our lives in ways that matter to us' (Herford 2004: 6). The phrase 'Words flatline' evokes the image of the heart monitor that goes from waves that tell us the person is living to the flat line that tell us he is dead.

The fact that the death was random, avoidable or intentional brings fury as well as disbelief for the family, friends, colleagues and community of the deceased (Riches and Dawson 1998). Very often there is secondary trauma as those left to grieve deal with the police, press, criminal justice system and the onlookers who watch the reactions of their neighbours as they move through the notoriety, embarrassment and shame experienced by some people who are the other victims of traumatic death (Conrad 1998). Doreen Lawrence, whose son was stabbed to death in London, wrote of her experience in *And Still I Rise* (2006). In it she charts the anguish, and emptiness caused by his murder, but also the intricacies of failed bureaucracy, police mismanagement and racism which dogged the investigation. This fuelled her campaign for changes in the law and 'Justice for Stephen'. In the aftermath of her son's death, her marriage broke down, as it does for many couples who are subject to such traumatic loss (Riches and Dawson 1998; Rosenblatt 2000b; Schwab 1992; Victim Support 2006).

In 1968, Eileen Corrigan's son Brian Howe was murdered by 11-year-old Mary Bell. Subsequently, Eileen suffered enduring grief. Her words reflect what happens to so many who have experienced the trauma of murder to a loved one: 'sometimes now I do feel happy – but it is not the same kind of happiness as I knew before. When your child dies you don't get over it; you survive. The pain doesn't go away, you live with it.' June Richardson's son, Martin Brown, was also the victim of Mary Bell and she explains how she reacted to his loss: 'I used to wait for Martin to come through the door. For months and years after it happened I would wait for him. The shock, you think it can't be happening to you … I've even gone out looking for Martin, night after night. I knew he was gone, yet I thought I could find him' (both quoted in *Observer* 1998: 5). Both women still dreamed of their sons thirty years after their deaths.

Post-traumatic stress reactions following murder or manslaughter

Poussaint (1984) found that grief reactions to death caused by murder are often extreme. Anger, rage and an urge to seek revenge or justice were present in the bereaved, as well as sadness and despair. Anger is usually directed at the murderer and all associated with him or her (Bucholz 2002). The bereaved often felt vulnerable and let down by police and the demeaning criminal justice systems that became involved in their lives (Victim Support 2006). Difficulties are intensified where the murderer is not caught or not brought to justice. In addition a family bereaved by murder generally 'have an uncertain status in that they are not themselves the direct victim, but the victim once removed' (Oldham and Nourse 2006). They suffer too.

Trauma impacts on the body as well as the mind and it is useful to consider this when working with anyone who has suffered a traumatic bereavement. A major contributor to expertise in this area is Bessel van der Kolk, Professor of Psychiatry and Director of the Trauma Centre in Boston. He reports on the way trauma becomes somatised or stored in the body. In his words, 'The body keeps the score' (van der Kolk et al. 1996: 214).

Van der Kolk and colleagues (van der Kolk et al. 1996) use brain scanning equipment to show how the memory of traumatic events influences the brain activity of previously traumatised patient volunteers. Images taken while the patient remembers a traumatic incident show how areas of the right hemisphere of the brain – the parts associated with emotional states and autonomic arousal – are activated. The 'imprint of trauma', he says, is found mainly in the limbic system, the part that interprets what is safe or dangerous in the world. It is also found in the brainstem, whose function is to modulate arousal levels: sleeping, breathing, urinating and chemical balances. At the same time, parts of the frontal lobe that deal with the capacity to plan, to rationalise, to inhibit inappropriate behaviour, and specifically one area associated with speech, are shown to shut down. This work led van der Kolk to conclude that when people relive their traumatic experiences, the frontal lobes become impaired and as a result the person has trouble thinking and speaking. They are no longer able to tell others what is going on. Nor, he argues, are they capable of imagining how things could change so they become locked in a rigid cycle of remembering but being unable to find a way out of their psychological distress.

A bereaved client may feel guilt if they were present at the death, for instance if the death was caused during an attack and the bereaved did not cry out for help or intervene in some way. Margaret Wilkinson advocates greater understanding of how the function of the brain affects our action or inaction, especially in trauma. During a traumatic event 'the hyper-arousal of trauma functionally inactivates the left hemisphere where the speech centre is located' making it impossible to cry out (Wilkinson 2006). Explaining this to the client may alleviate feelings of guilt and inadequacy.

The nature of the person's 'fight or flight response' to threatening situations or memories is also affected (Wilkinson 2006). For example, some people may well resort to freezing, numbing or dissociating as their only options for 'leaving' the distressing event. Dissociation involves the person cutting off from connections to their experiences so they become unable to recall events, or become distant. This is an unconscious process over which the person has no control (Kenney 2002).

Where a person has experienced traumatic loss he may feel unsafe in his body as well as in the wider world (Gilbert 2005). The therapeutic work of van der Kolk and colleagues (1996) have shown that working to regain a sense of well-being involves the person actively reasserting his belief in his body. Van der Kolk believes that the most important thing that all mental health professionals need to know is not how to interpret complex behaviour, but how to help people stay on an even keel because then they are in a physiological condition where they can think and have quiet space which is vital for the recovery process. At the Boston centre he uses yoga and Tai chi to help people remain grounded and embodied and to be still, even when in distress. He says telling the story can help but it's the imprint in the body that he is most concerned about.

Babette Rothschild (2005) has researched extensively into the impact of trauma on the brain and the significance this holds for therapeutic support and interventions. She explains the importance of the client being able to 'put on the brakes' before exploring deeply traumatic experiences in order to prevent re-traumatisation and to avoid the client being flooded with the memory, bodily sensations and emotions of the event. A trauma survivor's primary need in counselling is to feel safe. Many practitioners share the view that recovery from trauma starts when those left behind feel they are in a safe place which is predictable and trustworthy (Herman 1992).

Symptoms of PTSD can include:

* Hypervigilance, which involves scanning the environment for possible sources of threat
* Heightened startle response
* Blunted feelings, emotional numbing
* Flashbacks or intrusive thoughts that cause distress
* Sudden eruptions of anger, rage and aggressive behaviour
* Controlling behaviour towards others
* Poorer memory and the inability to concentrate
* General anxiety
* Depression
* Abuse of alcohol, drugs and other substances
* Dissociation: feeling outside one's body, including dissociative flashbacks
* Insomnia or disturbing nightmares
* Thoughts of suicide
* Survivor guilt

Grief in those who cause death

An area of traumatic loss which is often overlooked is that of the person who has caused a death, for example the driver in a fatal accident (Connor 2005). In many ways their grief is disenfranchised yet knowing they have caused the death of another person is often traumatic and life changing. Kelly Connor, who killed a 77-year-old woman in a road traffic accident states, 'My life wasn't taken from me, but my identity, my future, my past, and in many ways, my family, were lost to me as a consequence of this catastrophic moment in time' (2005: 20). In our work with the bereaved it is important to remember the impact on those who cause deaths as well as those who suffer the dreadful impact of traumatic bereavement.

The families of those who have caused death may also be affected. They may suffer secondary or vicarious trauma, they may be ostracised by their community and experience disenfranchised grief. Cho Seung-hui shot thirty-two people dead at Virgina Tech in the USA before shooting himself. The following day Seung-hui's family apologised for his actions which, they said, 'had made the world weep' (Goldenberg 2007). Their words convey the utter devastation that they experienced. In a statement read by his sister, the family said: 'Our family is so very sorry for my brother's unspeakable actions. It is a terrible tragedy for all of us. We pray for their families and loved ones, who are experiencing so much excruciating grief. And we pray for those who were injured, and for those whose lives are changed forever.' She added, 'We feel hopeless, helpless and lost. This is someone that I grew up with and loved. Now I feel I didn't know this person.' The family had to move to an undisclosed location for their own safety.

The struggle for knowledge – finding meaning

The bereaved want to know why death happened and the circumstances surrounding the death (Jacobs 1999). They need to seek until they have sufficient knowledge or are satisfied with partial knowledge. They need to find a story that describes what has happened and gives some kind of meaning to the event and this is usually done by telling the story to an interested listener, often a counsellor (Caverhill 2002). People need to 're-order their reflexive self narrative to make sense of what is currently happening in their lives' (Giddens 1991; Riches and Dawson 2002: 219).

Death of a child

The death of a child brings a sense of traumatic loss since it is out of the natural order. Children are expected to outlive their parents so when a child dies it has a profound impact on the survivors – parents, grandparents and siblings in particular (McKissock and McKissock 1985). The loss is complicated because it involves the loss of the child, loss of self as a parent, loss of the child's anticipated future and often brings a feeling of annihilation (Dijkstra and Stroebe 1998; Ironstone-Catterall 2004–2005).

For parents the death of a child is unnatural and untimely. Wheeler's study of parents' grief found that they found meaning in connections with others, which often involved helping others with similar experiences, and cognitive mastery of the event (Wheeler 2001). Personal beliefs, values and personal growth all featured during the crisis of finding meaning in their child's death.

'When my daughter was run over and killed, the driver didn't just kill her, he killed the family we'd made. He destroyed our complete family and left us smashed apart.'

(Leah)

Where a child is murdered, killed in an accident or in other tragic circumstances parents often feel they have failed to protect the child. The mother quoted above berated herself because she thought she should have stopped her daughter going out with her friend, even though it was a normal activity. Her 'failure' devastated her and the concurrent crises of the grief in her other children added to her distress.

The poet Rudyard Kipling's only son, John, was killed in the First World War, known as the Great War. After he had received a telegram informing him that his 18-year-old son had been killed in action, a letter arrived from John: 'We marched 18 miles last night in the pouring wet ... This will be my last letter for some time. Well, so long my old dears' (Imperial War Museum 2007–2008). Shortly after he wrote the letter he was shot in the head at the Battle of Loos and though his sergeant pulled him into a shelter, his body was never found. Kipling was devastated and spent the rest of his life looking for his son. In part this was driven by guilt because Kipling had used his connections to get his son a place in the Irish Guards after his son had been rejected because he was so short sighted.

There may be greater social isolation following a violent death because those bereaved by suicide, murder or manslaughter may be seen as contaminated in some way, or because their social group does not know what to say or how to offer support. There is an increased likelihood of isolation within the marital relationship following the death of a child since many marriages break down after such a bereavement (Forte et al. 1996; Riches and Dawson 2000; Rosenblatt 2000b). Intervention in the form of support by a grief worker in a specifically designed programme can prevent long-term mourning difficulties (Murray et al. 2000).

Finding meaning following the death of a child can be harrowing especially if the cause was intentional, due to neglect and/or where the child suffered violence or pain. In a study by Murphy and Johnson (2003) into parents' reactions following bereavement they found that by twelve months post-death only 12 per cent had found meaning in their child's death. Sixty months post-death 57 per cent had found meaning whereas 43 per cent had not. However, parents who had attended bereavement support groups were four times more likely to find meaning than parents who did not attend. Religious beliefs were significant, as those who believed it was 'part of God's plan' experienced some relief in that view. Support groups and religious beliefs were the two most important factors in finding meaning in the child's death. There are implications for bereavement counselling in Murphy and Johnson's work. They state: 'the education of bereavement counselors, health care providers and the general public cannot be overemphasised. Evidence is mounting to suggest that parents do not return to "pre-bereavement states"' (2003: 401).

For some people bereavement inspired a greater appreciation of each day, of friends and family, and brought about a re-ordering of priorities (Braun and Berg 1994; Janoff-Bulman and Franz 1997; Neimeyer 1998).

Suicide

The response to the death of anyone who is close brings intense grief and mourning but the reaction to and emotions arising from death by suicide elicits an intense array of emotions (Wertheimer 1999). It is claimed that for every suicide, on average six people suffer intense grief (Clark and Goldney 2000).

> 'It is impossible to describe the devastation suicide leaves in its wake. There were times in the first few months when I thought my body would explode with the pain of grief. I could hardly believe I was alive, it hurt so much.'
>
> (Wolfy Jones, whose boyfriend died by suicide, Jones 2007: 15)

The fact that the person seemed to have an element of choice raises painful questions which death by natural causes or as a result of accident does not (Jordan 2001). Research indicates that following death by suicide the shock, social isolation and guilt are greater and continue for longer (Dyregrov 2003–2004). Repeated questioning about motives, and self-blame for not preventing the death ring with recriminations against self and the dead person and this response may mask feelings of anger and powerlessness (Kalischuk and Hayes 2003–2004). One person described her reaction:

> I felt like he had committed murder, and in a sense he did. He took the life of the person I loved most. I am furious at what he has done to his life and mine. Then I short-circuit that feeling with self-blame that somehow I could have saved him. If only I had been a better wife; if only I had listened closer and picked up the clues; maybe something I did or said caused him to take his own life. Then I feel his agony. I realize how much he must have been suffering to decide this was his only option.
>
> (Jordan 2003: 2)

Having suicidal thoughts is not uncommon and the bereaved may need to be assured that this does not mean they will act on those thoughts. Bowlby (1980) highlights the frequency of death by suicide, and other violent deaths of young adults, following the sudden death of someone close. Obviously, as counsellor, befriender or grief worker, you need to check out how significant, repeated or serious these thoughts are and to discover what support is available in the bereaved person's life. You may have to help identify who and what these supports are and ascertain whether or not they are being used.

Like other sudden, unanticipated loss, those bereaved by suicide have no time to say Goodbye and no time to make preparations for the loss. Suicide, or death by other unexpected causes, draws attention from the media, which may further distress relatives and friends. After a suicide, despair and fear abide. If a loved one kills himself, especially if this comes 'out of the blue', it undermines personal security. If he did that, can I?

Should I? Contemplation of one's own suicide is not uncommon in the aftermath of the suicide of a loved one (Wertheimer 2001). Some people bereaved by suicide feel abandoned and rejected by the deceased. Harry's close friend took his own life. Harry said, 'How could he do this to me? He was my best friend. Why didn't he talk to me?' Initially he felt intense shock as well as disbelief.

Jon and Sue Stebbins, whose only son died by suicide, have been running support groups for suicide-bereaved parents and have devised a system of working with groups (Stebbins and Stebbins 1999). 'Consistently, we have found that allowing the bereaved to tell their stories, and listening actively and empathically, without judgement, eventually helps them to regain autonomous control over their shattered lives' (1999: 52). They have found that the groups work best when the same simple format is followed each time. The newly bereaved speak first, and those who have been attending for longer periods speak later. The latter can be a source of hope for recovery for those struggling in the aftermath of suicide: 'In this context, the helper's task is to establish an atmosphere of care and support, to focus on listening to and clarifying stories. Change and re-growth will then take care of itself' (1999: 55).

Dyregrov et al. 'found no evidence proving that suicide survivors have greater difficulties in adapting to the loss compared with survivors of SIDS or accidents' (2003: 155). In fact, there was some evidence to suggest that those bereaved by accident might experience greater shock than suicide survivors. Where there has been a history of depression, poor mental health or suicidal ideation the shock may be reduced, whereas the impact of the loss of a child suddenly and in traumatic circumstances has a devastating, long-lasting impact (Janoff-Bulman and Berge 1998; Lehman et al. 1987; Vance et al. 1993; Yule 1999).

Recurring images of the death may preoccupy those bereaved by suicide as they search for the reasons for the death, to find meaning in what has happened and an answer to the recurrent question 'Why?'. Different members of the family or friendship group may have conflicting answers, which may lead to recriminations and painful verbal exchanges. Blame may be apportioned, causing deeper guilt and devastation as one member of the family accuses another of being partly to blame for the suicide. Research suggests that someone bereaved through suicide tends to experience greater self-blame, feelings of guilt and more self-questioning (Redfield Jamieson 2002).

Non fatal suicidal acts

Not all determined suicide attempts end in death. The person who survives is faced with both her own feelings, perhaps of failure or relief, but also with the reactions of those closest to her. They have the same reactions as others faced with a death by suicide, but they have the chance to ask the person who has survived why she tried to take her life. They can express their shock and pain. Anyone affected by a non-fatal suicide will struggle to come to terms with what has happened and relationships may be severely affected, particularly if there were no early indicators that suicide was being contemplated. As one very successful professional woman told me, 'I'd just had enough. I couldn't see any way to change my life then when I realised I could kill myself I was euphoric and so calm. But,' she went on, ' I couldn't even get that right. I failed again.' Outwardly, she looked as if her life was perfect: happy marriage, highly paid job, lots of friends and everything to live for. Her serious suicide attempt shocked her friends and family and the reverberations impacted on her relationships. A non-fatal suicide attempt has lasting repercussions (Hinton 1967; Jenkins and Merry 2005).

A non-fatal suicide attempt may leave the person who attempted suicide with lifelong disability or severely impaired health. This may be a complicating factor for both that person and her family and friends. Whilst many people bereaved by suicide feel they have been rejected by the deceased, those who live with a person who has survived their suicidal act may feel both rejected and burdened by the changes in their lives.

The response to non-fatal suicide acts is influenced by the perceived cause of the suicidal act (Dahlen and Canetto 2002). Where the precipitating factor is physical illness or a disabling condition, this is viewed less critically than relationship difficulty or achievement-related issues. There is also a gender issue: men are more likely to agree that people have the right to kill themselves (Marks 1988–89; Wellman and Wellman 1986).

Al Alvarez (1972) in *The Savage God* comments on a study by two psychiatrists in New York who identified a common element in the lives of those who had attempted suicide; Ninety-five per cent of the fifty had experienced the death or loss, in tragic circumstances, of significant individuals, usually parents or siblings, before the patients had finished adolescence. They named this pattern 'the death trend' (Carswell 2003).

Helping those bereaved by suicide

What can you do to help the person bereaved by suicide? It is crucial that the bereaved have the opportunity to vent feelings, particularly those that may be masked because they are considered to be illicit in some way. Suicide in a family puts others at greater risk (Jordan 2001) and the bereaved may experience thoughts of taking their own life as a way of avoiding their pain. They may experience stigma and be involved in lengthy police investigations or coroner's investigations, all of which impact on the process of mourning (Hawton and Simkin 2003).

We can help by encouraging survivors to remember the things they did to help the deceased as well as listening to feelings of guilt and abandonment. In the search to find the reason for the suicidal act, the good is often overlooked.

A Canadian study (Rogers et al. 1982) of people bereaved by suicide indicated that they needed help and support to:

- Get the suicide into perspective;
- Deal with family difficulties following suicide;
- Feel better about themselves;
- Talk about the suicide, especially since shame and stigma are associated with it;
- Obtain information about suicide and its effects;
- Have a safe place to vent and explore their feelings;
- Understand and deal with other people's reactions;
- Get advice on practical and social concerns.

Some people who are bereaved by suicide find help through talking with others who have been similarly bereaved. Some take up social advocacy or social action as a means of managing grief and continuing to hold bonds with the deceased, for example setting up self-help groups, campaigning groups and so on.

Families after traumatic loss – what helps?

Figley et al. (1997) identified a number of strategies to support the positive functioning of families following loss. These include:

- Moving away from blaming to a solution-focused approach;
- Tolerating other members of the family and recognising the need to grieve in different ways;
- Maintaining clear communication between family members;
- Showing caring and commitment in an overt way;
- Reinforcing strong family cohesion;
- Building and accepting flexibility in roles and functions within the family unit;
- Making full use of any resources within and outside the family;
- Avoiding the use of drugs;
- Not pressurising or bullying members of the family psychologically, emotionally or physically;
- Maintaining sensitivity to others' needs;

Whilst these strategies may be very helpful, there are some grievers who do not want to or cannot fit into the family grieving 'model'. They may want to grieve alone or express their feelings in a way that is unacceptable to the family.

As Kathleen Gilbert says, 'Families do not grieve. Only individuals grieve. This is done in a variety of contexts, one of which is the family' (1996: 273).

Reflective exercises

Case Study: 'Rebecca'

Rebecca's nine-year-old son died in a traffic accident when he was out with his twelve-year-old sister. Three years later Rebecca continues to talk about her guilt because she feels she should have kept them in the house, eventhough it was usual for them to go out together. Rebecca has low moods, and dislikes going out in her neighbourhood because everyone knows her and she feels judged by neighbours: 'They think I should be over it but to me it's like it happened yesterday.' She has problems sleeping and hints that she blames her daughter for her son's death because 'She could have taken greater care.'

- What role does guilt play in Rebecca's bereavement?
- How does the wider society feature in the grieving process?
- How might you help Rebecca address her losses? Where would you start?
- How could you help Rebecca to care for and mother the child she still has?

Rebecca's son died in traumatic circumstances. Her relationship with her daughter changed. She lost her own definition of herself as a 'good' mother. She lost relationships with her neighbours and the wider community. She lost the complete family that she had always wanted as one child was taken away by death and the other had witnessed the death of her brother. The event brutally destroyed the previous unity of the family.

Loss and transition

This exercise is designed to enable you to put yourself in the place of a person who has been forced to leave his country. Because of disaster, war, civil conflict, religious or political persecution he has had to flee. He becomes a refugee or asylum seeker if there is no safe person in his homeland who can take him in and shield him.

Imagine you are such a person. What losses might you experience? If you are someone to whom this has happened please list the losses you have experienced.

Losses may include:

- Death of family, friends, members of your community
- Separation from family, friends and members of your community
- Uncertainty about the fate of family, friends and community
- Loss of members of the family who are missing
- Loss of home
- Loss of language and cultural roots, cultural bereavement
- Loss of possessions

- Loss of social and economic status
- Loss of beliefs
- Loss of traditional activities and procedures of the home country
- Loss of personal identity
- Loss of stability and certainties
- Loss of professional qualifications and position
- Loss of hope
- Loss of ancestral connections
- Loss of certainty
- Loss of employment

> Transition is moving from a familiar place, where we know how things are done, what to do and what to say, where we take certain things for granted to a place where everything is suddenly different and strange and where we have no language. To be in transition is to occupy a limbo stage ... half in one world and half in another, not fully in one or the other.

(Boyles 2004)

In Memoriam

People choose to remember the dead in different ways. Immortality may be gained by leaving a legacy, as it was for William Wordsworth in his poem 'Intimations of Immortality' which celebrates the joy of the natural world:

> To me the meanest flower that blows can give
> Thoughts that do often lie too deep for tears.

If a person believes in an afterlife then this indicates a belief in immortality. What do you think?

Do you think there are ways in which we could be said to be immortal?

What legacy would you like to leave to those you care for?

Orpheus and the Underworld

This exercise, 'The Orpheus Exercise', was devised by existentialist psychologist James Bugenthal. Orpheus, in the Greek myth, was so devastated by the death of his wife Eurydice, that the dark powers were persuaded to let him go into Hades to sing for her release. They imposed one condition, which was that he did not look back to see her until they had both ascended to earth. At the last moment, he could not resist looking back and he lost her for ever.

The story of Orpheus symbolises the inability to accept loss which necessitates leaving the past behind and looking forward. I'm not sure that this fits in with the model of Continuing Bonds (see p. 10), but it demonstrates the importance of having some investment in the future.

Think of some important aspects of your life, your roles or your relation-ships. Make a list of those most important to you:

Parent
Sexual partner
Role at work
Friend
Cook
Gym member

Now, imagine you can no longer fulfil those roles. For example, you can no longer continue your work because of illness. Do you still value yourself if you are no longer in that role? Who can you be if you are no longer in that role?

Imagine you can no longer express your sexuality or that you can no longer have a fulfilling sexual relationship. Does that impact on your sense of self-worth? Consider how you could adapt to these changing roles.

In reflecting on these imagined changes can you see how you still have a valuable existence even without these defining roles? Are you more than the sum of your roles? Can you change the way in which you view your-self? Seeing yourself letting go of certain roles may allow you to see how you could invest in other areas of life.

In working with those who are bereaved or facing their own death, there is the possibility of seeing who they are as being more than the roles they have fulfilled in the past. This reassessment is an important aspect of adjustment in the grieving process.

As you imagine giving up these roles you may feel the pain of losing that part of yourself but you may also realise that a deeper part of you remains. You are more than the sum of what you do. Try to get in touch with the part of you that 'is' rather than the part that 'does'.

5

'She should be over it by now': Complicated Grief

People are much greater and much stronger than we imagine, and when unexpected tragedy comes ... we see them often grow to a stature that is far beyond anything we imagined. We must remember that people are capable of greatness, of courage, but not in isolation ... They need the conditions of a solidly linked human unit in which everyone is prepared to bear the burden of others.

(Archbishop Anthony Bloom 1969)

This chapter considers the aspects of grief under the umbrella term of complicated grief, which has also been termed difficult or abnormal grief (Raphael and Minkov 1999). As stated earlier, grief is a normal human response to a death or loss of someone we care about (Currer 2001). It is not pathological to experience the pain of loss; however, in some instances a person may become 'stuck' in their grief. The intensity of the grieving does not abate and the person has trouble functioning normally (Prigerson 2004; Walsh-Burke 2005). A classic example of morbid or 'pathological grief' is that of Queen Victoria, whose husband Prince Albert died of typhoid after a short illness. She secluded herself from the public, insisted that the court should be sombre, wore black mourning clothes until her own death and continued to idealise her dead husband.

Complicated grief is delayed or incomplete adaptation to the loss and the failure, over time, to return to pre-loss levels of functioning (Payne et al. 1999). Complicated grief is established over several months and is distinguished from other grief mostly by its relentless continuation and the disruption it causes to the everyday life of the bereaved. Previously healthy relationships may become troubled and work or studies affected. The bereaved may be preoccupied with thoughts of the dead person and constantly refer to the deceased. Those who are 'stuck' in the grieving process may be totally unaware of their behaviour or, if they are aware, feel powerless to change (Kushner 1982). Often a doctor, family member or friend may suggest that the bereaved seek counselling.

Complicated mourning was described by Rando (1993), who looked at the factors underlying its development. The Harvard Bereavement Project was a longitudinal study of widows and widowers who were followed for four years to discover why some people did well while others fared badly following loss (Parkes and Weiss 1983). It identified a number of risk factors which indicated the development of later problems. The first significant area was the mode of death: where it was sudden, violent or horrific and the bereaved was unprepared, there was increased propensity to complicated grief; as there was where the bereaved felt responsible for the death or viewed others as being culpable or where there were multiple losses.

The risk of complicated grief is increased where there is no body to bury or mourn, for instance where someone is missing but presumed dead (Glassock 2006). Complicated grief may occur where it is an unmentionable death such as a death that is caused by sexual misadventure or is drug related. Disenfranchised grief, which we will consider in detail later in this chapter, is another underlying factor influential in complicated grief.

The personal characteristics of the bereaved also play a part. As Mander states, 'Serious complications are certain to arise when there was a high degree of psychic ambivalence, unresolved hostility and unfinished business in the relationship with the dead' (2005: 42). In a dependent relationship in which the bereaved was dependent on the deceased, or vice versa, or where there was an ambivalent relationship, complicated grief was more likely to occur. Mander found that people with poor self-esteem or who lacked trust in others and those with a history of psychological vulnerability were more likely to develop complicated grief, as were those who lacked social support, felt isolated or had a family network that was absent or inflexible (Riches and Dawson 2000). Social isolation or exclusion was found to be a major factor in unresolved mourning. 'Isolation is the best predictor of psychosocial distress' (Dyregrov 2003–2004: 157). When working with those who have been bereaved it is helpful to establish if they feel isolated or excluded.

Key features of complicated grief

In a randomised control trial on the treatment of complicated grief Shear found the following characteristics of those who had been bereaved (Shear et al. 2005):

- A sense of disbelief about the death;
- Anger and bitterness about the death;

- Recurrent waves of painful emotions, intense yearning and longing for the deceased;
- Preoccupation with thoughts of the deceased and intrusive thoughts concerning the death;
- Absent grief or severely inhibited grief;
- Disturbed sleep pattern, persistent inability to sleep through the night;
- Inability to regain former competence, e.g. at work or in studies;
- Uncharacteristic behaviour such as increased risk-taking and self-destructive acts;
- Lack of social contact with friends, or impaired relationships;
- Drug abuse;
- Inability to talk about the person who has died or the death; or the opposite – focusing on the death to the exclusion of everything else.

Who is at risk of complicated grief?

People who have had difficulties in early attachments seem to be particularly vulnerable to complicated grief (Ribbens, McCarthy 2005; Neimeyer et al. 2002). People who have experienced early loss or loss for which they were not allowed to grieve may suffer emotional and physical effects which carry on into adulthood (Elliott 1999). Charles Darwin's mother died when he was a child but his father and sisters never spoke of her after her death. His feelings were suppressed and it is thought that his poor health as an adult was a psychosomatic manifestation of those buried feelings. As van der Kolk says, 'The body keeps the score' (van der Kolk et al. 1996: 214).

Following traumatic bereavement as described in Chapter 4, we may find that grief never completely goes away; rather it becomes woven into the life tapestry that is the bereaved person. It continues as a sound that echoes through their days, a 'white noise' whose volume increases as memories are triggered, anniversaries are passed: even in sleep, the noise continues in dreams and nightmares (Mallon 2005).

The sudden traumatic death by murder, manslaughter or accident, coming 'out of the blue' can rock the foundation of the bereaved person's world and complicate grief. Zisook, Chentsova-Dutton and Schuchter (1998) compared people whose spouses died of natural causes to others whose spouses had died as a result of suicide or accident. Those whose spouses had died as a result of accident or suicide had significantly more symptoms of post-traumatic stress disorder (PTSD). At 12 months the survivors of bereavement from suicide had more symptoms of psychological distress.

Some people withdraw because their assumptive world has been shattered. Their scale of values may be turned upside down so that other people's problems seem trivial in comparison to their own. They may withdraw from social contacts rather than say anything or become involved in speaking about their feelings. Frightening, intrusive images, memory impairment and lack of concentration also make social interaction problematic and the bereaved may become alienated from their social network (Gilbert and Smart 1992; Jordan et al. 1993). As one parent whose child had died said to me, 'I feel awful, but I don't want to hear about their bloody holiday plans with their kids. I can't go away with all my family now that one of them's gone. I just want to yell at them but I can't do that. It's not fair so it's better if I just keep out of the way.' She would go shopping in the evening so that she wouldn't bump into any neighbours and, where possible, she avoided all social situations.

In holding continuing bonds some bereaved people may find that they are speaking aloud to the deceased, or speak to them in their thoughts. Parents of dead children may find themselves continuing to refer to them in the present tense even though many years have passed since their child's death (Rosenblatt 2000a). This ongoing conversation often brings comfort and support (Dunn et al. 2005).

People with poor mental health, those living in dysfunctional families or in abusive relationships have greater risk of experiencing complicated grief (Raphael and Minkov 1999). This also applies when the death happened in an unfamiliar place where the bereaved felt isolated, for instance a sudden death on holiday. The bereaved may have had no immediate support, with the added difficulties of a foreign language, unknown procedures and customs. The situation may be exacerbated by anxiety about whether to leave the body there or bring it home, thus increasing the strain on the bereaved. As Lisa's experience confirms:

'My mother died earlier this year. It was a shock as she had been in remission from cancer for three years. One of the most sad things was that she died abroad. She was on holiday with my Dad and it took over a week to get her body back into the country, and it was hard for my Dad being there on his own and hard for me having to tell everyone and sort things out as I was also seven months pregnant.'

Complicated grief may have a number of causes, single or multiple. These may be to do with the nature of the relationship with the deceased: for example if there had been an unresolved conflict between parent and adult child, the bereaved may feel robbed of the opportunity to make the relationship whole once more. He may feel guilty that he did not have the opportunity to say sorry or goodbye. Guilt may inhibit his grieving to the extent that he can't focus on other aspects of his life.

Complicated grief and the death of a child

Gorer (1965) was one of the first to point out that the death of a grown-up child was one of the most severe losses and led to long-lasting grief. As Klass (1988) noted, there is a special meaning in parental loss 'The goal of grief, then, is not severing the bond with the child, but integrating the child into the parent's life and social networks in a new way.' (Klass 2000: 4).

Kay Talbot, an American psychotherapist, reiterates this view in saying that rather than breaking the bond with the dead child, the bereaved parents should be helped to reframe their role as that of the child's biographer and build a new relationship with their dead child's spirit (Talbot 2002).

Bereaved parents want to know if their grief is normal (Bissler 2005; Rando 1986). They want recognition that their planned future has been shattered and, as seen earlier, they want to keep the bond with their child. Bissler's research showed that 'bereaved parents felt creating a continuing bond with their deceased child was the most helpful aspect of assimilating the loss' (2002: 5). When a child dies the parents are left with a space in which their legacy would have continued in the world, which Erikson described as 'Generativity strivings' (Erikson 1963) When this does not happen, the family may grieve long after others think 'they should be over it by now' (Potts 2005). Genevieve Jurgensen's moving story of her attempts to manage after the death of her two daughters in a car accident, and how she fought to keep their memory alive, encompasses the devastation bereaved parents feel and the possibility of a gradual re-emergence into the world (Jurgensen 1999).

In essence, the parents of a dead child will always be parents: 'death does not cancel parent status' (Rosenblatt 2000a: 35). For parents who believe in life after death, physical death does not terminate the spiritual existence of their child (Bennett and Bennett 2000; Walter 2006).

Death is not the only cause of disenfranchised grief, as we have seen. It is also caused by loss through injury. If a child, sibling or parent suffers severe injury, such as head injury following an accident, there is grave loss. The person may lose normal body functioning or personality or character traits that were there prior to the accident. Carers may experience ongoing grief. They may feel conflict and ambivalence: 'He could have died so I should be grateful he's still here.' Another part grieves for the person who has gone for ever yet who is still physically present.

Other maladaptive or unresolved grief reactions

Maladaptive grief reactions include 'suppression, repression, denial, inhibition, prolonged or extreme grief reactions, mourning, depression or mania' (Miller and McGown 1997: 156).

Absent or **inhibited grief** is where grief does not appear at all (Deutsch 1937). The bereaved continue as if nothing has happened. There are no obvious signs of mourning. The bereaved may look stiff and be unable to speak about the death or their feelings. However, some people do not wish to display their grief and may grieve when they are alone, and in some cultures it is not the norm to grieve openly.

Exaggerated grief is disabling and can worsen over time. It may include clinical depression, anxiety, mania or post-traumatic stress disorder (Worden 1991).

In **delayed grief** the grief may be postponed, inhibited or suppressed. It is characterised by a rapid return to normal activities such as going to work and an avoidance of reminders of the death. A later loss may trigger a reaction out of proportion as the first loss is reactivated.

Distorted grief may be seen as an intense reaction, in anger or hatred for example, against others whose loved partner or child is still alive. Where it persists it may wreck relationships with others who cannot cope with the destructive behaviour and attitude towards them. This may show itself in punishment of others, as in the case of a woman who blames her mother-in-law for the death of her husband and punishes her by preventing her from seeing her grandchildren (Paul 2006). Sometimes the bereaved punish themselves by stopping activities that previously gave them pleasure.

Disenfranchised loss

'Disenfranchised loss' is a term that was introduced in 1989 by Kenneth Doka, Professor of Gerontology at the College of New Rochelle, New York and senior consultant to the Hospice Foundation of America. He defined it as the grief that people feel from a loss that is not, or cannot be, openly acknowledged, publicly mourned or expressed in the social setting of the bereaved. He describes those grieving as being outside the 'grieving rules' that attempt to specify who, when, where, how and how long, and for whom people should grieve (Doka 1989). The relationship is not recognised, the loss is not recognised and the griever is not recognised, thus the griever is marginalised and stigmatised. The circumstances of the death may also disenfranchise the grievers. Often this means that they are cut off from the social support network that is so important in the mourning process.

Disenfranchised grief is complex since it has social, psychological, spiritual, physical and interpersonal implications (Doka, 2002a). The rules or patterns of grieving are affected by the social or cultural milieu in which it occurs, which shapes the experience of loss and the process of mourning (Walter 1999). Losses which are not socially sanctioned leave the bereaved isolated. Where the griever is not socially recognised, for instance if they are perceived as too young, too old, mentally disabled or defined as being incapable of grief, then their response to loss frequently goes unrecognised or is ignored. Similarly, someone who has had an acrimonious relationship with the deceased may be seen as having no 'right' to sadness yet may still grieve for the part of the relationship that was significant. Non-finite loss occurs for parents of a developmentally disabled child who grieve as their child fails to reach milestones. Other people often fail to recognise the pain felt by such parents who do not speak of their losses.

Disenfranchised grief may be found in birth mothers whose child is given up for adoption, particularly where society 'blames' the mother for behaviour which is deemed socially unacceptable. She has no 'right' to mourn. Grieving is complicated by the fact that the baby is still alive somewhere though the birth mother has no knowledge of where that place is so there is not the same finality that comes with a death. In addition there are no rituals to mark the ending, no flowers, no cards, or expressions of sympathy. This may give rise to feelings of loneliness and abandonment. There is often a sense of ambiguity in disenfranchised grief. Those who judge the mother who gives her baby up for adoption may think she should be grateful that someone else has taken her baby on. The infertile mother may be told to adopt a baby without legitimising her feelings of loss and parents who have experienced miscarriage or still-birth may find their loss is not regarded as a 'proper' bereavement (Jenkins and Merry 2005; Lovell 2001).

'We describe Kiera coming into the world asleep – I don't like the term stillbirth.'

(A woman who had six miscarriages)

After miscarriage many women feel guilty, worrying about the fact that maybe they shouldn't have gone shopping or to the gym or that it is some form of pun-ishment. A sense of failure can linger long after the miscarriage (Pierce 2003).

'When the five month routine scan showed my baby was dead, the room took a sick lurch. It was two days before I could return to the hospital to 'complete' the mis-carriage ... I couldn't bear to be seen in public with my pregnancy bump, feeling a fraud because my baby was dead, and fearing casual conversations with strangers.'

(Sarah Anderson 2006: 12)

It is the personal significance of the loss which is important not the gestational age of the baby (Pierce 2003).

Attention has also been directed at the disenfranchised grief of the donor-conceived adult (Rose 2001). These adults may grieve as a result of their separation from biological relatives. Joanna Rose writes of her per-sonal experience. With her brother she was seeking 'the examination of international human rights standards in light of our request to access infor-mation concerning our identities, medical histories, ethnicity, information regarding ourselves which is linked inseparably to our biological fathers' (Rose 2001: 1). She describes the loss donor-conceived people feel in regard to blood relatives, and the need to become whole by making a reconnec-tion. The validation of such grief may help resolve some of the complicated grief issues involved.

Disenfranchised grief and abortion

Abortion is not a single, physical act. It involves not only the termination, but the conception, the reasons for the decision to terminate as well as feelings following the event. Underneath 'it's over and done with' may be a range of emotions which have not been dealt with. Post-abortion counselling works with the ambivalent feelings that many women have about termination and, as with any grief work, includes working with sadness, guilt, anger and, in many instances, shame about the event and the woman's shame about her inability to cope post-termination. Many women feel they have no right to grieve if they elected to have an abortion, which may lead to complicated grief that is unresolved for years after the abortion took place (Caleb 1998).

Ways to mark the end of the pregnancy are many. One couple, who reluctantly decided that a termination was their only option, planted a tree in a favoured spot and held a private ceremony of remembrance for the unborn baby. Jaspers (1954) calls abortion 'an ultimate situation': it shakes our everyday situation and may cause us to re-evaluate our lives and the way we live. In addressing, in counselling, the disenfranchised grief that is involved we may assist in that process of reappraisal.

Imprisonment and disenfranchised grief

The person whose partner, father, son, brother or sister has been given life imprisonment – or in America and other countries the death penalty – is frequently given little sympathy (King and Norgard 1999). Their shame prevents the seeking of support from others, particularly where the inmate is portrayed as some kind of monster (Jones 2005). Their grief is both disenfranchised and non-finite: they do not know how long the person will be incarcerated or when he will die. The use of victim impact statements may set up a 'hierarchy of victims' in which the family of the perpetrator have no opportunity to express the impact of their loss (King and Norgard 1999).

'You know the judge ordered my son to death, but he actually sentenced me to death.'

(Mother of man given the death sentence, USA, in Jones 2005)

Death which takes place in prison brings its own trauma (Jerrom 2004).

Disenfranchised grief causes great distress to the bereaved. It may occur where same-sex couples have kept their relationship secret from family and/or friends and the bereaved partner is not invited to the funeral or included in any customary rituals following death. It may occur where a married person is having a clandestine relationship or where an ex-partner is assumed not to care about the person with whom she has spent many years. Sometimes there is the assumption that parting means no longer having a history of a shared life or many deep experiences about which ex-partners grieve. The marital relationship may have ended but the memories do not. In addition, where children were born in the marriage the bonds between the parents are not automatically severed at death.

Non-finite loss

Non-finite loss refers to situations in which losses are manifested over time and are continuous. There is no opportunity for the individual to recover from the loss since it remains ongoing, she is unable to leave her known world and the future world is bleak, as is the case with prison inmates. Non-finite loss involves loss of one's hopes and ideals; it follows a major loss and is continuous, and what was expected for the future of the loved one cannot be realised. The mother who rang the London police following the 7 July 2005 bombings in London, to say her son was missing, later found out not only that her son was dead, but that he was one of the bombers. Her loss was unlikely to be met with sympathy yet she was a traumatically bereaved mother with other children whose loss was also disenfranchised. Where stigma is attached to the loss, disenfranchised grief is more likely to occur and such devastating events leave a terrible legacy for those involved.

A central task in counselling someone who has experienced disenfranchised grief is to validate the loss. Van der Wal's (1989) work with family members in mourning following a suicide emphasises three basic tasks that are essential in the grieving process. He described the first as recognition of the loss, mourning the loss and detaching from it. The second task for the bereaved is to maintain a supportive social network. The third basic task is to maintain a satisfactory self-image while being able to reinvest in future attachments.

Ambiguous loss

Ambiguous loss comes in many forms and may lead to disenfranchised grief. It is loss which lacks clarity and which may cause some to question whether a loss has actually taken place. It includes:

- Infertility
- Adoption
- Perinatal death, miscarriage, stillbirth
- Termination of pregnancy
- Adoptive parents whose child wishes to discover the identity of the birth parent(s)
- Death of a pet

- Suicide
- Alzheimer's Disease
- AIDS, HIV
- Death of an ex-lover or spouse
- Stroke victims who are still alive though dramatically altered
- Mental illness
- Having a child with mental or physical impairment

The theory of continuing bonds is important in this aspect of grieving, as is Pauline Boss' idea of 'ambiguous loss' (Boss 1999). The ambiguous loss model demonstrates how family boundaries are disrupted by the unfinished business of some losses, for example where someone in the family is psychologically or neurologically absent, as in dementia, or where someone is missing, presumed dead (Killick 1996; Meuser and Marwit 2001). There is no finality and those closely associated to the person are not sure how to act or what to do. In the counselling role we have to help the client live with the inherent stress of their situation and tolerate the ambiguity (Boss 2006).

Infertility is much commoner than many people realise. One in six couples worldwide seeks assistance to conceive and 80 per cent of couples undergoing fertility treatment are currently unsuccessful. Infertility can provoke a major life crisis (Burns and Convington 1999). As well as affecting marital and sexual relationships, it undermines each person's sense of power, personal and sexual. The grieving involved is often disenfranchised as people feel disinclined to speak of it (Henderson 2008). Men and women react differently to infertility (Perkins 2006). Women tend to feel isolated, that their femininity is threatened, that their body has failed them, which in turn has a detrimental effect on their self-esteem. Men often feel marginalised in the infertility treatment programme and it may threaten their sense of masculinity (Gannon et al. 2004). Involved in infertility loss is the anticipated future as a parent, loss of status within the wider family and society and loss of stake in the future that will live on after the death of the infertile person (Monach 2006). Depression is often observed in the involuntary childless and is linked to the grief of being a failure as well as to the aspects already covered (Domar et al. 1992; Hunt and Monarch 1997).

Grief and the missing person

'The not knowing is the very, very hardest thing, it really is.'

(Mother of a missing child)

The tsunami of 2004, the bombings in England in 2005, the attack in New York on 9/11, like so many other man-made and natural disasters, left many people grieving with no body to bury. In other situations a family member suddenly disappears, leaving no note or indication of their whereabouts; a son does not come home after a night out, a mother does not come back after work or a friend leaves his flat and disappears into thin air (Franks 1990).

Are they missing because they wanted to start a new life? Have they been killed or abducted? After a time the missing persons are presumed dead, yet for those left behind there is a lurking doubt that the person may not have died. There is the hope that the missing person will once more walk back into their ordinary life. Hope may be the lifeline that allows existence to continue (Larsen et al. 2007).

> One of the strongest predictors of getting better after a disaster was hope.
>
> (Raphael 2005)

Since the tsunami in 2004 people from fifty-two countries have been left wondering about a loved one who has not returned or has not been traced (Glassock 2006). Most missing people do return home but for tracing agencies, which deal with named people who are reported missing, the return rate is much lower. Families of missing people often feel disenfranchised as if, with no body to mourn, they cannot complete the rituals that mark death. They move between despair and hope, they search places the missing person used to frequent and mistake others for the one who is no longer there.

Chronic sorrow

> Death mingles and fuses with our life throughout.
>
> (Michel de Montaigne 1533–92)

The concept of chronic sorrow was introduced in the early 1960s by Simon Olshansky (1962). He worked as a counsellor with children and young people with 'mental retardation', now termed developmental delay or impairment, and was aware of the pervasive sorrow experienced by parents who lived day by day with their ongoing loss. Later Susan Roos (2002) developed the concepts of 'self-loss' and 'other loss'. She describes it thus:

> A set of pervasive, profound, continuing and recurring grief responses resulting from a significant loss or absence of crucial aspects of oneself (self-loss) or another living person (other-loss) to whom there is deep attachment … The essence of chronic sorrow is a painful discrepancy between what is perceived as reality and what continues to be dreamed of. The loss is ongoing since the source of the loss continues to be present. The loss is a living loss.
>
> (2002: 29)

Chronic sorrow is often present in elderly people who have lost a spouse and who may still be profoundly distressed many years after the death

(Doka 2002b). Frequently they wish that their life was over too, though they are rarely suicidal; instead the bereaved may withdraw from social events and display lack of self-care. They may stop eating or eat very little. Chronic grief 'follows the termination of a relationship characterised as highly dependent or clinging' (Stroebe et al. 1993: 34) and is more common than delayed grief (Anderson 1949).

This ongoing loss serves as a daily reminder of what is missing: the child whose mental age will never progress beyond that of a three-year-old, the husband who no longer remembers the time prior to his accident. Some parents of children with developmental disability will never get over their sorrow though they love their child dearly. Other significant predictors of chronic sorrow are having no other children, having little education, not working outside the home, and being a woman. Surviving children act as a protective influence on the bereaved (Dyregrov and Dyregrov 1999).

One helpful way to break out of this isolation, parents found, was to tell their social network how they wanted to be supported in their grief. They often express relief at being 'allowed' to be sad rather than being defined as neurotic and so their grief is granted some 'normality' as Teel found (1991).

In chronic loss those who grieve may be faced with years of crisis and adaptations, whether related to ongoing medical crises or where a family member is missing, killed in a car accident or murdered. Support – emotional, financial and social – is needed in any of these cases as the person struggles with chronic sorrow.

Sudden Infant Death (SID)

The impact of Sudden Infant Death is profound (London Foundation for the Study of Infant Death 2001). For the parents and family, the death is unexpected and often unexplained. It gives no time for preparation and no period of anticipatory grief. Often the parents of a child who dies suddenly may be young and it is their first experience of death; this is intensified if they have discovered the dead baby. The loss becomes even more problematic if the police have to investigate the cause of death and take away clothing, bedding and other items to assure themselves that no intentional harm has taken place. Jen, whose young son died in the emergency room in Accident and Emergency, said, 'When I got back from the hospital, I couldn't believe that there was a policeman in my house and Ian's cot had been stripped and his pyjamas taken away. What did they think I'd done? I'd told the doctor that afternoon that he was ill but he just told me to give him Calpol. They thought I'd murdered my own son, it couldn't make things worse but I wanted to scream, "Don't you have a heart?"'

Parents of a child whose has died suddenly are plagued with doubts and 'if onlys' – 'If only I had checked him sooner', 'If only I hadn't put him for a nap when I did'. They need facts as well as emotional support. The results of the autopsy may give reliable information that reassures parents that there was nothing they could have done to prevent the death. The pathologist who performed the autopsy will answer their questions, and this may clarify the cause of death (Valdes-Dapena 1995).

In conclusion, complicated grief may occur because of the nature of the loss, the personality and previous life experiences of the bereaved and the response of the social network in which they live. In working with complicated grief we need to take all these factors into account as we sensitively try to unravel the threads that tie the bereaved to their continued distress and to assist them to find ways to release their pain.

Reflective exercises

A newly born baby

Take a few minutes to think about how you would feel if you were told that your newly born baby had a serious condition which means he will not develop in the same way that your first baby developed. On questioning the paediatrician, she says that most children with this condition do not live beyond seven years of age.

* What might be your first reaction?
* What are your feelings following your first reaction?
* What impact does this news have on other relationships?
* What do you think you need at this point?

Make some notes for consideration later.

Now consider how you might respond if someone in this situation came to you for support or counselling six months later because of persistent feelings of sadness.

* How would you begin the session?
* What issues would you explore?
* What emotions might you anticipate would emerge in the session?
* If the person asked 'Is what I'm feeling normal?' what would you say?
* How might you end the first session?
* How would you feel if the same issue recurred over and over with seemingly no resolution?

It is useful to help clients to feel compassionate towards themselves and to enable them to see the value of convalescence, a word that comes from the Latin *con*, 'altogether', and *valescere*, 'grow strong'. This is an old-fashioned term today yet it encompasses the wisdom of the bereaved giving themselves recovery time and allowing others to help in the rebuilding of their strength.

Personal reflection on bereavement

Think of an experience of bereavement or loss in your own life. This may have happened in childhood or more recently. You may use this as a chance to reflect on this event and the impact it had on you or choose to use it as a basis for discussion with others who are completing this exercise.

Complete the following statements.

1 The person who died was..
2 The person who told me that my loved one died was....................................
   ....
3 When I found out that my loved one had died I was in/at..............................
4 What I know about how my loved one died was that.......................................
   ....
   ....
5 At the time when others found out about the death other people acted.................
   ....
   ....
6 When I found out my loved one had died I ....
   ....
   ....

Was there any way in which you felt that you were disenfranchised in your grief?

Look back over your answers. Can you think of anything that feels unresolved?

What might you do to help resolve any issues that still concern you?

6

Spirituality, Religion, Culture and Rituals

All that live must die,
Passing through nature to eternity.
(*Hamlet* I.ii)

In this chapter we will explore how the strands of spirituality, religion, rituals and culture interrelate and how they feature in supporting bereaved adults (Cobb 2001; Walsh et al. 2002). This is by no means an exhaustive exploration of spiritual, religious and cultural responses following bereavement; however, I hope it recognises the diversity in grief responses (Klass 1999b). The importance of valuing and respecting difference in each person's unique reaction to bereavement cannot be overestimated (Boyd-Franklin 1989; Despelder and Barrett 1997). In working with those from different cultures to your own it is helpful to discover how their beliefs, core values, social and philosophical ideas influence their lives and their deaths (Laungani 2004; Morgan and Laungani 2002; Walter 2003). Spirituality is a significant dimension of the human experience.

The spiritual dimension of grief

Never perhaps have our relations with death been as barren as they are in this modern spiritual desert, in which our rush to a mere existence carries us past all sense of mystery.

(François Mitterand in Introduction to Hennezel's *An Intimate Death*, 1995)

Spirituality is concerned with the search for the meaning and purpose of life. It concerns a sense of oneself in relation to that which is transcendent, and is not necessarily associated with a religious faith (Mahoney and Graci 1999; Sulmasy 1999). In death, or journeying with someone who is dying, we come face to face with mortality. What happens after death? What is the meaning of life? Why are we here? These questions lead to the exploration of belief, which may further involve religious, philosophical or spiritual concerns (Pargament and Park 1997). In this process the person seeks the meaning of existence or the ultimate meaning of life (McGrath 2003).

Death anxiety is a fundamental part of human existence. When a person is faced with their own imminent mortality or that of someone close, the personal closeness of death becomes all enveloping. It goes from impersonal to personal in a moment and life changes at that point. Handzo states that a life-limiting diagnosis 'evokes a patient's ultimate existential and spiritual concerns' (1996: 45). It is hard to face the idea of non-being, of the world continuing when we are no longer present (Klass 1999b). In working with grief and in end of life care, we need to offer a holistic approach that addresses physical, emotional, psychological and spiritual needs (NHS 2007; Speck 2000; Walsh et al. 2002).

Born in 1889, Harry Patch, aged 107, recalled his experiences in the First World War, in which a spiritual dimension played a significant part. In the Pilckem Ridge battlefield, he said,

> 'I came across a Cornishman who was ripped from shoulder to waist with shrapnel ... As I got to him he said. "Shoot me." Before I could draw my revolver, he died. I was with him for the last sixty seconds of his life. He gasped one word – "Mother". That one word has run through my brain for eighty-eight years. I will never forget it. I think it is the most sacred word in the English language. It wasn't a cry of distress or pain – it was one of surprise and joy. I learned later that his mother was already dead, so he felt he was going to join her.'

Such experiences of transcendence, a sense of something beyond the here and now of life, often provide comfort when we are facing our own death or the death of others. They can bring a belief in something beyond death:

> 'When I think of death it makes me sad but I believe that we live on in others, so that belief in life after death helps me.'
>
> (Stella)

> 'When I think of death I feel excited, curious and quite comfortable, it's a big adventure. My spiritual path helps me greatly.'
>
> (Ian)

Spirituality is important in bereavement care on many levels, not least because of its potential benefits to mental well-being and emotional health (Galanter 2005). A study in the United Kingdom (Walsh et al. 2002) concluded that people with stronger spiritual beliefs resolve their grief more quickly and completely after the death of someone close. Within palliative care, the spiritual needs of patients and their families play an integral part in the holistic patient pathway (Marie Curie Cancer Care 2003; Wimpenny 2007; Wright 2002). Many patients view spirituality as a mechanism for coping with their health (NHS 2007: 102). In recognising the spiritual needs of people who are dying we honour their values and beliefs (Bregman 2006; Stanworth 2004).

What is spirituality?

Spirituality is something that every person possesses and it is not dependent on religious belief. It relates to the meaning and purpose of our existence.

Spirituality brings a deep sense of meaning and purpose in life accompanied by a sense of belonging. Murray and Zentner (1989) describe the spiritual dimension as that which tries to be in harmony with the universe and seeks answers about the infinite. It comes more sharply into focus at times of emotional stress, physical and mental illness and at times of loss, bereavement and death. The following seems to capture this deep sense of belonging as well as the spiritual dimension of existence:

I believe in the sun even when it does not shine;

I believe in love even when it is not shown;

I believe in God even when he does not speak.

The words were scratched on a wall in a Jewish ghetto in Poland (McCormick 1997: 86).

The most basic spiritual needs include hope, a sense of meaning in our existence, a sense of being in relationship with others, forgiveness or acceptance and transcendence, 'to know the life that transcends death' (Campbell 1972: 21):

I have come to view life as a spiritual experience, that is to say, a search for meaning, purpose and personal connection to something greater and more enduring than the self.

(Mount 2003: 94)

Spirituality can be experienced by anyone, including those with learning disability, since it is not related to intellectual ability (Swinton 2002). The emotional and spiritual needs of people with learning disabilities are frequently overlooked and they are left outside the loop of care that other bereaved people are given (Blackman 2003). This discrimination disables and devalues them and the long-term consequences of this disenfranchised grief are significant.

The spiritual is not dependent on a religious creed or belief system; rather it links that which is deeply personal to the universal and often relates to a power greater than the self (Culliford 2002). Such a power is viewed as being able to help the person transcend their present state and re-establish hope in the face of grave difficulties (Speck 2000; Wright 2002). The role of spirituality relates to that part of ourselves which moulds our identity and sense of purpose (Cox et al. 2003).

Grieving as a spiritual journey offers a transformational experience. In *A Grief Observed* (1961), the diary C.S. Lewis kept after the death of his wife, he recounts how he struggled to reconcile her death with his strong religious faith. Finally, his beliefs were strengthened and he felt himself to be a transformed man.

Salma Khalid (2007) argues that in Western counselling and psychological therapies too little attention is paid to the spiritual dimension. 'The Greek word "psyche" means soul or spirit.' Psychology, she points out, is therefore literally the study of the soul, yet soul is notably absent from much Western psychological thinking. In the Islamic tradition, to understand the self has to include understanding the spiritual aspect (Khalid 2007: 34). Spirituality needs to be included in our work with different cultural groups if we are to address the diversity of beliefs and values.

An important aspect of both spiritual and existential care is to provide what Busch calls an 'Open Frame' (2001). This will enable the bereaved to tell their narrative while expressing the 'letting go' and 'keeping hold', simultaneously, for example, expressing pain of loss and the joy of having known the deceased. In providing spiritual and existential support we need to listen to the person's experience and respond to questions that arise, even when there are no immediate answers. We need to affirm the humanity and self-worth of the individual and respond as their spiritual needs change over time. A helpful way of opening a dialogue about spirituality or religious beliefs can be simply to ask:

> 'What sustains you at difficult points in your life?'
> 'What supports you through this experience?'
> 'Is there anything that gives you a particular sense of meaning in your life?'
> 'Are there any beliefs or traditions that would help you at this point?'
> 'Are there any cultural or spiritual considerations it would be helpful for me to know about?'
> 'Do you belong to a particular support or faith group?'
> 'Is there a spiritual dimension that is important to you?'

It may help to be aware of different spiritual practices, which may include some of the following (Culliford and Powell 2005: 3):

- Belonging to a faith group and taking part in community worship
- Pilgrimage and retreats
- Prayer and meditation
- Ritual and symbolic practices
- Acts of compassion
- Reading sacred literature or spiritual material

- Contemplation
- Yoga, Tai chi or other disciplined practices
- Enjoying and respecting the natural world

There is extensive evidence that there are positive gains in mental health in belonging to a faith community, holding spiritual beliefs and associated practices (Koening et al. 2001). There is also a greater emphasis on including spiritual concerns in assessments of patients (Bregman 2003; Post et al. 2000). Unmet spiritual needs can be a threat to those who are dying or those who are bereaved.

In research carried out with people close to those in hospice care Professor Michael King found that those with strong spiritual beliefs coped better with bereavement than those without (King 2002). He said, 'Most spiritual beliefs whether or not associated with religious practice contain tenets about the course of human life and existence beyond it' (Walsh et al. 2002). Research has suggested that spiritual belief is associated with a decrease in death anxiety and an increase in psychological well-being (Ardelt 2003; VonDras and White 2006). Belief that death is not the final act, and that there is some form of continuity, may bring much comfort (Bennett and Bennett 2000).

Illness is a spiritual event. Illness grasps a person by the soul and by the body and disturbs them both.

(Sulmasy 1997: 1003)

Religion

Religion comes from the Latin *religare*, meaning to tie together. Religions provide a community-based worship and each faith has its own sacred practices and beliefs to which the communicants adhere. It is in the set of beliefs that the members find meaning. Religious worship is usually allied to specific rituals and culture (Emblen 1992; Sulmasy 1999). Many who are bereaved find solace in their religion or spiritual practice and seeking spiritual comfort, from whatever source, does not indicate that grief is being suppressed. We need to include the client's view of spirituality if we are to provide a holistic bereavement counselling service.

Within different religions there is a continuum of variations: not all Muslims will grieve in the same way, neither will Christians, so it is important that we recognise that the broad brushstrokes here do not give the detail that we may need. As always, it is vital to ascertain what the individual we are working with or supporting feels and believes. The duration of bereavement as a period of mourning is limited in many cultures, for example in Muslim cultures, and where this is the norm there do not appear to be examples of prolonged grief (Rosenblatt et al. 1976).

'Religion is in part what glues societies together' (Walter 2003: 219). The death of one person affects the family, the community and in some cases, for example the death of a spiritual leader or high profile person, the whole society. Rites hold the group together as they attend to the necessary demands that follow the death. However, for many people in Western secular societies there is no religious tradition to follow. In Europe only about 40 per cent believe in the afterlife, though 75 per cent of Irish people believe in it and there is a continuing rise in belief in America (Walter 1996a). As we saw earlier, a person may not belong to a religious group and still have a spiritual belief which may encompass its own rites and rituals.

Death and loss can act as a catalyst for spiritual development (Batten and Oltjenbruns 1999) by leading the person either to develop a new spiritual or religious path, or return to a known one but with greater depth and commitment. Belief in God may bring comfort when it cannot be found elsewhere, as Leana Peltier records following the death of her brother in a climbing accident: 'I turned to my spirituality often during the months around my brother's death and the years following. I asked God for guidance, strength, comfort and wisdom. When Chris was missing I felt the very fabric of my world being frayed at all the edges. The only small escape in those painful days were the moments I was praying' (Peltier 2006).

Culture, rituals and customs
following death

Death is deeply personal and shaped by the society and culture in which we live (Parkes et al. 1997). It reveals individual and societal values and beliefs. Farrell (1982) points out that death is a cultural event and societies as well as individuals reveal themselves in their treatment of death. The rituals and customs surrounding dying and death are highly informative.

Bereavement responses are common across cultures (Bowlby 1980; Rosenblatt et al. 1976; Steele 1977), and there is an overlap between cultural groups as well as universality in the grieving process (Averill 1968). In almost every group, women cry or keen after death, anger is common, as is fear of the dead body and the deceased's spirit. The research of Janice Reid with Yolngu Aboriginal Australians found a complex response to bereavement which included women keening, men acting out their anger in a ritualised way and burial and purification rites being performed to drive away the spirit of the dead person (Reid 1979).

Cultural factors influence not only the rituals around dying and death but also the way in which we grieve. In bereavement counselling we need to ensure we respect the cultural mores of whoever we are working with, otherwise we may make mourning more difficult. As Maqsood says in *After*

Death, Life!, for Muslims only Allah has an awareness of the life and death of every person. Each must entrust his fate to the will of Allah, which eases his ability both to contemplate his own mortality and to accept the death of others (Maqsood 1998).

In some cultures death is not seen as the end but as a stage on a journey to another place. In the Mexican tradition, for example, death is embraced, as is evidenced by El Dia de los Meurtos, the Day of the Dead, a joyous occasion when the souls of the dead return to reunite with living relatives. Across the world people find ways of examining the meaning of life and death.

Rituals

Rituals allow us to mark significant events or transitions. In some cultures it is customary for the family to 'lay out' the dead, to wash the body and prepare it for burial. In the West this has all but disappeared and is seen, by some, as distasteful. However, such acts can honour the dead and reinforce the bond of kinship. A nurse on an oncology ward told me of a situation in which a man was close to death. His son and wife took it in turns to be with him, sleeping on his bed in the last nights before he died. Finally, in the early hours of the morning, he died. When the nurse said she would lay out the body his son said he wanted to help her. She was in a dilemma: this was not hospital practice. He said, 'This is the last thing I can do for my father. My Mum and I said whoever was here when he died would help to prepare him for his burial.' She agreed to allow the 17-year old son to lay out his father and felt it was the right thing to do. Her colleagues, when they learned what had happened, were shocked, yet her actions allowed the grieving and healing process to begin under the best circumstances.

Funeral rituals bring people together to provide support for the bereaved and let us acknowledge the loss, and share thoughts and memories of the deceased. As Gamino states, 'Funeral rituals appeared to enhance mourners' comfort at the time of death, both by facilitating social support and by connecting the griever with deeper levels of meaning with which to understand and frame their loss experience' (Gamino et al. 2000: 91). Funeral rituals allow us to explore spiritual responses to death and gain solace in the process. Research carried out by Australian David Richie found a consistency in people's beliefs about the purpose of life and the continuity of the human spirit and the need to keep connected through public rituals – shrines, eulogies at funerals, music to reflect the spirit of the deceased and so on (Richie 2003).

In traditional Indian culture there are many rituals associated with death and dying, purification being essential, ensuring that the soul will find rest (Laungani 1997). The *karyam* is one ritual in which prayers are said by priests. Lamps or candles are placed in front of a picture of the dead person, as are incense, flowers and religious offerings. The rituals let the bereaved confront their loss and bring families and the community together to mark the process of grieving. Death is not seen as a private affair of the individual: instead it is a community affair which reinforces the idea of interconnectedness, common bonds and interdependence. Grieving is for all the community and so funerals are public events where loud expressions of grief are the norm.

Cultural rituals help the bereaved to recognise their loss and their altered relationship with the deceased and the change of roles within the family. In 'Grief as a Family Process', Shapiro (1994) notes the place of the family within the wider culture. She says, 'In the dominant North American culture, which emphasises the centrality of the isolated individual; minimises the importance of spiritual, as compared to scientific, explanations; and stresses the value of "letting go" and "moving on", social sanctions are likely to pressure the bereaved into re-entering the flow of ordinary life before [the bereaved] feel psychologically ready' (1994: 221).

Rituals play an empowering role in reducing survivor guilt, which is often found after disasters or traumatic loss (Erikson 1963). Where a person feels that someone else prevented her death at the cost of his own life, she may feel intense guilt that she did not die (Rubin et al. 2003). In aiding the grieving process, leave-taking rituals – such as visiting the grave if the person could not attend the funeral or saying ritual prayers for the dead according to cultural or religious demands, such as reciting the Kaddish, the Jewish memorial prayer for the dead – help the bereaved to reassess a death, which can facilitate separation (Van der Hart 1983; Witztum and Roman 2000). As Rubin points out, the lack of opportunity to engage in grieving for the deceased can delay or derail the mourning process (Rubin and Yasien-Esmael 2004).

Death rites

Each culture and religion has its own form of ritual to honour the dead and dispose of the body. Disposal of the body holds great significance. Sophocles in his play *Antigone* shows how vital it is to treat the body with respect. Antigone's dilemma has is how to honour her dead brother's body when she has been forbidden to bury him.

> ... My brother's burial I will make, and if for making it I die 'Tis well.
>
> (Sophocles, *Antigone*, 1963: 20)

The city state he took arms against had refused to allow her brother to be buried and Antigone would rather die than have him so dishonoured. Antigone spreads 'a coverlet of dust' (p 29) over his body in a symbolic burial and knows my life is past long since, free given in service to the dead.

(1963: 44)

The ancient play emphasises the profound need of humans to honour their kin in burial because to do otherwise undermines the powerful nature of relationships that go beyond life. To abandon the dead is to deny humanity.

'Those who do not honour death cannot understand the meaning of existence.' This was posted on the website of Lu Youqing, who wrote frankly about his cancer in an on-line diary, unusual in China where discussion of death is taboo (Youqing 2000). Rituals honouring the dead are a kind of punctuation in the life journey to show that something highly significant has occurred. Many are carried out as a socialising process, and we may take part in rituals in order to belong to our chosen community. Many cultures have post-burial funerary rituals, such as those of the Jewish and Chinese traditions.

In some cultures the coffin is kept open so the corpse can be viewed prior to burial or cremation and it is customary to photograph the deceased. It may cause discomfort for some counsellors when a bereaved person wants to bring photographs of the deceased in their coffin to the counselling setting. In some traditions the body, wrapped in a thin shroud, is carried through the streets to the place of burial. The rituals following death may include symbolic elements such as the colour of clothes worn at the funeral. In Buddhist funerals white is the colour of mourning, whilst black is often worn in the West. In Indian Hindu funerals rice is thrown into the pyre while Buddhists offer food to the statue of Buddha.

There are social considerations following bereavement which have to be negotiated. In Britain, in the past, it was expected that the bereaved would wear black, or black armbands, which alerted others to their loss. In recent years football teams have worn black armbands to commemorate football disasters such as the anniversary of the multiple deaths at Hillsborough stadium in 1989. Such outward signs of mourning are not the custom now, which makes revelations about death more complicated. It is not so simple now as, Jane Seaton described:

> But being bereaved is like being the Ancient Mariner, the ghastly guest at any feast. You leer into the sight of some unsuspecting person with a great albatross around your neck. You try very, very hard not to embarrass people. There is nothing you can do about it. At some point, a family reference comes up – it always does, in any number of ways – and you, the bereaved, have to explain to the shocked mistake-maker what has happened.

Death. (2006: 24)

Whatever our beliefs, values or cultural norms, death impacts on us as individuals and as members of a wider community. In working with the bereaved we must respect and honour each person's right to follow the way that feels right for them in their mourning. The diversity of paths allows us each to find our own way in making sense of that which will come to each of us at some point. Death is the only certainty in life.

Spiritualism

Spiritualism may offer some comfort to the bereaved. In Britain there are 400 churches dedicated to spiritualism (Walsh 2007) and round the world people seek contact with deceased family and friends through spiritualist mediums (Walter 2006). According to a USA Today/CNN/Gallup poll in 1994, almost seventy million people in America believe it is possible to communicate with the dead (Grubbs 2004).

The passionate desire not to 'let go' of the deceased, particularly after the death of a child, may cause some bereaved people to seek continued connection through these channels. Indeed as Richie and Dawson's qualitative research shows, it was only after long periods of time, when trust was built up, that bereaved parents felt safe enough to disclose their visits to spiritualists and clairvoyants, as well as relating their dreams and visions of the deceased (Riches and Dawson 2002). Justine Picardie's book, written following the death of her sister Ruth aged 32, describes the search for contact with her sister through visits to mediums (Picardie 2001).

Whilst some bereaved people would not seek out mediums or others who claim they can contact the deceased in the afterlife, others do report situations they find hard to explain. Melvyn Bragg, the noted British television journalist and writer, had an unusual experience. Writing after the death of his father he said,

> About two months after he died I had a very strange experience. While I was asleep there was what felt like a clamp on my left hand, as fierce as a vice. It was his hand trying to pull me out of bed. I don't believe in spirits or anything like that, but it was so vivid and strong I can't deny it happened. That was the worst time of all, because somehow it proved he had really gone. For two years, I was kind of frozen in that bedroom where he died; it winded me, psychologically and emotionally. Now I see him all over the place, and it's fine. I have conversations with him in my head, things I would have told him, or would have told him had I been the man that I am now.

(Bragg: 15)

> Love is not changed by Death,
> And nothing is lost and all in the end is harvest.

(Edith Sitwell, in Whitaker 1984: xiv)

Religious beliefs and practices

It is helpful in bereavement counselling to have knowledge about different faith groups to ensure that we are sensitive to differing practices and the needs that ensue from them. In this section we will explore some major faiths (Laungani 2004). The different faith groups are arranged in alphabetical order to ease access, and a brief outline is attached in each case. I would like to point out that having been brought up by Irish Catholics who emigrated from Ireland just before I was born, and living my life in a secular tradition in England, I cannot represent the true depths of different religious groups. However, as I lived in a Muslim country for a number of years and worked with all faith groups, I hope I do no disservice to any group. If I have not reflected your faith group's beliefs or practices accurately, please let me know so that corrections may be made in the next edition of this book.

Baha'i

The Baha'i religion was founded in Iran by Baha'u'llah (1817–92). The Baha'is believe in the oneness of God and the oneness of humanity and religion. Baha'u'llah brought a message of peace and justice on earth and love, hope and forgiveness for every person. Instead of clergy or priests there is a locally elected group known as the Local Spiritual Assembly.

The Baha'i believe in one Creator who can be worshipped in many ways and known by many different names. Belief in the equality of religions and people is central to the faith, and followers work to overcome all kinds of prejudice and intolerance and actively promote inter-faith activities. Most Baha'i are vegetarian and abstain from alcohol.

There are no specific requirements for the dying though the body of the dead person must be treated with great respect. Baha'i law prescribes that burial should take place no more than one hour's journey from the place of death, and embalming is not allowed. Cremation is not permitted in the Baha'i faith. Friends and relatives pray for the dead person. The Baha'i believe that life begins at conception and a miscarriage is seen as a great loss. The remains, wherever possible, should be returned to the parents for burial.

There are no objections to post-mortems or autopsies, should this be necessary. The donating of organs is regarded as a positive act.

Buddhism

Buddhism began in the sixth century BCE and was founded by Gautama Siddartha, the Buddha or 'Enlightened One'. He was the son of King Suddhodana who sheltered him from the realities of pain and death in the world. At the age of 29, he visited the world outside his palace and discovered the sick and dying. He renounced his worldly comforts and lived as an ascetic in order to understand the meaning of life and suffering. After many years of meditation and self-denial he became enlightened and his teachings spread throughout the world. Buddhism teaches tolerance and acceptance of life by following a middle way, neither extreme asceticism nor self-indulgence.

The basic tenets of Buddhism are:

- All sentient beings suffer. Birth, illness, death and other separations are all aspects of life which cannot be avoided.
- The cause of suffering is desire which is manifested by attachment to others, material objects and to security.
- In order to end suffering, people need to relinquish their desires.
- Desire can be stopped by following the Eightfold Path. This comprises:

  1 Right belief
  2 Right intent
  3 Right speech
  4 Right action or conduct
  5 Right work
  6 Right effort
  7 Right mindfulness
  8 Right meditation

By following the Eightfold Path, Buddhists believe they can achieve enlightenment or nirvana, Sanskrit for 'a blowing out, as of a flame', and avoid rebirth.

Buddhism is a faith based on the life of the Buddha, who is not revered as a god but as a model for how to live a moral and right life. Buddhists believe in reincarnation and condemn killing, abortion and euthanasia. They believe in the precept of no-harm to others, including all sentient beings, and so are vegetarian. As with many other faith groups, there are many variations in the practice of the faith. There are a number of forms, including Theravada Buddhism, Mayahana Buddism and Zen Buddhism. Each is influenced by nationality and ethnicity.

The principle of karma is central to Buddhist belief. Karma states that if you live correctly and take right actions you will be reborn to a higher state. If you carry out wrong actions, you will be reborn into a lower state. This is based on the idea of cause and effect rather than on reward and punishment.

As a person is dying their state of mind is particularly important because this will influence the rebirth or reincarnation on the karmic journey which each Buddhist believes will happen. This influences the response to the use of drugs to ease the dying process, since drugs may reduce consciousness. When dying, a Buddhist will aim to have wholesome thoughts which include the awareness of the transient nature of life, the recollection of good actions and letting go of life rather than striving to remain attached to it. Quiet time for meditation and peaceful reflection is required. The presence of another Buddhist is important, to aid the dying person and to give spiritual guidance. The dying person may gain comfort from a visiting monk or nun who can help in the process with meditation, chanting and reading from scriptures and *The Tibetan Book of the Dead*. Whilst different Buddhist sects perform different rites at death, each will observe chanting, the burning of incense and post-funeral memorial services. Images of the Buddha may be placed near to the dying person.

Buddhists refer to death as 'blissful rest' and after death the body is left undisturbed for as long as possible so that the mind can separate from the body. The body is then wrapped in a plain cloth with no decoration or emblems. Buddhists believe that viewing the dead body is an important reminder of the impermanence of life.

The funeral usually takes place three to seven days after the death and cremation is preferred to burial. White is the colour of mourning and in some traditions close relatives may shave their heads as a sign of mourning.

Memorial services begin seven days after the death and then every seventh day until the forty-ninth day after the death. The service takes place in the family home or in a Buddhist temple. Close friends and family normally gather together on the first and the second anniversary. The third anniversary is particularly significant because it marks the end of the three-year grieving period for the family.

There is no religious objection to post-mortems and no injunctions against organ donation, which may be regarded as an act of charity.

Chung Yuan is a Buddhist festival in which objects for use in the spirit world are offered for those deceased who have no descendants or resting place. It is believed such offerings will ease the path to nirvana.

Ching Ming is a family festival for many Chinese people, where the family visits the graves of the deceased. The graves are cleaned and swept and the families have picnics by the grave as a way of sharing meals with their ancestors.

American Buddhists in particular have made a significant contribution to death awareness (Bregman 2003). In 1982 Steven Levine's classic *Who Dies?* was published. It examines Buddhist themes of mindfulness, impermanence and no-self and greatly helps in understanding the Buddhist view of dying, death and grief.

Christianity

Christians believe in Jesus Christ as the Son of God and in the resurrection of the body. An essential belief is in the Trinity: God as Father, Son and Holy Spirit. There are many varieties of Christianity. In the UK there are an estimated 220 different Christian denominations, including Roman Catholicism, Methodism, the Anglian Church, Baptists and the United Reform Church. Each has its own organisations and its own specific rituals. Baptism is a sacrament in Anglicanism, Catholicism and many forms of Christianity. Baptism into the Catholic Church is a fundamental rite for a child as it cleanses the child of Original Sin and marks the entrance to the spiritual life.

Christians believe death is a release from life which gives the deceased the chance to be with God in His heavenly home where Jesus is 'sitting at the right hand of God', as stated in the Nicene Creed and the Apostles' Creed. Hell is the place of utter damnation where sinners are punished after death. At the Last Judgment all humans and the fallen angels, those who defied God and were cast out by Him, will be judged by Jesus Christ and a final assignment to heaven or hell will be decided.

As a person is dying there is usually a desire to have priest or chaplain present. Roman Catholics normally wish to make a confession and receive absolution, forgiveness of sins and wish for the 'last rites', extreme unction, which is the anointing of the person with consecrated oil by a priest. This can be done just prior to death or up to one hour afterwards. After the death, according to Catholic funeral rites, a mass is offered on behalf of the dead person's soul and mourners may take Holy Communion (Houben 2006). This recalls the last supper that Jesus Christ shared with his disciples before his death. In other Christian traditions prayers and religious services mark the passing of the body from the physical to the spiritual domain.

It is the custom in most forms of Christianity that after death the body is washed and prepared for the funeral. The corpse is dressed in their usual clothes or clothes of special significance, then placed in a coffin. A service is normally held in a church, chapel or at a chapel in the crematorium. There are prayers, readings from the Bible, hymns, blessings and contributions from friends and family. A eulogy, a speech praising the dead person, is often made by someone close to the deceased.

In the Christian tradition there are no strictures about burial or cremation: both are allowed.

Christian Scientists

The Church of Christ Scientist was set up by Mary Baker Eddy in 1879 with the aim of reinstating primitive Christianity and the ministry of healing. Prayer is used to bring cure and relief from illness and disease in continuance of the healing practised by Jesus Christ.

There are no last rites for the dying, though privacy is required for prayer and access to religious literature such as the King James Bible and *Science and Health with Key to the Scriptures*.

Christian Scientists will agree to a post-mortem if required by law but generally they prefer to keep the body complete without any interventions such as organ transplant. They prefer cremation to burial but ultimately it is up to the family to choose.

Jehovah's Witnesses

Jehovah's Witnesses worship Jehovah and live their lives according to biblical tenets and the Ten Commandments. There are no formal rituals for the dying, though last rites may be performed at the point of death.

Burial or cremation are equally acceptable.

Transfusions of blood are unacceptable to Jehovah's Witnesses, though organ transplants or organ donation are a matter of individual choice. Post-mortems are acceptable.

The Society of Friends

The Society of Friends, also called the Quakers, have a number of views about life after death since they have no formal creed that stipulates what will happen. Generally, they believe that there is no personal survival after death but the good that people have done will live on in the lives of those who come after them. Some Quakers believe in rebirth or reincarnation, while others hold a similar view to Christians: that the soul goes to heaven or hell, depending on our actions when we are alive.

The funeral or memorial meeting may follow the customary 'unprogrammed' tradition in which members sit in silence until they are inspired by divine guidance to speak. This is known as 'vocal ministry'. In a programmed funeral meeting, the pastor will lead prayers, readings, hymns, silent worship and address the members of the meeting.

Hinduism

Hinduism is at least 3,000 years old. The five main principles of Hinduism are:

Parmeshaw – God
Prarthana – prayer
Punjarna – rebirth
Purushartha – law of action
Prani Daya – compassion for all living things.

In the Hindu perspective on death, dying and bereavement there are significant factors which contribute to the whole experience (Luangani 1996). The importance of the involvement of the whole community is central. All who have known the deceased are involved, including children. Death is viewed as a force of destiny rather than a matter of chance. The social

91

mores of the caste system and the Law of Karma all have their place in the rituals of the dying and after death.

Hindus believe in the unity of all things. They believe in one God who can be worshipped in many forms so there are numerous deities, such as Shakti, Rama, Krishna and Shiva, each with a specific aspect. The sacred text is the Veda. They believe in karma, which means that each person's status in life is determined by actions in a previous life and that actions taken in this life and past lives bring consequences. Hindus believe in transmigration, which is the passing of the person's soul or being into another body after death. They believe in reincarnation or union with Brahma and do not see death as being utterly final; instead death is accepted as part of each person's journey.

Hindu society is divided into four main groups or castes. Brahman, the priestly caste, perform religious rites and teach others to follow the correct spiritual path. The Kshatriya is the military caste which governs, rules and enforces the laws of the country. The Vaishya are the business, trade, agricultural and commercial caste. Finally, the Shudra, the lowest caste, are involved in manual labour.

At the point of death Hindus prefer to be as close to Mother Earth as possible and may wish to lie on the floor or on a mattress which has been placed on the floor. A dying person may wish to be washed with running water as bodily cleanliness is linked to spiritual purity. A Hindu priest and the presence of the family is important as the person is dying. The priest will administer the last rites and tie a thread around the person's neck or wrist as a blessing. Water from the Ganges is sprinkled over the dying person and a sacred tulsi leaf is placed in the mouth. Money or property may be touched by the dying person, and it is then distributed to those in need. Hindus prefer to die at home as this holds religious significance.

At death the family wash the body and perform the last rites. Jewellery and sacred threads are not removed and the body is wrapped in a plain sheet. Adults are cremated but holy men, and children under five years old, are usually buried. The cremation is carried out before the first sunset following the death but where this is not possible the corpse should be kept in a lit room. The soul cannot leave the body until the prayer for the dead is recited (Pollack 2003). Caring for the deceased earns religious benefits for the living, which Bringa describes as a 'spiritual exchange which ensures the continuity and indivisibility of life and death' (1995: 195–6). In Hindu teachings the soul of the dead does not go straight from earth to heaven; there is an intermediate stage known as Barzakh, a form of barrier between the two (Smith and Haddad, 1981). At the cremation food is symbolically offered to the deceased before the body is cremated (Firth 2003).

Cremation releases the spirit and the flames represent the presence of the God Brahma, the Creator. During the funeral ceremony dirges are played on drums and the eldest son walks ahead of the procession and carries a lamp. He recites the sacred word OM and lights the funeral pyre to free the soul of the deceased. If there is no son the eldest male relative lights the pyre. In Western crematoria the eldest son will press the button that makes the coffin disappear from public view and go below to ignite the cremator. Usually offerings of rice balls and milk are made.

After ten days, if all rituals have been correctly carried out, it is believed the soul of the deceased is free. The ten days after the funeral are days of seclusion for the family because it is believed that they and the corpse are impure. Relatives take care of any outside matters that they would normally deal with, ensuring that the bereaved can concentrate on their loss and on religious duties. In this period specific ceremonies and rituals are carried out so that the soul of the deceased can find a new spiritual body which will enable him to pass on to the next life. The eldest son performs all funeral ceremonies and rituals. Sometimes the eldest son of the deceased will shave his head as a mark of respect; other male mourners may do likewise. After cremation the ashes of the deceased should be thrown into a flowing river. Shirley Firth (2003) provides an excellent map of death rituals in India and in Britain.

Hindus believe in ghosts often known as *bhuts*. These can cause problems as they are believed to seek revenge, particularly if death was caused in unusual circumstances such as by murder, suicide or sudden traumatic accident. To avoid such ghostly malevolence, funerals and the attendant ceremony are carefully conducted to ensure that the person's soul is not angered. Hindu belief states that every soul stays as a lingering shadow, or *pret*, until all the ceremonials are completed, thirteen days after death (Smith and Haddad 1981). If this is not done properly then the *pret* may become destructive. It is also important that ghosts do not touch the body. They are believed to come in different forms, such as wasps or flies, so mourners stand around the body to protect it. In some rural communities, a bar of iron is laid close to the body as it is believed that it will cause the *bhut* to burst into flames and disappear.

Post-mortems are allowed, though they are disliked by Hindus.

Humanism

The British Humanist Association (BHA) developed from the Ethical Union in 1967 (Norman 2004). Secular Humanists believe this life is the only one we have, it is not a 'dress rehearsal' and it should be lived by following moral precepts that respect people, promote happiness and fulfilment in life. They believe in using reason and knowledge to resolve difficulties and solve problems, and decisions are based on available evidence and assessment of outcomes, not on any dogma or sacred text. The BHA is committed to human rights, equality, democracy and mutual respect.

Humanist officiants, accredited by the British Humanist Association, are non-judgmental, open minded and have wide life experiences which they bring to their empathic funeral ceremonies. Funerals can take place in ceme-teries, crematoria and woodland burial grounds. Prior to the funeral, the Humanist officiant will visit the family to get to know as much about the deceased person as possible. This enables him or her to provide a highly per-sonal declaration about the dead person's life. The family will also have the opportunity to stipulate what they want from the Humanist service, which will then be written down. A printed copy of the ceremony is given to the family to send to people who are not able to attend the funeral and to keep as a memento. Humanists believe we live on in the memories of other peo-ple, the work we have done when we were alive and in our children.

Humanist funerals celebrate the life of the deceased and acknowledge the loss without following any religious rituals. The funeral ceremony will open with a welcome and an outline of the proceedings which usually includes favourite pieces of music, poetry and prose readings and a tribute to the deceased made by friends and family. There will be quiet meditation or the opportunity for quiet reflection, followed by the committal or some form of farewell.

Islam

God is the Light of the heavens and the earth.

(Qur'an 24: 35)

The Muslim religion is based on the articles of faith, commands and teach-ings revealed through the Prophet Muhammad (Armstrong 2000). These beliefs include the prophecies of Muhammad, the afterlife, belief in angels, the belief in the divinity of holy books and belief in fate (Maqsood 1998). Islam is not only a religion but a complete way of life. There are many branches of Islam, including Sunni and Shiah, as well as different influences that operate in the many countries where Islam, the fastest-growing world religion, is found. The five duties – known as the Five Pillars of Islam – of a devout Muslim are:

- Faith in God
- Daily prayer, five times a day
- Fasting during Ramadan
- Giving alms
- Making a pilgrimage to Mecca

The word 'Islam', in Arabic, means 'surrender', specifically to Allah (God).The acceptance of the will of Allah is a basic tenet of Islamic belief and it is Allah who determines the time of death. The Qur'an states that all creatures, including humans, come from Allah and return to him. Birth and death are perceived as divine decrees and death is not regarded as the end of existence but as a step back to Allah, who said, 'People are asleep, and when they die they wake up' (Chittik 1992: 136). The body ceases to function but the spirit continues, so prayers are said for the mercy of Allah (Abdesselem 1991).

As death approaches a relative will give the dying person some holy water, *zam zam*, to drink. Visiting the sick is regarded as a basic duty of Muslims. 'For a Muslim, visiting a sick brother or sister in faith is a basic form of worship to bring one closer to God' (Sajid 2003: 6). The visitor should comfort the sick or dying person, offer hope and help to keep his spirits high. However, all Muslims are encouraged to contemplate death and to prepare for it by good deeds and living according to the laws of Islam (Al-Awwal 2007).

At death a Muslim may wish to lie in a position which faces Mecca, the south-east. As death approaches the 'shahadah', the creed is recited, as are prayers from the Qur'an. The thirty-sixth surah, Ya Sin, is spoken into the ear of the dying person by the eldest male present. The last words heard should be 'There is no God but Allah, and Muhammad is his prophet' and 'la ilaha ella allah' which means 'There is no God but Allah'. When the person dies, Muslims present say, 'To Allah we belong and to Allah we return'. A baby which dies before birth or dies at birth has to be given a name (Sajid 2003).

The Qur'an, the Hadith, the sayings of Muhammad or words attributed to him and the Sira, the story of the life of Muhammad, all contribute to the Islamic beliefs about life and death and the way in which people should behave at various points on the life journey. Rubin and Yasien-Esmael (2004) provide a detailed account of Muslim responses following bereavement, including gender differences which are echoed in other faith groups: women are perceived as being more sensitive and so can express their grief more overtly while men are expected to show constraint and express grief in a controlled manner. It is believed that 'Weeping aloud and wailing cause pain and suffering in the dead person' (Sajid 2003: 17).

Most of the customs related to death, dying and burial are laid down in the Shariah (Muslim laws) which are based on the Hadith rather than the Qur'an. The Islamic religion defines a clear period of mourning, the *iddah*, which is usually three days. In that time grief is expressed within traditional controls so that by the third day the bereaved will have accepted their loss and be ready to return to their community. However, prayers may be said for a period of forty days. Public rites after death are attended by males only. Religious laws dictate that a Muslim wife should stay at home for four months and ten days following the death of her husband, or if she is pregnant, until her baby is born. However, if the woman is the main breadwinner she can have a religious dispensation to continue to work. It is not customary to send flowers or wreaths. The religion encourages the sharing of grief with the extended family network and any feelings of guilt are also shared.

Continuing bonds with the deceased are expressed personally and privately: they continue to live on in hearts and minds (Kasher 2003). The continuing bond is also maintained by giving charity in the deceased's name.

After death the body is never uncovered but is ritually bathed by family members of the same sex with perfumed water. Deceased males are draped in three robes and females in five. If the dead person has made a pilgrimage to Mecca and returned with sheets worn there, then the body is draped in those. Burial should take place as soon as possible after the death, preferably within twenty-four hours (McDermott and Ahsan 1980). Prolonged public expression of grief and mourning is not encouraged in Islamic practice, which emphasises the acceptance of Allah's will with restraint (Rubin and Yasien-Esmael 2004). However, grief is recognised as an acceptable response to the death of a loved one; in fact, the Prophet Muhammad wept over the death of his son Ibrahim. As Ibrahim was dying, the Prophet, picked him up and tears fell from his eyes. A person present at that time asked why he was crying and his reply was that the heart is sad and the eyes weep at the prospect of being separated though it is the will of Allah.

During the mourning period, members of the extended family or the community bring food and look after the bereaved (Neuberger 2004). Islamic belief states that the grave of the deceased is visited by two angels who ask questions to ascertain whether the deceased is fit for the afterlife and the Day of Judgment.

The Qur'an is read as a blessing for the deceased and to bring comfort to the bereaved. The body is taken to the local mosque or an open space where the imam leads the prayer, though a family member may also lead the service. The body is not encased in a coffin but placed directly in the hole that has been dug to fit the size of the deceased. According to the Shariah law, the burial should take place without a box or coffin though in many countries this is not accepted practice, but it is important for Muslims to have direct contact with the earth. According to different Islamic traditions sometimes a stone structure will be erected later or there may be a simple grave with a headstone (Jonker 1997). The local mosque or community centre will arrange for Janazah, the Funeral Prayer, to be said. Prayers for the dead *salat*, are said after the funeral, to ask for forgiveness for any wrong deeds and for mercy for the deceased.

Post-mortems are forbidden unless ordered by a coroner. Organ donation is acceptable to some who follow the Islamic tradition and unacceptable to others.

Sharia Law, Islamic law, is a code for living that governs all aspects of life including food, which has to be halal, donations to the poor, and the proper way to dress and it provides day to day guidance for daily living (Bell 2007). Muslims consult the Islamic Shariah Council for guidance so that they can live correctly according to their faith.

Judaism

The origins of the Jewish people go back 4,000 years. The Jewish faithful believe that all life is created by God and that each person survives death in an afterlife. In early times when the Bible was written Jews believed that the soul entered *sheol*, hell, where the good and the bad lived as shadows. This idea developed over time so that heaven and hell were defined. The person who had completed good deeds was rewarded by going to heaven, whilst others were punished by going to hell. All take part in the resurrection for the final Judgment. Following the teachings and laws of Judaism is believed to bring reward from God in the next life.

The Jewish Reform movement, unlike the Jewish Orthodox movement, does not believe in the idea of a physical resurrection after death but does believe that every soul is immortal and will return to God. Orthodox Jews believe that bodily resurrection will occur when the Messiah comes. Traditional Jewish law forbids cremation but it is acceptable to Reform Jews.

In the Jewish tradition it is very important to ensure that the dying person is not alone. After death the body is never left alone until it is buried.

After a person dies the eyes and mouth are closed by a close relative and the body is washed and wrapped in a shroud, though men may have the addition of their prayer shawl. As a mark of respect, if possible the burial should take place within twenty-four hours of death. From death until burial the body is 'watched over' by community members and psalms are recited. Prior to the funeral mourners tear or rend their clothes, *keriah*, as a symbol of their pain at being torn from their loved one. (Ludman 2000)

The funeral service is usually brief and mourners accompany the body and say prayers at the graveside and sing psalms. The Kaddish prayer, an ancient prayer of sanctification, is recited in Hebrew before the mourners fill the grave with earth. The Kaddish may be recited later, in the service at the synagogue. Following the interment there is a symbolic washing of hands before everyone returns home.

Every Jewish community has a holy burial society known as Chevra Kadisha who prepare the body for burial and help to make the arrangements for the funeral. The body is ritually prepared, *Taharah*, by washing and being placed in a shroud and a simple pine coffin which symbolises the equality of all people. Public viewing of the body is not usually acceptable nor is embalming of the body.

Traditional Jewish mourning begins with intense expression of grief, and over the space of twelve months there is a series of marked rituals. Four stages of mourning are traditional:

- The first stage covers the period between the death and the funeral. During this period, the mourner, known as the *onan*, is relieved of all duties and responsibilities. A symbolic small tear may be made on the clothes of the mourners: this symbolises a broken heart.
- The second stage covers the week of mourning that follows the funeral. It is known as 'Shiva', and the mourners stay at home, sitting on small stools or low chairs and receive visitors. This is described as 'Sitting Shiva'. Mirrors in the home are covered; mourners wear slippers. These symbolise the idea that the mourners need to focus their thoughts on their loss and to remove themselves from worldly interests. Personal friends as well as members of the community visit the family during the period of Shiva.
- The third stage covers the following twenty-three days as the mourners re-engage with their usual activities.
- The fourth stage covers the next eleven months where there is less intense grieving.

On four occasions over the twelve months of every year, there are rituals for remembering the deceased, including the anniversary of the death. Remembering is a communal activity in the context of religious ceremonies in the synagogue.

Once the earth has settled on the grave it is customary to erect a headstone and have a special memorial. An annual ceremony of remembrance, known as *yahrzeit*, is held for the deceased in the synagogue or temple. At home a *yahrzeit* candle that burns for twenty-four hours is lit.

Yom Hashoah is a day of remembrance for all those who died in the Holocaust. Memorial candles are lit in special services to mark the day.

Post-mortems are not permitted in Jewish law unless it is required under civil law. Donations of organs is acceptable if they are to be used immediately.

Sikhism

The word 'Sikh' comes from the Sanskrit and means disciple. Sikhism was founded by Guru Nanak in the early sixteenth century CE. Originally Nanak's faith was Hinduism but after a revelation he believed that to find God people had to look into their own heart and meditate on their relationship to the divine.

Sikhs believe in one God and each individual makes their own personal relationship with God and finds their own way to worship. Male Sikhs observe the five religious symbols of their faith, the five Ks: Kesh – uncut hair; Kangha – the wooden comb; Kara – the metal bracelet, worn on the right wrist; Kirpan – a short sword worn underneath outer clothing; and Kaccha – knee-length underpants. Traditionally the hair of Sikh men is always covered and remains uncut.

A dying Sikh will be attended by family who recite hymns from the Sikh holy book and, if possible, the dying person himself will also recite the hymns. After death the body of the deceased is washed and dressed in clean clothes before being put in a coffin. The five Ks remain on the body. After death, cremation takes place as soon as possible and in some countries a relative lights the funeral pyre. For ten days following the cremation readings from the Adi Granth, the Sikh scripture complied by Guru Arjan (1604 CE) take place in the homes of relatives. After the final passages are read, all who are present share *prashad*, which is holy food made from equal amounts of wheat, sugar and clarified butter.

Though Sikhs do not believe in rebirth, they do believe in an afterlife and that the soul leaves the body at the time of death for eternal life and joins God, Akal Purakh. As death is seen as an act of God, it is written in the scriptures that emotions should be kept under control. Sikhs believe that the soul never dies and there is no expectation that mourning will take place; the soul is on its journey back to God. As in Hinduism, the button to make the coffin disappear from public view in the crematoruim will be pressed by the next of kin. The ashes are scattered on running water.

Funeral rites are important and the body is accompanied with a procession to the crematorium. The whole community will attend the funeral rituals. Women mourners wear a white head covering. At the beginning of the funeral service an *ardas* or community prayer is recited, two Sikh daily prayers, Japli and Kirtan Sohila are said and the cremation begins. After the funeral service another service may be held at *gurdwara*, the Sikh place of worship. It is customary for the faithful to chant the word 'akal' which means 'undying' as it is believed this helps the soul to be released into the infinite. There is no religious objection to blood transfusions, organ donation or transplants or to post-mortems.

Rastafarianism

The Rastafarian movement began in Africa. Haile Selassie I is regarded as the New Messiah, who, it is believed, will lead black people to freedom. Their sacred texts are the Holy Piby, the Kebra Nagast and the Bible, which is interpreted by Rasta Soul, to give guidance and direction to the faithful.

Rastafarians do not cut their hair and wear their hair in dreadlocks which are a symbol of their faith.

There are no specific rituals which are carried out as a person is dying. Burial is preferred to cremation.

Rastarfarians will not agree to a post-mortem unless required by law. Organ transplants are similarly disliked though it is acceptable if it is the exchange of organs between family members.

Reflective exercises

What supports me?

Where do you draw your strength to cope?

Do you have a religious or spiritual belief that informs your work with those who are bereaved?

Do you belong to a support or faith group?

What experience do you have of other people's spiritual lives?

How comfortable do you feel talking about spiritual matters?

The Epitaph

The Churchyards Handbook contains instructions for vergers and stonemasons. According to the handbook, the purpose of epitaphs is 'to identify the resting place of the mortal remains of a dead person' (Bayliss 1999: 221). However, many people are given much more elaborate epitaphs than the bald facts of name, date of birth and date of death. You can see from the following examples how diverse epitaphs can be. Some include reference to religious or spiritual beliefs:

Here lies a miser who lived for himself,

who cared

For nothing but gathering wealth.

Now where he is and how he fares;
Nobody knows and nobody cares.

(Leamington, England)

Here lies

Ezekiel Aikle

Age 102

The Good
Die Young

(East Dalhousie Cemetery, Nova Scotia)

Hereabouts died a very gallant gentleman, Captain L.E.G. Oates of the Iniskilling Dragoons. In March 1912, returning from the pole, He walked willingly to his death in a Blizzard, to try to save his comrades, beset By hardship.

(On a cairn and cross erected in the Antarctic, November 1912)

Sacred to the memory of Anthony Drake
Who died for peace and quietness sake;

His wife was constantly scolding and scoffin;
So he sought for repose in a twelve-dollar coffin.

(Burlington Churchyard, Massachusetts)

Some epitaphs describe the history of the dead person:

Blest in every domestic relation, in her father's house
In her own, and those of her sons, she yet
Endured lasting trials with courage and patience.
Her grandchildren who learned their
Letters at her knee remember her as a
Serene and serious presence, her sons
Regarded her with entire love and reverence
And in the generation to which she belonged
It was said of her that she resembled
A vessel laid up unto the Lord
Of polished gold without
And full of heavenly manna within.

(Ruth Emerson, mother of the poet Ralph Waldo Emerson, Sleepy Hollow Cemetery, Concord, Massachusetts)

George Washington
Blue Mountain,
Linglestown, Pennsylvania
Died April 8, 1868
Looking into the portals of eternity teaches that the brotherhood
Of man is inspired by God's word; then all prejudice of race vanishes away.

Dear is the spot where mother sleeps
And sweet the strain which angels pour
Oh! Why should we in anguish weep?
She is not lost but gone before.
God calls our loved ones, but we lose
Not wholly what He has given
They live on earth in thought and deed
As truly as in Heaven

(Charlotte K. Means, Blue Hill, Maine)

On the 22nd of June
Jonathan Fiddle
Went out of tune.

(Hartscombe, England)

Here lies the body
Of Margaret Bent
She kicked up her heels
And away she went

(Winterborne Steepleton Cemetery, Dorset)

…….. He was a good Dad.
Always tried his best.

(Hobart cemetery, Tasmania)

How far do you think these epitaphs reflect the culture and beliefs of the epitaph writers?

Write an epitaph for yourself.

Rituals and rites

This is an opportunity to consider the rituals around dying and death that influence your thoughts and behaviour. Write down your responses to the following questions.

- Do you think of death as the beginning or the end?
- Do you mourn death or celebrate it or is there a mixture of both?
- What traditions do you have that help at the end of life as a person is approaching death?
- How do you mark the death of someone close to you?
- Do you think feelings about death are influenced by culture or are they universal?

7

Creative Approaches to Expressing Grief

Much bereavement work concentrates on talking, however there are times when it is too difficult to say what has happened. There do not seem to be the words to say it or the person we are working with prefers a different way to express their grief. Just as there are different preferred modalities in learning so there are different ways of communicating and exploring grief (Bertman 1999). In this chapter we will review some creative activities that can be used with those who are bereaved and those who are dying (Gordon 1978). The importance of creativity in health and well-being and as a means of overcoming distress is well documented (Bolton 1999; McLeod 1997; McNiff 1992).

Grief has its own rhythm, pace and refrains, which differ from person to person. There are pockets of time where the pain of bereavement can be set aside – when making a picture, cooking food, creating a collage of the person who was loved, making a scrapbook, mending something or writing down thoughts and feelings (Ellis 1998). It may be in the small, mundane things that people find a moment of stillness that eases an aching heart (Frampton 1986). Many people find that they express their deepest thoughts and emotions in their creative acts. For some it will be in making and playing music, in building a memorial, in creative writing or in gathering objects and making mementos for a memory box that they can express their feelings. Reading or bibliotherapy can also provide insights into the grieving process, offer hope and reduce the sense of isolation a bereaved person often feels, which is why 'Book Prescription' schemes are being introduced throughout the United Kingdom (Frude 2005). In this chapter we will consider a variety of creative activities which facilitate grieving.

One of the most creative acts related to meeting the needs of a terminally ill patient that I have ever come across was revealed by the Right Reverend

Kevin Dunn, chaplaincy co-ordinator of hospital chaplains, who spoke of celebrating diversity in death rituals at the end of life. He told the moving story of an acrobat who was terminally ill in St Christopher's hospice, the first hospice established in Britain. The acrobat longed to reconnect with his circus life and the animals he had loved but was too ill to move. He was close to death. One day, one of the staff said to him, 'Look out of the window.' The acrobat was overjoyed when he saw an elephant. The staff had arranged for the animal to be brought so that he could have a last connection with a life he had been passionate about. I thought this was an extremely creative response to meeting the needs of a dying person, and while we cannot all do the same we can think creatively about meeting the needs of those we care for. Creative therapies help people find expression of feeling beyond words or traditional therapy.

Writing

> When we give testimony to experience through writing our stories, we bear witness to the past and challenge the idea that terrible experiences are too awful to be told.

(Etherington 2003: 35)

Writing is a very effective way to release emotions and explore feelings around loss and bereavement (Bolton 1999; Brimacombe 1996; Mallon 2005). Whatever the form of writing, whether it is a diary or journal, fiction or factual, it can significantly enhance the grieving process and bring healing too (Lyons 1997). Creative expression can be used with those who have life-limiting illness as well as those with dementia (Frampton 1986; Killick 1996; McLoughlin 1985). It can also help the dialogue between health care practitioners and patients. 'When practioners and educators use the principles of creative writing – plot, imagery, character, sensations – they are listening differently and expressing their understanding in narrative form' (Maultsaid 2007: 157). In telling our own stories we make a link to the larger stories that are found throughout the world, and in doing so reduce our sense of isolation.

Keeping a journal may help chart the territory of grief. Eva Lager (Lager and Wagner 1997), whose daughter died by suicide, wrote *Knowing Why Changes Nothing: Diary of Sorrow and Survival*. Begun just one month after her daughter's death, it provides deep insight into the desperation, hurt, love and pain of such a loss. It also includes literary quotations and specially written poetry by Sascha Wagner, presented in beautiful calligraphy. Wagner's daughter also died by suicide. Penelope Ironstone-Catterall wrote an 'Auto-ethnographic meditation on mourning a toddler' and described it as 'my need to produce a narrative that might both acknowledge the rupture in my life-story and work to repair it' (2004–2005: 3). It gives particular insights into the value of writing by including personal accounts of her son's life and death, self-analysis to make sense of her loss and meditations on what it is like to mourn a toddler.

> The joyful will stoop with sorrow, and when you have gone to earth I will let my hair grow long for your sake, I will wander through the the wilderness in the skin of a lion.
>
> (Mitchell, *The Epic of Gilgamesh,* 2004: 155)

In response to grief the creating of stories to make sense of loss is what Figley (1988) calls 'healing theory'. Psychologist Marie de Hennezel who works with the terminally ill writes of the importance of narrating life stories:

> To tell the story of one's life before one dies. The telling of it is an act, and for any-one whose autonomy is diminished, this act takes on full importance. There is a need to give shape to one's life and to show this shape, which gives it its meaning, to someone else. Once the telling of it has been accomplished, the person seems to be able to let go, and to die. (1995: 111–12)
>
> The stories people tell have a way of taking care of them.
>
> (Lopez 2003: 5)

The story which is told acts as a bridge between what was the norm before the loss and what makes sense after the loss. Stories allow us to bring order back into our lives (Bruner 1990) and the teller can understand what happened in their lives by creating a meaningful narrative. The story a bereaved person writes may be a factual account of before and after the death, a story told from someone else's perspective or a series of scenes of the most critical events. It may be a tale about what the future holds (Gersie 1997). Joan Didion, when asked how she was able to write after the death of her husband, replied, 'There was nothing else to do. I had to write my way out of it' (Brockes 2005: 15).

In working with clients we can help them identify rituals which may reflect the bond with the deceased. Writing letters, poems or a list of shared experiences can integrate the event into their new biography. Though these may be painful, it helps the person to recall time past and experience the grief instead of suppressing it or denying it. Here is Chloe's piece:

> 'We shared holidays in France. Bottles of wine, crusty bread and fresh cheese on river banks. We used to share the bath when we were younger before he got arthritis. We shared time with the kids, reading stories and playing in the garden. When they grew up and left home, we shared the gardening and made pots of tea to drink in the afternoons. We shared our lives ... and now he's gone.'

Our lives are a series of chapters which carry our story line. Some of those early chapters reveal our past and others are, as yet, unwritten. In bereavement counselling we will hear stories that are sad, tragic and in some instances have the quality of a horror story. Most therapeutic interventions enable the client to tell the story that needs to be told; in telling the story the bereaved person can reflect on the meaning of the person's existence and their own relationship and construct a healing story (Parker 1993; Philipp 1996; Riordan 1996). In working with adults, in listening to their stories , unconditional positive regards brings out the least guarded or censored accounts (Bearison 1991).

Poetry

> But the living are wrong in the sharp distinctions they make.
>
> Angels, it seems, don't always know if they are moving among the living or the dead.
>
> (Rainer Maria Rilke, *Duino Elegies,* 1992: 25)

Poetry is associated with the expression of profound emotion and much of it originates in the experience of loss. In writing poetry the bereaved can give vent to feelings in a highly personal way and gain much comfort from doing so (Bolton 1999; Fuchel 1985; Morrice 1983).

Michael Rosen's son died at 18 years of age from meningitis. In *Carrying the Elephant: a Memoir of Love and Loss* (2002) he writes of his grief and experiences after the death, including the fact that one of his neighbours on hearing of the death said, 'Rather you than me.' Rosen charts the journey through shock and despair in a way that may help grieving parents.

Anyone whose partner has died may find Nell Dale's book *What Colour is Grief: A Journey* of particular value. In drawings and poems she writes, 'This book is for all those like me who suddenly found the future they thought was there – is no more' (2007: 10).

> 'The colour of grief'
> What colour is grief?
> Grief is a dark still grey foggy day
> It is November in June
> It is the colour of gloom.
> It is the starless night of the black moon.
> Grief is lost on a boggy moor.
> Grief is drowning in the cold sea.
> Grief wades through the oceans of time and goes nowhere.
> Grief is a stopped clock.
> Grief you were not invited in – you have invaded my space.
> Grief you were not invited in – you have invaded my spirit.
> You have overtaken my brain and body
> Grief you have no direction

Grief you are too heavy – you drag me down
Grief I never wanted you as my partner.

(Dale 2007: 7)

Song-writing may also be used to express grief. Eric Clapton composed 'Tears in Heaven' after his son died following an accidental fall from a hotel bedroom in New York. Paul McCartney wrote 'Here Today' after John Lennon was murdered. As part of his grieving process McCartney also wrote *Blackbird Singing*, a series of poems and lyrics after the death of his wife Linda.

Letter-writing

Letter-writing can play a therapeutic role in the grief process (Ellis 1998). As part of bereavement counselling clients sometimes write a letter to the deceased person, particularly when they have not had the opportunity to say goodbye before the person died. One young woman whose father had died wrote, 'Dear Dad, I miss you so much, I'm so sorry that we couldn't sort out the things we argued about even though I know you loved me. I dream of you over and over and we make plans. You tell me how to look after the baby. You can see her in my dreams but I'm sad that you'll never see her any other way.'

Letters give the bereaved the opportunity to say what they could not say before death and can communicate how the bereaved feels at this point in their lives. Arline, the wife of the American Nobel Prize winning physicist Richard Feynman, died three years after they married (Feynman 2005). He wrote her a letter a year after her death; here is part of it:

You only are left to me. You are real.
My darling wife, I do adore you. I love my wife. My wife is dead.
Rich
PS Please excuse my not mailing this – but I don't know your new address.

The bereaved person can choose to keep the letter, perhaps in a memory box, bury it near the grave, burn it or dispose of it in whatever way feels most appropriate. Writing letters can also be helpful for women who have had abortions (the male partner may also wish to do this). The woman can write a letter to the foetus expressing her feelings and the reason and circumstances in which she took her decision. This often brings clarity and self-forgiveness.

Reg Thompson's 13-year-old daughter was killed crossing a railway line at a station where there was no footbridge. He wanted a way to remember her and to maintain some kind of contact with her and so he began writing a series of letters which were published in *Dear Charlie* (Thompson 2006a). They reveal the raw emotion of loss and the impact it has on his wife and their two younger sons. He describes the despair, disbelief and agony immediately following his daughter's death. 'When I write I am with her, surrounded by her presence, immersed in memories of her' (Thompson 2006b: 25). At first these were private letters but he was persuaded to publish them in order to help others who had lost a child in tragic circumstances.

Making and remembering

Anything good you've ever been given is yours forever.

(Rachel Naomi Remen, in Redwood 2002)

Activities in this section can include the use of clay, paper, twigs, shells, rocks and pebbles; in fact any materials that can be found. Using these the bereaved person can create something that reflects their feelings. One activity is to gather whatever material the person chooses and then using clay or paper create a base as a landscape. On the surface of the landscape they can place their story, their feelings and thoughts. The materials symbolise their emotions and the events of their narrative. They may choose something to symbolically represent the person who has died, perhaps from a collection of different coloured gemstones or seed heads, and place this in the landscape they have made.

The aim of these activities is not to create a pretty finished work of art: it is the process that is important (McNiff 1992). It allows the person the have time to play and explore without thinking too much and it can have a truly healing effect. As one person in a group project I was involved with in Cumbria said, 'I liked that [creating something from feathers, sheeps' wool and moss] because I used to make things when I was young, it brought my childhood back a bit and I was just feeling a safe place, to rest in ... I completely switched off from everything ... You could actually tell people's feelings from what they made – you could see how that person was feeling – and there wasn't a word spoken' (Mallon et al. 2005: 25). There was no need to tell their stories yet each member of the group found ease in the making process. As my colleague Miranda Tufnell wrote in 'When I Open My Eyes' (Mallon et al. 2004: 3), 'The medicine of the arts means that no matter how frail and troubled we may be, some small act of creating, of making, brings us into life within us. It brings us to the wholeness which is health.'

After completing the creation it can be helpful to ask the person about the process, how they felt about it, what the starting point was, what different parts represent, and so on. This gives them an opportunity to voice their feelings and to talk about any insights they have gained if they wish to.

Life Map

Grief only becomes a tolerable and creative experience when love enables it to be shared with someone who really understands.

(Simon Stephens 1972: 53)

This is a way to enable the bereaved to become more aware of losses in their lives. It helps people open up about life events that have been distressing and can help to show patterns of response, such as reactions to setbacks or actions that have influenced their emotional and physical health. It is also a way of reassessing resilience in response to adversity.

The person draws a line to chart the course of their life, indicating highs and lows and including any significant events. They can write these or draw their own symbols to represent the events – a cradle to indicate a birth, a coffin to represent a death – or choose different colours to signify their emotional response.

Once they have finished, they take the counsellor through the Life Map, talking through their experiences. It is useful to ask if they can see any patterns and to point out any patterns that you can see. These are offered rather than imposed: 'I noticed that each time you moved house you felt lonely. Is that how it was for you?' or, 'When your grandmother died you were sent to stay with your aunt and after your father died you weren't allowed to go to the funeral, that looks like you were left out. Does that reflect how it felt?' In this process you are helping the bereaved to explore a range of feelings and thoughts. It is also helpful to ask if there were any gains from the losses, for example: 'I was eight when my sister left home and I really missed her.' In response to 'Were there any gains when she left?' came the response, 'Well, I was so miserable that my Mum and Dad finally let me have a dog and that was brilliant.'

Memory boxes

Memory boxes are so called because the bereaved collect objects that remind them of their dead loved one. Objects that have been chosen by adults I have worked with include the dead person's mobile phone, photos, pieces of clothing and jewellery, letters from and to the deceased, perfume or aftershave bottles, DVDs and CDs with special music or a favourite film and personal items of significance. The box can be decorated on the outside and stored to be brought out when the bereaved wants comfort from past objects and memories.

Memory boxes may also be made by someone who is dying so that they can leave their own legacy of letters, videos, messages and special items for those who live on after their death. Sometimes a memory box is made when the person has a life-threatening illness and parent and child use it as a letter box, writing about the things they feel are too difficult to raise face to face.

The Memory Box Project (Mendel 2006) began as a way of encouraging Ugandan women with AIDS and HIV to prepare for death by making memory books to leave for their children. It developed into 'memory work' and is used by HIV organisations throughout Africa.

'The memory box is important because if I die my child will see what I have written for her, and my photos are there, my birth certificate is there, and her drawings are there. It will help her to remember me when I have gone. For now she is very young – she is unable to understand the memory box.'

(Zamathembu Mthembu, in Mendel 2006: 6)

As part of the project, creative activities are important. The participants make memory boxes, memory books, hero books that trace their lives, their problems and body mapping drawings. These give the participants the opportunity to tell their stories, reflect on the lives and pass their stories on to their children

Memory quilt

'The Fabric of Life' can be collected into a patchwork memory cushion or quilt. Pieces of fabric from the deceased's clothes – shirts, blouses – are cut up and sewn together. Friends or family members can work together, sharing their feelings, thoughts and hopes. The finished quilt could be used as a comforting quilt or cushion. The AIDS Memorial Quilt has become a national symbol in America.

Love Wraps

I am grateful to Trudy Hanson for this creative idea. Trudy is the co-ordinator of the Centre for Loss and Grief in Dubbo, New South Wales. She works with indigenous Australians whose ongoing history of loss is deeply disturbing. She and her colleagues run camps for bereaved Aboriginal children to help build resilience. At the end of each camp each child is given a Love Wrap. These are blankets made with individual knitted squares representing the individual nature of grief. Many are knitted by people who have been bereaved. No two blankets are the same, which emphasises that each experience of grief is unique. At the end of the final gathering a leader 'wraps the recipient with love' with the presentation of the Love Wrap. They hope this keeps out the chill of grief and once back home, whenever the young person wants to feel connected to the love and warmth of the group, he can wrap himself in it (Hanson 2005).

Balloons

The bereaved write a message, which includes the words they long to say to the dead loved one, and tie it to a helium balloon. They then release it with their message attached. This helps them to reach out to the loved one and reconnect with the bond within. This can be done alone or with a group of family or friends to mark special anniversaries.

Collages

Collages can be made using photographs, drawings, poems, postcards, proverbs, or anything that has a visual connection to the deceased. These are arranged on a flat sheet of paper and stuck down once the creator is happy with the completed arrangement. Collages can be made at various points following the bereavement. The finding of images, including those from magazines, can act as a meditation as the person connects to thoughts and feelings that may have been suppressed. Collages can be made individually or by a family group or a group of friends.

Celebrating special days

Many bereaved feel a surge of memory and attachment at times of public holidays, such as Christmas, Thanksgiving, Eid, Passover and so on. When wreaths are placed on doors, or trees decorated, one ribbon in the deceased's favourite colour may be included as a visual reminder of her place in the heart of the family.

In some traditions, for example in South East Asia, the release of paper lanterns and boats marks special anniversaries. Lit paper lanterns were held aloft at Khao Lak in Thailand on the anniversary of the 2004 Tsunami.

Anniversary table

This idea was given to me by a little boy whose father had died suddenly in a walking accident. On the anniversary of his father's death his mother had arranged to have a small table set aside so that the family could remember their father. On it were placed a bowl of water with salt in it 'to represent the tears we've cried', a star painted blue on one side, 'the colour of sadness' according to my small client, and yellow on the other side, 'the colour of happiness', 'because though you can be sad it's nicer to be happy'. They also had photographs of the family before his father's death and others of them without their father.

To extend this activity the bereaved could leave pens and strips of paper for the family and selected friends to add their thoughts, feelings and memories. There may need to be guidance on this: perhaps the bereaved want positive affirmations rather than negative comments.

Screensaver and Trash

This is an activity to help the bereaved to think about memories they want to keep, the 'Screensaver' and those they want to get rid of, 'Trash'. It helps them to look at memories they treasure but also to consider those characteristics of the deceased and their relationship which were negative. In the 'Trash' they can metaphorically dump what is unhelpful and retain what feels positive. It allows them to see the complete relationship in a realistic way.

Iceberg

Very often, when we work with the bereaved we see their surface actions or behaviour, but not what swirls below the surface. In this activity the person draws an iceberg with one tenth showing above the surface, which represents what everyone can see. Then they write or draw, below the water line, what people can't see. Some examples of what clients have said to me that are below that surface line are: crying when no one else is around, drinking on my own to help me forget, watching videos of my son again and again as a way to keep the memories, putting on my husband's shirt to be close to him, and lying on my daughter's bed to smell her scent. The iceberg lets people explore anything that seems shameful or unacceptable. It can help to air the secrets that can lock the person in their loneliest grief.

Parting gifts

Often we don't actively recognise what gifts have been passed on to us by those who have died. I adapted this activity from the plot of *Badger's Parting Gifts*, a children's book by Susan Varley about a badger who knows his time is limited and gives a gift to each of his friends – not a physical object but something he taught them, such as kite-flying. I use it with adults and children to identify some of those sustaining legacies that help us to keep continuing bonds. Here are some that I have been told about:

- 'My Dad taught me to whistle.'
- 'She gave me a love of the countryside.'
- 'He gave me the kids. I look at them and see his expressions. It's such a comforting thing, knowing that part of him is still here.'

Gardens

Creating a garden can bring joy and it can be a garden of remembrance. It can be planted with flowers that symbolically connect to the person who has died. Some that might be included are: snowdrops, the first flowers of spring that represent beginnings after a period of bleak darkness; pansies, whose name comes form the French *'pensée*, thought; forget-me-nots and rosemary for remembrance.

There is healing power in the natural world, as Richard Mabey (2006) reveals in *Nature Cure*, and being in natural surroundings as well as planting and tending can bring both emotional and physical benefits. The bereaved can make a living shrine, for example by planting a wood or building a dedicated feature in a garden.

Shrines and memorials

A shrine is a place of worship or of commemoration. It can take many forms. American writer Clay Carmichael and sculptor, Mike Roig devised a four-week programme to enable grieving people to create their own memorials (Carmichael and Roig 2003). They discussed Mexican *retablos* (small oil paintings on tin, wood or copper made to venerate saints and placed behind an altar), altars, videos, songs, plaques and murals, and encouraged the participants to create their own. One man made a bird-bath in memory of his son who loved birds; another made a cabinet in which he could keep his father's treasured possessions.

Roadside Memorials

Throughout Britain there is a growing trend to create roadside memorials after the death of a loved one in a road traffic accident (Clark and Franzmann 2006). In creating such roadside shrines or memorials the bereaved are often challenging local authority rules or religious norms, since these memorial-makers are setting up their own sacred sites. The authors state that some bereaved people believe that the spirit stays at the place of death so these memorials must be placed at the scene, not somewhere that might be more convenient for others. The memorials are a public expression of grief that the bereaved want to share with the rest of the world (Doss 2002). In some instances, they are warnings to others about the risk of that particular place.

Dreamcatcher

Dreamcatchers originated in North America, there Native Americans constructed a circle with a web of strings across it which were then decorated with beads and feathers. They believed these trapped bad dreams and protected people from nightmares. In making a dreamcatcher with a client you give the opportunity to talk about disturbing dreams and help them to recognise that they can exercise an element of control over them. By talking about them, by trying to understand their message or the waking events that triggered the dream, you enable the person to feel more empowered.

Using the internet

On-line cemeteries or 'virtual cemeteries' were founded by Michael Kibee in Canada. His site www.cemetery.org gave rise to many others used by various communities, including Chinese and Americans as described by Chang and Sofka (2006). These offer internet memorial halls, e-temples and on-line grave-yards and many of the sites have message boards (Martin 2000). According to a report from the Funeral Administration Office of the Bureau of Civil Affairs in Peking (Guo 2006), more than 30,000 people used online services to mark Tomb Sweeping day, a memorial day on which Chinese people remember their ancestors. One site offers the opportunity to post a letter from 'beyond'. Here a message can be left before death to be 'posted' after death has occurred (www.mycemetery.com/pet/index. html) (Chang and Sofka 2006).

Web cemeteries offer those who are bereaved the opportunity to create memorials, and provide somewhere to 'place' the dead and to visit, just as physical cemeteries do (Roberts 2006). Web memorials may give the bereaved the chance to express their feelings, which might otherwise be suppressed, and they often include personal tributes to the deceased (Golden 2006). A Taiwanese virtual temple, www.8k.com.tw/baby.asp, acts as a memorial for aborted foetuses, providing a place which allows those whose grief may be disenfranchised to be marked, especially since many Chinese are Buddhists who believe that the spirit of an aborted baby needs a name and a place.

An American site, www.empty-cradles.com/index.html, allows on-line users to leave messages for a deceased child as well as the chance to choose a tiny star in a 'cyber galaxy' to represent the child. They create continuing bonds to ensure the dead are not forgotten (Walter 1996a) and the majority of web memorials are written as letters to the dead (Golden 2006; Roberts 2006). Guest-book entries, which invite visitors to the site to write comments, elicit shared communication and an ongoing knowledge of the stories of those who died (Walter 1996b). This creation of the 'story' of a person's life and death is an important part of the grieving process, as Tom Golden, grief therapist, illustrates through his site www.Webhealing. com, which he set up following the death of his father.

MySpace.com is an online networking tool and the second most visited site after yahoo.com. It provides instant communication between friends and allows users to contact other groups. Whilst common interests such as music and sports are widely shared users also share information about grief and suicide. The use of MySpace accounts allows a swift response to death and is heavily used by adolescents in particular (Oltjenbruns and James 2006). Friends can leave tributes, send respects and messages following a death, and this happens particularly when the death has been sudden and tragic, for example following a gang-related death. People may also write blogs, create shrines and deliver bulletins. The internet is also used to research information about a death which has been in the news.

The internet has its downside as well, since some groups discuss and encourage such acts as self-mutilation and suicide and no one can be 100 per cent sure of the identity of the person who is communicating. Predators stalk the internet and there is no guarantee that someone offering advice and support is what he says he is (Oltjenbruns and James 2006).

Reflective exercises

A pillow journal

This is an exercise you can do for a week, a month or for ever. You could also consider inviting someone you are working with to do the same.

At the end of each day, just before you go to sleep, write one positive statement about your day in a small journal (Waines 2004). Take a new page for each entry. It does not matter how unimportant it may seem: if it feels positive to you, then write it down. It could be something somebody said to you, something you are proud of achieving or something you observed that made you feel good.

Ask yourself:

- What made me smile today?
- What did I enjoy?
- Which of my senses were stimulated today?
- What lifted my spirits?
- What made me glad to be alive?

After you have been collecting these statements for some time you will have accumulated a journal of private, uplifting memories. Read it when you need a positive input – when you are feeling low, for example.

Decorating the gap

English politician and diarist Tony Benn wrote movingly of his wife's death after a long illness. In an interview (Driscoll 2007), seven years after her death, he said: 'I think about her every day, every hour. You can never fill the gap, the gap is always there, but you can decorate the gap with flowers and happy memories. I'm trying' (Driscoll 2007: 10).

Think about a loss in your life and the gap it has left.

How have you 'decorated' the gap?
What happy memories sustain you?
What more could you do now to fill that gap?

My Poem

Refer to the poem 'The colour of grief' (pp. 106–7) and consider how you might write your own poem about loss or death. Begin one line with the word you have chosen and on the next line begin with 'It'. Consider it in the following ways:

- What is the colour?
- What is the texture?
- What is the sound?
- What is the taste?
- What is the feeling?
- What is the temperature?
- What does it bring?

You can add other things as well.
    Here is one I wrote:

Death is indigo blue.
It feels like grit on velvet.
Death is the sound of the snipe, calling in despair.
It tastes metallic, bitter on the tongue.
Death is feeling bereft.
It chills every corpuscle.
Death brings me to a standstill.

You are not trying to create a polished poem but intuitively responding to the images that arise. Trust the process and write what comes into your head.

After you have completed your poem reflect on the words you used and the images you have chosen. What connections can you make?

Writing a condolence letter

After a death it may be appropriate to send a letter or note in which you offer your genuine thoughts and feelings about the person who has died and offer kind words of comfort to the bereaved.

Think of someone who has died and compose a letter to the person's parents or to one of their friends.

Think about the nature of your relationship with the deceased.
Was it close or distant? Formal or informal?
Was the person a friend or a colleague?

Is there a special event that you shared with the deceased that would be helpful to the person you are writing to?

Write a note that expresses your feelings. Keep it short, as people who have been bereaved may find difficulty in concentrating on longer letters.

Clumsy clichés to avoid:

'It's part of God's plan.'
The bereaved may wonder what kind of God let their child have cancer and die at a young age. Some people find their belief in God vanishes when they experience what is perceived as an unfair death.

'She's in a better place.'
Such statements feel like hollow platitudes. The bereaved want their loved one with them and may resent the idea that the place they had with them was not the best. Also, the bereaved may have their own views on whether there is an afterlife, so it's important not to make assumptions.

'He's at peace now.'
This again feels like a platitude. The family may still be tormented by images of a less than peaceful death or a suicide which left them reeling.

'He had a good innings.'
No matter what the age of the person who died, the bereaved don't need clichés in the aftermath of death. Instead, talk about some of the events in his life, showing your genuine affection and positive regard.

'I know exactly how you feel.'
Grief is different for each of us. If you have had a similar experience – had a cot death, for example – you might say, 'I too have had a cot death and I'm really sorry for your loss.'

Try not to say 'you should' or 'you ought' or 'you will'. Avoid being directive and telling people what will happen. What happened to you or helped you may not be helpful to the person you are writing to.

Keep it simple and make sure the feelings you express are honest.

'I was so sorry to hear of John's death.'
'You are in my thoughts at this sad time.'
'I would like to call in to see you if that is all right with you. I'll give you a ring on Tuesday to find a convenient time.'
'Your son was such a special man. I will never forget his kindness when ...'

8

Dreams in Dying, Death and Grief

'Dreams are a very important way to continue my relationship with my father since he is not here physically. It is something I don't take lightly. Our culture is one that believes in dreams as a way to see things, to understand and to communicate with the past. Many of our ancient prophets communicated through dreams.'

Ziggy Marley, son of musician Bob Marley, in *Gay*, 2006: 10)

Our dreams reflect our lives, our culture and the events that influence our thoughts and feelings (Bynum 1993). Those of us who work in bereavement care can use dreams as part of the process of addressing emotional aspects of loss. Learning about dreamwork is a deeply satisfying process which empowers those with whom we work (Barrett 1992; Garfield 1997).

What is a dream?

The dream cries out to each of us. Look at this and be attentive, for you must learn from me as best you can.

(Artemidorus, *The Interpretation of Dreams*, 1975)

A dream is mental activity which occurs when we sleep (Hobson 1989; Moffitt et al. 1993). For most people dreams are an imagined series of events that may form a coherent story whilst for others they are a series of surreal images or shapes with no overt narrative thread. Dream imagery changes as we mature, though some people have consistency in their dream 'themes' which last throughout life. At times of great stress or when emotions are heightened, we are likely to have dreams of greater intensity, which impinge on our waking world.

That all things are changed, and that nothing really perishes, and that the sum of matter remains exactly the same, is sufficiently certain.

(Francis Bacon 1604)

In cases of trauma dreams can play a part in 'achieving a calming of the storm' (Schredl 2000: 247). In my practice as a counsellor and in research (Mallon 2000a; Orbach 1999) I have found that those who are grieving recall their dreams more readily than those who are not. People anticipating bereavement, those who have been bereaved and those who are dying may well experience heightened intensity in their dreams (Goelitz 2007; Grubbs 2004). Dreaming is generally responsive to experiences that precede it during the day. Emotional arousal affects the intensity of dreams rather than their length or specific content (Hartmann and Basile 2003).

Dreams of the deceased facilitate the grieving process (LoConto 1998). The deceased returns in dreams, and dreams allow the past and present to be integrated. They enable individuals to complete acts that were unfinished (Bulkeley 2000). Dreams permit us to work through specific traumatic episodes and traumatic grief and to attain some form of resolution (Mallon 2006). However, this is not always the case. Some nightmares following a traumatic incident may allow the person to review the incident and find some meaning for themselves. On the other hand, such nightmares may further traumatise the individual so that they are reliving the trauma rather than reviewing it. In the latter case, the nightmares may also serve as a signpost to the need for skilled therapeutic intervention, particularly when post-traumatic nightmares impair waking life (Barrett 1996).

The nature of dreams

I dreamed one night that dear More was alive again and that after throwing my arms round his neck and finding beyond all doubt that I had my loving son in my embrace – we went thoroughly into the subject, and found that the death and the funeral at Abinger had been fictitious. For a second after waking the joy remained – then came the knell that wakes me every morning – More is dead! More is dead!

(Samuel Palmer in a letter to a friend, in Cecil 1969, quoted in Bowlby 1980: 112)

Normal grief reactions such as anger, guilt, sadness and helplessness are reflected in dreams of the bereaved (Davidson et al. 2005). This is shown in the following examples told to my by bereaved clients:

'When I was much younger I dreamt of my father who died when I was ten. He appeared in army clothes and was looking for my mother. I was annoyed as I thought he did not want us children. He told me he would go away and I have never dreamt of him since.'

'In this dream my father has grown very old and is really ill. He later dies. I feel it is my fault and get really upset.'

'After the death of a very close friend I had terrible nightmares in which I saw his shooting and the scenes afterwards as his father and medical staff tried to revive him. Then the operation, his death and the funeral.'

The dreamer of the last dream worked on her dreams over many months since they were so disturbing she was afraid to sleep. However, she recognised that she needed to face the pain captured in the dream images, which she did. She concluded, 'These dreams helped me to get rid of pent up feelings and to accept that he was gone and nothing would bring him back.' Grieving is not a linear process and emotions may need to be re-experienced (Belicki et al. 2003). The dreams may recur and force us to face unhappiness repressed or avoided in waking life.

Working with dreams: good practice

It is very helpful to discover something about the dream life of people we work with and the subject is easily introduced by asking how they are sleeping and then asking if they recall any dreams. You can then work with whatever they bring to the session.

In working with dreams the essential aspect is to listen to the dream, to explore the connections the dreamer makes between the dream images and waking life; to ask the person to describe images in greater detail and to collaborate with the dreamer to construct an interpretation. Using the core counselling skills described in Chapter 3 will facilitate this process. The aim is not to offer your own interpretation but to enable the dreamer to make her own interpretation. The person who holds the key to the meaning of the dream is the dreamer. There are many more techniques you can use in dreamwork but the first step is to be open to your clients' dreams, invite them to tell their dreams and to listen to the dream narrative (Mallon 2001).

People often have a strong sense of what the dream means. When I was researching material for *Dreams, Counselling and Healing*, a woman wrote about two dreams which were particularly significant to her: 'Six months ago my Granny died. We were very close and I miss her very much. She was the best thing around me in an unhappy childhood. Recently in my dream, she came to me and we hugged. This made me feel that she was alright and that she is still around me.' Another dream was not quite so direct but intuitively she knew it had meaning for her: 'Recently I dreamt about blue irises. Although I am a florist, I am not fond of blue irises as they remind me always of my Granny's funeral when I was a teenager. Even on waking the image of these flowers filled my head and remained with me throughout the day, bringing my Granny "around me". By tea time I was curious about whether it was a significant date, maybe Granny's birthday? When

I telephoned my parents to ask, I was told it was the anniversary of her death.' Dreams sometimes remind us of what we already know but have forgotten.

Dreams may be used in anticipatory grief work. For example, in working with cancer patients and their carers dreams are discussed and related to the impact of the illness on the emotional lives of those concerned (Goelitz 2001). Dreams may be used in conjunction with visualisation, healing imagery and relaxation techniques (Lyons 2003; Mallon et al. 2005). Wanda Easter Burch (2004) writes of the important role her dreams played from the time she was diagnosed with aggressive breast cancer and through her surgery, chemotherapy and in the depression that accompanied the process. She charts their significant healing aspect on the spiritual as well as the physical level.

Dreamwork is a valuable therapeutic tool which can be used with all ages and in a wide variety of settings (Bynum 1993; Garfield 1991). As Cartwright and Lambert point out, 'In our times of trouble, when we suffer loss of self-esteem or have our belief in our competence knocked out from under us, dreams help repair our damaged sense of self' (1992: 269). In bereavement care dreamwork enables us to gain insight into the world of the bereaved, to understand the emotional issues facing them and helps us to identify appropriate support (Bulkeley 2000). The dreams also enable the dreamer to access dream thoughts and dream feelings. By discussing, working with and reflecting on these dreams you will enable the bereaved to explore their feelings more extensively (Mallon 2000a).

Dreams facilitate movement through the grieving process. In a presentation at the International Manchester Area Bereavement Conference in 1999, Ruth Harrison spoke of 'The impact of murder on families'. She recounted the experience of an eight-year-old girl who was having trouble sleeping following the murder of her sister. In her nightmares Sally knew her sister was there though she couldn't see her face. She was terrified of these nightmares yet none of the professionals who saw the child asked her about them. It was only later when Harrison helped Sally and her mother to work on the dreams by drawing, listening and making a dreamcatcher that Sally was able to move on from her 'stuck' grieving position. The disturbing nightmares disappeared, allowing the bereaved girl to sleep in peace once more.

Working with a dream

I worked with Jamie, whose father had died from cancer.

'My Dad died four years ago. It was cancer and there were three weeks between his diagnosis and his death. He came home and my Mum and Auntie, who was a nurse, were there and I was there. We were with him when he died. I'm glad about that but it was so quick. It's just that I have these dreams sometimes and, well, I wonder if it's normal.'

I asked Jamie to describe his dream:

> 'It's different situations really, but usually it's upstairs in our house and I'm hugging him. It's more the sensation of being close and hugging him. He's saying things like "I was kidnapped, that's why I was away" or "I was a spy so I had to leave." And I'm saying, "It doesn't matter, it doesn't matter." I'm reassuring him and hugging him. It feels so good. When I wake up I'm a bit sad but it is good to have that feeling of being with him.'

In working on the dream – I asked Jamie to draw it as he talked – he said how when his father was dying he would put his arm round him as he lay in the bed, and hug him. It was a very special feeling and in his drawing of the two stick figures, he drew a circle that encompassed them both. 'It was like we were together again and it was such an important feeling.' Jamie found the dreamwork reassuring and felt much more positive about his dreams as well as appreciating the fact that dreaming about the deceased is 'normal'.

Dreams about bereavement are not rare (von Franz 1986). They may come prior to the death of person to whom the dreamer is close as a form of anticipatory grief, shortly after a bereavement in reaction to the loss, or for the rest of a person's lifetime, reflecting the nature of continuing bonds. Adults who have experienced the death of someone they loved may long for a dream in which they are reunited yet may feel heartbroken on awakening because, 'It was only a dream'.

A woman was referred to me following the death of her husband after a short illness. During one session, the client described a dream image. It was a hand with what initially seemed to be water dripping from the palm and fingers. She began to cry and said, 'No. It's happiness slipping through my fingers.' After a period of intense grief, she still found it extremely difficult to hold on to any happiness. She felt that without her husband there was no longer any room for joy in her life. The hand trying to hold water symbolises the impossibility of containing her emotions. Happiness slips away because she feels she has no control, the symbol of the open hand indicates she cannot grasp and keep what she so desires. Also, she felt that by allowing herself to enjoy herself she was betraying her husband: it just didn't seem 'fair'. After talking about the lack of joy in her life she explored simple ways in which she might find more contentment and decided to join an art class with a friend. Painting was a hobby she had given up some years before and, as she continued to see me for a year, she brought paintings of her other dreams which we then worked on together.

Nell Dale's husband died and some time later she had a dream which she records in *What Colour is Grief? A Journey* (2007: 8). She wrote, 'I dream I go into a shoe shop full of very high heeled shoes. I take off my comfy flat shoes, I try many pairs on. I keep falling over. I cannot walk on them and now my own shoes are missing. I am stranded. I cannot walk anywhere.' Dreams often include symbols and metaphors which can be used to interpret the dream (Mallon 2007). In this dream the 'comfy shoes' come off and then go missing. Nell is 'falling over', 'stranded' and she cannot go anywhere. The new 'high heeled shoes' are all that are on offer but they don't work for her. If we relate this to Nell's situation without her dearly loved partner we can see the dream as a metaphor for how she was feeling at the point she had the dream. She doesn't want the image that she can take on if she accepts the new shoes. They don't suit her, in fact they are dangerous. However, her previous comfortable flat shoes have gone, as has the life she had with her husband. Somehow, she has to find a way to stand on her own two feet so that she is no longer stranded.

The spiritual dimension of dreaming in relation to death

All of the dreams of people who are facing death indicate that the unconscious, that is, our instinct world, prepares consciousness not for a definite end but for a profound transformation and for a kind of continuation of the life process which, however, is unimaginable to everyday consciousness.

(Marie-Louise von Franz 1986)

In many cultures dreaming is highly valued and dream reporting is the norm (Bulkeley 2002). For example in the Gazan and Galilean Arab culture children grow up thinking about and narrating their dreams and many studies have shown the efficacy of working with dreams (Garfield 1996; Gogar and Hill 1992; Keller et al. 1995).

Dreams offer spiritual solace to those have been bereaved. Elisabeth Kubler-Ross (1975) called dreams of the dead 'true contacts on a spiritual plane'. Such dreams can bring people closer to the sacred and the transcendent that inspire and guide waking life (Bulkeley 1995). They can bring some comfort after a seemingly meaningless, random event such as accidental death or murder. Where the dead person is cared for by God or angels or other revered beings in dreams, then the bereaved often feel relieved. It is important to take spirituality, faith and belief into account when working with dreams and the bereaved.

As we saw earlier, it is not unusual for people to remark that the dead appear in dreams just as they were in life which furthers their belief that life does not end here on earth. Symbolically, the deceased is often on a journey, as in the following dream which was told to me by a client:

'Shortly after my father's sudden death I dreamt that I stood on a river bank watching my father preparing for a boat trip. In the dream my father was about twenty years younger than his actual age at death. I felt happy about his trip and he departed cheerfully. When I woke up I felt much more at peace about my father's death – it seemed to mark a turning point in the grief process.'

In some instances the dead person appears but there is no longer the opportunity to touch the loved one:

> 'I dreamt I was on a golf course I know well. My son, who died seven years ago, was walking towards the green but somehow I couldn't get to him.'

I have noted a pattern of dreams of the bereaved in which the deceased goes further away and cannot be touched, they have gone to 'the other side', where the living gain no access. This is not always the case of course, there are no iron-clad rules about what will or will not happen in dreams, but it is something I have found regularly. The dreamer above sees her son on his own journey; she cannot accompany him. Dreams of an afterlife in which the dead live on often help those 'left behind' to move through their grieving (Garfield 1996). They indicate the bonds between the deceased and the bereaved are intact yet allow the bereaved to carry on with their own life (Norbury 2004).

Visitation dreams

Many mourners feel that they have been visited by the deceased and there has been much investigation of such dreams (Bulkeley 2000; Moody 1993; Rees 1971; Vickio 1998). These visitations maintain the bonds that were so strong before the death. Suzanne Gingell's partner of fourteen years died of heart failure in his sleep. After some months she had this dream:

> I was sorting out some clothes when a dark shape came through the door. It was David, looking so happy. He kissed me and said he'd come back for the sweater I'd spun and knitted for him on one of his trips. He picked it up, smiled and then he faded away. I felt really happy and I felt at peace.
>
> (Gingell 2005: 58)

Not all dreams of the deceased are so pleasant. One of my clients dreamt of her friend who had died of cancer. 'In my dream,' she said, 'she appeared as a corpse and had her hand up as if she wanted to strike me. She seemed to be mad at me for some reason and she was saying something that I couldn't hear.' The dream was disturbing but it provided the impetus to talk about the physical changes in my client's deceased friend, which she had found distressing but had been unable to mention to anyone. We also looked at ambivalent feelings that she had towards the deceased. The old saying 'Don't speak ill of the dead' may prevent the bereaved describing the nature of their true feelings.

In the following example we can see how dreams reflected the process of grieving, as the bereaved moves from disbelief to acceptance:

> 'After my father died I had a series of dreams about him. First I dreamed he wasn't actually dead, then that he wouldn't accept that he was dead. Finally, I dreamed

that he was getting better in the other world. Then a lovely dream where I met him. He was wearing a light blue shirt and looked years younger than when he was dying of cancer. He put his arms around me, told me he was fine now, that he loved me and told me not to worry about him any more. I felt good when I woke and have felt good about him ever since.'

The final meeting in the dream marks the resolution: the dreamer accepted her father's death and had no further feelings of remorse.

While grieving, many of us long for a 'sign of life' from the dead person, some indication that they are not suffering or that they are looked after (Devers 1997). One of my clients, whose seven-year-old daughter had died, found comfort from a dream in which she saw her daughter with her own mother who had died several years previously. For my client this was a healing dream.

'It seems that the dreams I remember are very significant, as if someone, often someone I know, a relative who has passed on is emphasising I am being looked after. I remember them for years after. They are imprinted on my memory.'

(Tricia)

Dreams of guidance, of being 'looked after', have ancient roots in beliefs that the ancestors continued to watch over and care for the bereaved from beyond the grave. This is evident throughout the world in ancestor worship, prayers for guidance, shrines erected to the deceased and in spiritualism and mediumship (Picardie 2001; Walter 2006).

Taylor (2005: 56) writes of counselling clients who see loved ones in dreams. She quotes Dee, whose partner had died three years prior to the sudden death of her husband:

Dee described her sense of the presence of her 'boys' in her dreams and used this in order to gain information and guidance from them. She was also aware of G's. [her partner's], presence throughout the house through objects moving around. She found the sense of G's presence reassuring, often speaking to him. However, she later expressed the fear that the two men might talk to each other and compare details of the relationship with her. This reinforces the fact, that when counselling or supporting someone in bereavement, we need to give plenty of time and opportunity for the exploration of emerging feelings. Nancy, in the same study said, 'It's as if he's walking next to me and giving me strength.'

It is important to ask those we work with about their culture and beliefs because this influences a person's response to the sense of presence of the deceased. A spiritualist will not be surprised by this. As Shirley, a medium, explained in Taylor's study, the presence is 'just something that comes to me, like opening your text messages' (2005: 59). However, some people who sense the deceased, like Dee (above), may feel fear that the deceased is watching everything they do, including having sex. This may lead to problems for the bereaved and can cause the breakdown of a newly formed relationship.

Dreams of the dying

The dreams of those who are approaching death offer a valuable healing resource (Mallon 2005; von Franz 1986). Decathexis, the process of letting go as death approaches, may bring dreams in which companions come to assist the dreamer to the 'other side'. These 'companions' are usually people who were close family members or friends who, in dreams, may sit beside the dying person's bed or explain that it is time to go (Mallon 2000b). They may appear to be ready to set off on a journey with the dying person. Seeing former friends once more in dreams often brings comfort and pleasure.

Traditional symbols of light and rebirth are often found in the dreams of the dying. Marie von Franz, a noted Jungian analyst, found that travel images are common in the dreams of the dying. She states, 'In my experience the image of the journey in dreams is also the most frequently occurring symbol of impending death' (von Franz 1986: 64). This does not mean that all people who dream of travel are about to die; just that it is a common image.

Asking clients about their dreams – whether they have life-limiting illness or are the bereaved – can open up a rich dialogue and give the opportunity to explore many dimensions, including the spiritual. 'A light in the darkness of mere being' (Jung 1973: 326) for me encompasses the process of counselling and the therapeutic relationship on which it depends. Initially the client and counsellor are, metaphorically, in the dark. The healing process illuminates 'the darkness of mere being'. The journey taken together includes the world of dreams as well as recalled experiences of loss and psychological insecurity. The reality of day to day grief and suffering is the tip of the iceberg below which the world of deams and the unconscious are submerged. In this sea the counsellor often needs to be the anchor that holds the steady line. By appreciating the vastness of the dream world we can plumb the depths where danger may lurk, understand how it may be circumvented and even enjoy the beauty of the awesome territory in which we travel. And, in counselling, travel is what we must do because it is a process not a still, fixed point.

Reflective exercises

Dreams you never forget

Some people find dream recall easy, others find it more difficult. Think about the Life Map exercise you did earlier and try to remember any dreams you had during the time you have covered. Write down one vivid dream from childhood. Write down another that sticks in your mind and, finally, write the most recent one you can recall. When you have done this consider the following questions as applied to each dream:

What was so memorable about the dream?

Did it reflect current events in your life?

What was the message of the dream?

Was there a significant person in the dream? If so, in what way was the person important to you?

Did any of the dreams involve loss? If so, what was that loss and how do you feel about it now?

Can you see any recurring themes or patterns that link these dreams?

Finally, complete this sentence:

From these dreams I have learned …

Your dream journal

An uninterpreted dream is like an unopened letter.

(The Talmud)

This is a longer-term project than the exercises you have already completed. It concerns your developing self-awareness and will enable you to work more confidently with dreams in the support or counselling setting. Keep a notebook by your bed: this will be your dream journal.

Every morning give yourself a few minutes to focus on your dreams. Let the images from your dreams form a bridge between your sleeping and waking life.

Write down your dreams – unedited – and include as much detail as you can.

Give your dream a title as this will help you to recall it later.

Draw dream images, especially if it is hard to put the dream into words.

When you have time, return to your dream and see how it relates to your life right now. Was there an event that triggered the dream? Did something happen during the day to influence your unconscious mind? Think about other connections and record them in your journal.

Ask yourself, 'Why did I choose this image in my dream?' 'What importance does this colour or shape have for me?' Allow memories or associations to emerge in your answer. Over time you may find a pattern in your dream life which you can explore to gain greater insight into yourself and issues that concern you (Mallon 2000a).

You never know what is in store for you when strange events or dreams come to you. You may not know if they are enlightening or tragic. Destiny, in one form or another, may be a large part of them and if you are in tune with your dreams, you may certainly find that their calling comes from the depths of your soul.

(Grubbs 2004: 169)

Resources

'Resources' is divided into the following sections:

Bereavement
Cancer-related organisations
General resources
Mental health organisations
Miscarriage and early infant death
Traumatic injury and death

Bereavement

The Bereavement Register
Tel. 0870 600 7222
www.thebereavementregister.org.uk

The organisation aims to supply the names of the recently deceased to mail order companies to ensure that their names are deleted from databases so that mailings are not sent out which would otherwise cause distress to the bereaved. Register to stop direct mail being sent out.

Childhood Bereavement Network – CBN
8 Wakley Street
London EC1V 7QE
Tel. 020 7843 6309
www.ncb.org.uk

The Child Bereavement Network is a national multi-professional federation of organisations and individuals working with children and young people. They produce a directory which aims to put people in touch with children's bereavement support services in their local area. They have a database of information about sources of support for bereaved children. CBN is supported by all the major bereavement care organisations in the UK.

Child Bereavement Charity
Aston House

West Wycombe
High Wycombe
Bucks HP14 3AG
Tel. 01494 446 648
www.childbereavement.org.uk

The Charity provides training and support for professional carers and supplies information and resources for bereaved families and professionals.

Child Death Helpline
The Alder Centre
Alder Hay Children's Hospital
Eaton Road
Liverpool L12 2AP
Helpline: 0800 282 986
Tel. 0151 252 5391
www.childdeathhelpline.org.uk

The helpline is a listening service that offers emotional support to anyone affected by the death of a child.

The Compassionate Friends – TCF
53 North Street
Bristol BS3 1EN
Helpline: 0845 123 2304
Tel. 0117 966 5202
www.tcf.org.uk

The Compassionate Friends offers support and friendship to bereaved parents and their families, and to friends and professionals who are helping the families. It has self-help support groups throughout the United Kingdom. They offer a listening service and will provide details of local contacts who can offer ongoing support. (See also listing for Shadow of Suicide on p. 148.)

The Compassionate Friends also offer Support in Bereavement for Brothers and Sisters (SIBBS). This provides telephone support and advice, and arranges meeting for bereaved siblings. It has a contact network and a newsletter.

Crocus
Tel. 01463 704 000

Crocus offers support to bereaved children in Inverness and the Highlands of Scotland.

Cruse Bereavement Care
Central Office
Cruse House
126 Sheen Road

Richmond
Surrey TW9 1UR
Helpline: 0844 477 9400
Day by Day helpline: 0845 758 5565
Young Person's Helpline: 0808 808 1677
www.crusebereavementcare.org.uk

This is a national organisation with local branches and over 7,000 volunteers. It offers counselling, support and advice to those who are bereaved and training for volunteers and professionals working with the bereaved.

Cruse Young People's Helpline
Tel. 0808 808 1677

The helpline offers a listening and support service for bereaved young people. Cruse Bereavement Care Scotland www.crusescotland.org.uk

Daisy's Dream
PO Box 4738
Twyford
Reading
Berkshire RG10 9GT
Tel. 0118 934 2604
www.daisysdream.org.uk

Daisy's Dream offers a number of services to cater for individual family needs following bereavement. It provides training for professionals such as teachers, who may find themselves working with bereaved children.

Epilepsy Bereaved
PO Box 112
Wantage
Oxon OX12 8XT
Tel. 01235 772 850
www.dspace.dial.pipex.com/epilepsybereaved

Epilepsy Bereaved offers emotional support and advice to those who have been bereaved by a sudden death in epilepsy (SUDEP). It produces a news magazine and information on SUDEP.

The Grief Centre, Manchester Area Bereavement Forum
362 Manchester Road
Droylsden
Manchester M43 6QX
Tel. 0161 371 8860
www.mabf.org.uk

A charity that provides one to one counselling, telephone support and advice as well as running an annual international conference related to an aspect of bereavement. It also offers training in helping young people to manage loss and courses on bereavement care.

Hospice Information
Tel. 0870 903 3903
www.hospiceinformation.org.uk

Publishes a directory of hospice and palliative care services.

Lesbian and Gay Bereavement Project
Vaughan Williams Centre
Colindale Hospital
London NW9 SHG
Helpline: 020 7403 5969 (Tuesdays)

The Lesbian and Gay Bereavement Project offers emotional support and advice to anyone bereaved of their same-sex partner. The group also provides speakers and has prepared a free will form to encourage life partners to write a will. Send an SAE if you require a copy.

London Bereavement Network
www.bereavement.org.uk

The LBN maintains a list of bereavement services in London.

Lone Twin Network
PO Box 5653
Birmingham B29 7JY
Contact by post only

The Lone Twin Network offers support to lone twins over the age of 18 whose twin has died. This does not have to be a recent bereavement; the loss could have occurred at any stage of life.

Merrywidow.me.uk
www.merrywidow.me.uk

Online support and message boards based on one woman's account of being widowed at a young age.

National Association of Widows
National Office
48 Queens Road
Coventry CV1 3EH
Tel. 024 7663 4848
www.nawidows.org.uk

The self-help organisation offers telephone support and advice and may put widows in contact with others in a similar situation in their local area. The befriending service is accessed from the national office.

National Bereavement Partnership
National office:
Office No. 6
2 Bear Street
Barnstaple EX32 7DB
Tel. 0845 226 7227
www.natbp.org.uk

The national helpline is staffed by people who have experienced bereavement and organ retention. The helpline offers support and answers to relatives' queries about organs that might have been retained as well as offering practical support.

Rainbows
Tel. 0114 256 6445

Rainbows helps children and young people who are suffering bereavement or other forms of loss. It works through schools and family centres.

The Sand Rose Project
PO Box 70
Hayle TR27 5WY
Tel. 0845 607 6357
www.sandrose.org.uk

The Sand Rose Project organises breaks in Cornwall, free of charge for bereaved families.

St Christopher's Candle Project – London
Tel. 020 8768 4500

This bereavement service offers support to children and young people under 18 by telephone support, one to one and group counselling. It also runs training courses for professionals and volunteers involved in bereavement support.

WAY Foundation
PO Box 6767
Brackley NN13 6YW
Tel. 0870 011 3450
www.wayfoundation.org.uk

Self-help social and support network for men and women under 50 who have been widowed. The main aim is to help young widows to rebuild their lives by helping one another.

Winston's Wish
Clara Burgess Centre
Bayshill Road
Cheltenham GL50 3AW
Helpline: 0845 203 0405
www.winstonswish.org.uk

Winston's Wish offers practical support and guidance for bereaved children and young people and their families. There are weekend events which bereaved parents and family members attend, to work with their grief and take part in activities to build resilience after loss. Winston's Wish also sells materials, such a memory boxes, to use following bereavement.

Yad b'Yad
c/o Louise Heilbron
8 Grove Avenue
London N10 2AR
Tel. 020 8444 7134
Email: heilbron@cheerful.com

Yad b'Yad is Hebrew for Hand in Hand and is a Jewish child bereavement project which advises professionals and agencies about the needs of Jewish children.

Cancer-related organisations

The British Association of Cancer United Patients (Cancer BACUP)
3 Bath Place
Rivington Street
London EC2A 3JR
Tel. 020 7696 9003
Freephone: 0808 800 1234
www.cancerbacup.org.uk

Cancer BACUP provides a Cancer Information Service which gives practical advice and emotional support to patients, their family and friends and to those bereaved by cancer. The website has more than 4,500 pages of cancer information.

CALL – Cancer Aid and Listening Line
Tel. 0161 205 7780

CALL offers emotional support and home-based practical help for people living with cancer as well as their carers and families.

Cancer Counselling Trust
Tel. 020 7704 1137
www.cctrust.org.uk

The Cancer Counselling Trust has specially trained psychotherapists and counsellors who are experienced in working with people affected by cancer.

CancerHelp UK
www.cancerhelp.org.uk

CancerHelp UK is a free service which provides information on cancer and cancer care.

Cancerlink
11–21 Northdown Road
London N1 9BN
Tel. 0808 808 0000
Email: cancerlink@canlink.demon.co.uk

Cancerlink provides information and emotional support to people with cancer, their families and friends and those who work with them.

Cancer Research UK
General enquiries: 020 7242 0200
Support services: 020 7121 6699
www.cancerresearch.uk.org

Researches the causes, prevention and treatment of cancer and provides information on different types of cancer as well as addressing practical issues, including how to reduce the risks of getting cancer.

Chai Cancer Care
Helpline: 0808 808 4567
www.chaicancercare.org

Chai Cancer Care offers emotional, physical and spiritual support, advice and care to Jewish cancer patients and their family and friends.

Macmillan Cancer Relief
89 Albert Embankment
London SE1 7UQ
Helpline: 0808 808 2020
Head office: 020 7840 7840
www.macmillan.org.uk

Macmillan offers life support by providing expert care to ease the pain and discomfort of those with cancer. It provides a range of innovative cancer services and is dedicated to improving cancer care in the UK.

National Cancer Alliance
Tel. 01865 793 566
www.national canceralliance.co.uk

The alliance represents the concerns and interests of cancer patients, their families and carers. It works to raise awareness of cancer services, diagnosis, treatment and care.

Marie Curie Cancer Care
Tel. 020 7599 7777
www.mariecurie.org.uk

Marie Curie Cancer Care has a national network of Marie Curie nurses who provide palliative care in patients' homes and at Marie Curie Centres. These services are free of charge to the patients.

New Approaches To Cancer
Tel. 0800 389 2662
www.newapproaches.co.uk

This organisation for patients and their families promotes the use of alternative therapies in cancer treatment and care. It emphasises holistic treatment to meet their physical, emotional and spiritual needs. It provides information and a referral service.

Tenovus Cancer Information Centre
Tel. 029 2048 2000
Helpline: 0808 808 1010
www.tenovus.com

The Tenovus Information Centre funds support and counselling services for cancer patients and their families through a team of nurses, counsellors and social workers.

General resources

ACT Association for Children with Life-Threatening Terminal Conditions and Their Families
Orchard House
Orchard Lane
Bristol BS1 5DT
Tel. 0117 922 1556
www.act.org.uk

ACT is a national organisation which offers advice and support to familes.

ADEC
Association for Death Education and Counselling
111 Deer Lake Road
Suite 100

Deerfield
Illinois 60015, USA
email: info@adec.org
www.adec.org

ADEC is a non-profit organisation devoted to issues and education in dying, death and bereavement. It publishes a monthly newsletter and a journal which covers research in thanatology.

Age Concern
Astral House
1268 London Road
London SW16 4ER
Tel. 020 8765 7200
Information Line: 0800 009 966
www.ageconcern.org.uk

Age Concern Scotland
113 Rose Street
Edinburgh EH2 3DT
Tel. 0131 220 3345
Helpline: 0800 009 966
www.ageconcernscotland.org.uk

Age Concern Cymru
4th Floor
1 Cathedral Road
Cardiff CF1 9SD
Tel. 029 2037 1566
Helpline: 0800 009 966
www.accymru.org.uk

Age Concern is a registered charity that provides information and support to people aged over 50 and practical help for older bereaved people. Local branches may offer counselling support. It is open 365 days a year from 7 a.m. to 7 p.m. It also publishes information leaflets, policy papers and a range of books.

Alzheimer's Disease Society
Gordon House
Greencoat Place
London SW1P 1PH
Tel. 020 7306 0606
www.alzheimers.org.uk

The Society offers support and advice to those suffering from dementia, and to their families and carers. Local support agencies can be found on the national website or by telephoning the Society.

Animal Samaritans
PO Box 154
Bexleyheath
Kent DA16 2WS
Tel. 020 8303 1859
www.animalsamaritans.org.uk

The Animal Samaritans offers a Pet Bereavement Scheme, a telephone service where bereaved pet owners can find support, help and a sympathetic listening ear.

Asian Family Counselling Service
Suite 51, The Lodge
Windmill Place
2–4 Windmill Lane
Southall UB2 4NJ
Tel. 020 8571 3933
www.2-in-2-1.co.uk/services/asianfam/

The Service offers advice and support to Asian families.

BACP – British Association of Counselling and Psychotherapy
35–37 Albert Street
Rugby
Warwickshire CV21 2SG
Tel. 0870 443 5219

BACP has directories of counsellors and psychotherapists throughout the United Kingdom. It also conducts research, issues a monthly journal to its members and runs training and accreditation courses.

Befriending Network
Claremont
24–27 White Lion Street
London N1 9PD
Tel. 020 7689 2443
www.befriending.net

This is a befriending network of trained volunteers which is active in north and west London, though it does refer on to other agencies in other areas. Members offer support to people suffering from terminal or life-threatening illnesses as well as providing support for family and carers.

British Humanist Association
1 Gower Street
London WC1E 6HD
www.humanism.org.uk

The non-religious Humanist Society offer services to mark the death of a person in the form of a highly personalised, empathetic ceremony carried out by accredited officiants.

British Organ Donor Society (BODY)
Blasham
Cambridge CB1 6DL
Tel. 01223 893 636
www.argonet.co.uk/body

BODY is a self-help organisation that offers support to families of organ donors and those who have received organs. It also helps people waiting for organs and those whose relatives have died following a transplant or while waiting for one.

British Red Cross
Tel. 0870 170 7000
www.redcross.org.uk

The British Red Cross cares for people in crisis throughout the UK. Volunteers provide local services, including transportation and escort services if needed.

Buddhist Hospice Trust
1 Laurel House
Trafalgar Road
Newport
Isle of Wight, PO30 1QN
Tel. 01268 741 419
www.buddhisthospice.org.uk

Offers a befriending service and runs courses for Buddhists and those interested in the philosophy of death, dying and bereavement.

Campaign Against Living Miserably – CALM
Helpline: 0800 585 858
www.thecalmzone.net

CALM offers support to young men suffering from depression.

Crossroads Association – Caring for Carers
10 Regent's Place,
Rugby
Warwickshire CV21 2PN
Tel. 0845 450 0350
www.crossroads.org.uk

Recognising the stress of caring for others, Crossroads provides care and advice for carers. It has local contact numbers throughout the UK.

CRY – Cardiac Risk in the Young
Unit 7, Epsom Downs
Metro Centre
Waterfield
Tadworth KT20 5LR
Tel. 01737 363 222
www.c-r-y.org.uk

CRY is a national charity which was set up in 1995 to raise awareness of cardiac risk in the young, including sudden cardiac death and Sudden Death Syndrome. The website lists regional contacts.

Department for Work and Pensions: *What to do after a Death in England.*
www.dwp.gov.uk

A guide to what you must do and the help you can get is contained in the form D49 April 2006
This gives all the information related to legal procedures following a death and practical advice for the bereaved.

Depression Alliance
Tel. 0845 123 2320

The Depression Alliance offers information and support for people affected by depression.

Disabled Living Foundation
Helpline: 0845 130 9177
Tel. 020 7432 8009
www.dlf.org.uk

The Foundation focuses on making everyday life easier for disabled people, older people and their carers. It provides information and support.

Gingerbread
Sovereign House
Sovereign Court
London E1W 2HW
Telephone Advice Line: 0800 018 4318
Tel. 020 7488 9300
www.gingerbread.org.uk

Gingerbread provides friendship, support and advice to lone parents, including those new lone parents who have been bereaved.

Help the Aged
207–221 Pentonville Road

London N1 9UZ
Tel. 020 7278 1114
www.helptheaged.org.uk

Help the Aged provides advice and leaflets on housing, welfare rights and benefits following bereavement.

Hospice Information Service
St Christopher's Hospice
51–59 Lawrie Park Road
London SE26 6DZ

Offers care for the terminally ill in a hospice or at home with support from their families. Directory of local hospice services available. It also runs training courses for people working with children and adults on dying, death and bereavement.

Institute for Complementary Medicine
Tel. 020 7237 5165
www.i-c-m.org.uk

The Institute supplies names and addresses of practitioners of a wide variety of complementary medicine.

Islamic Cultural Centre
146 Park Road
London NW8 7RG
Tel. 020 7725 2213
www.iccuk.org

Advises on local services in the United Kingdom for those of the Islamic faith.

Jewish Bereavement Counselling Service
8–10 Forty Avenue
Wembley
London HA9 8JW
Helpline: 020 8349 0839
Tel. 020 8385 1874
www.jvisit.org.uk

The JBCS offers a confidential counselling service for the bereaved to any member of the Jewish community as well as advice on bereavement rituals and customs.

Metropolitan Police Family Liaison Team
Tel. 0800 032 996

The Liaison Team offers a telephone service for people affected by bereavement, including information on the role of the coroner, how to register a death, the role of the Foreign & Commonwealth Office when death happens overseas, and advice on wills and estates.

The Muslim Council for Religious and Racial Harmony
8 Caburn Road
Hove BN3 6EF
Tel. 01273 722438

The Imam, Dr Adjuljalili Sajid, offers advice and information on all aspects of Muslim law including those which relate to dying, death and mourning.

National Council for One Parent Families
Tel. 0800 018 5026
www.oneparentfamilies.org.uk

Offers information and support to lone parents.

Muslim Health Network
www.muslimhealthnetwork.org

The Muslim Health Network works with support networks throughout the UK to assist in the research, promotion and dissemination of health information to the Muslim community. Schools, community projects businesses and mosques all offer support and advice to the health network including that which relates to bereavement.

National Missing Persons
PO Box 28908
London SW14 7ZU
Helpline: 0500 700 700
www.missing persons.org.uk
www.missingkids.co.uk

The national charity offers support and advice to family and friends of people who have gone missing from home.

Natural Death Centre
6 Blackstock Road
London N4 2BT
Tel. 020 7359 8391
www.naturaldeath.org.uk

The Natural Death Centre aims to support people dying at home, and their families and carers. It helps them to arrange inexpensive, family-organised and environmentally friendly funerals. It aims to improve the quality of dying and events following death.

Natural Endings Funeral Services
151 Northenden Road
Manchester M33 2HS
Helpline: 0161 962 4141
www.naturalendings.co.uk

Natural Endings provides environmentally friendly coffins made from sea grass and willow for burials in woodland and natural burial sites.

Nightline
www.nightline.niss.ac.uk

Nightline is a national student telephone helpline run by students to help and support their peers. It is an active listening service which does not aim to give solutions but provides an empathic understanding of difficulties, including bereavement support.

Parkinson's Disease Society
215 Vauxhall Bridge Road
London SW1V 1EJ
Tel. 020 7931 8080
www.parkinsons.org.uk

The PDS offers support and advice to those who have Parkinson's disease as well as their family and friends.

Pet Bereavement Support
c/o The Blue Cross
Shilton Road
Burford
Oxon OX18 4PF
Tel. 0800 096 6606
www.scas.org.uk

Pet Bereavement Support offers help following the death of a pet. Trained volunteers listen and provide empathic comfort to the bereaved and provide a befriending service.

Rainbow Centre for Children (Seriously ill)
27 Lilymead Avenue
Bristol BS4 2BY
Tel. 0117 985 3343

The Rainbow Centre offers free professional support and help to children who are seriously ill, and their families. It also provides bereavement support following the death of a parent or sibling.

Refugee Action
The Old Fire Station
150 Waterloo Road
London SE1 8SB
Tel. 020 7654 7700
www.refugee-action.org.uk

Refugee Action provides counselling and impartial information to refugees who are considering return to their country of origin. They assist with travel arrangements if appropriate.

Refugee Council
240–250 Ferndale Road
London SW9 8BB
www.refugeecouncil.org.uk

The Refugee Council supports asylum seekers and refugees as well as offering training for support service providers across the United Kingdom.

Samaritans
Tel. 08457 90 90 90
www.samaritans.org.uk

Offers support on the telephone and face to face, twenty-four hours a day, seven days a week. It has branches throughout the country and provides confidential help to anyone in distress or despair.

Sue Ryder Care
2nd Floor, 114–118 Southampton Row
London WC1B
Tel. 020 7400 0440

Sue Ryder Care offers support to people with disabilities and life-shortening illnesses, as well as family and friends. It works in the community and aims to fill gaps that are found in the National Health Service. It has care homes and hospices throughout the UK.

Teen Issues
www.teenissues.co.uk

Teen Issues features articles on a variety of aspects, including living with loss.

British Deaf Association
1–3 Worship Street
London EC2A 2BA
Tel. 020 7588 3520
www.signcommunity.org.uk

The British Deaf Association offers bereavement counselling and support to the deaf.

> Stonewall
> Tel. 020 7593 1850
> www.stonewall.org.uk

Provides legal information for lesbians, gay men and bisexuals.

> The Terrence Higgins Trust
> 52–54 Gray's Inn Road
> London WC1X 8JU
> Helpline: 020 7242 1010
> General: 020 7831 4605
> www.tht.org.uk

A charity which provides practical support, advice and counselling for anyone concerned about AIDS or HIV infection and anyone bereaved by AIDS.

Mental health organisations

> Depression Alliance
> 212 Spitfire Studios
> 63–71 Collier Street
> London N1 9BE
> Information Pack Request Line: 0845 123 2320
> www.depressionalliance.org.uk

Depression Alliance has a network of over sixty self-help groups and a website that includes creative pages for people to contribute to (creative@ depressionalliance.org).

> ICAP – Immigrant Counselling and Psychotherapy
> 96 Moray Road
> Finsbury park
> London N4 3LA
> www.icap.org.uk

ICAP offers culturally sensitive counselling, including bereavement counselling, for the Irish community in Britain.

> Mencap
> Helpline: 020 7696 5593

Mencap is a charity which provides advice, support and information to people with a learning difficulty.

MIND – National Association for Mental Health
Granta House
15–19 Broadway
Stratford
London E15 4BQ
Tel. 0845 766 0163
http://mind.org.uk/

A national charity with branches throughout the UK. It provides information, individual support and support groups for those with mental health
concerns. It also publishes literature related to mental health concerns.

Miscarriage and early infant death

ARC – Antenatal Results and Choices
73 Charlotte Street
London W1T 4PN
Helpline: 020 7631 0285
www.arc-uk.org

ARC is a national helpline for parents who have had a termination for an
abnormality. It offers advice and support.

Babyloss
PO Box 1168
Southampton SO15 8XZ
Email: support@babyloss.com

Babyloss provides information and support for bereaved parents and their
families who have lost a baby at any stage of pregnancy, at birth or because
of neonatal death.

Foundation for the Study of Infant Deaths (Cot Death Research and Support)
Artillery House
11–19 Artillery Row
London SW1P 1RT
Helpline: 0870 787 0554
General: 0870 787 0885
www.sids.org.uk

The Foundation for the Study of Infant Deaths offers support to families of
a baby who has died suddenly and unexpectedly. It provides a twenty-four-
hour helpline, a national network of befrienders and holds meetings as
well as providing advice and leaflets to aid the bereaved.

The Miscarriage Association
c/o Clayton Hospital

Northgate
Wakefield
West Yorkshire WF1 3JS
Tel. 01924 200799
www.miscarriageassociation.org.uk

The Association offers support and information on any loss related to pregnancy, including ectopic pregnancy. It has a UK-wide network of telephone contacts who have experienced pregnancy loss themselves and who give support, understanding and an empathic listening ear.

Missing GRACE Foundation
www.missinggrace.org

The Missing GRACE Foundation offers pregnancy and infant loss support as well as support for those struggling with infertility and those seeking to adopt a child.

Stillbirth and Neonatal Death Society (SANDS)
28 Portland Place
London W1B 1LY
Helpline: 020 7436 5881
Tel. 020 7436 3715
www.uk-sands.org

SANDS offers support for bereaved parents and families following the death of a baby who dies at birth or shortly afterwards. It has a national telephone helpline and a national network of support groups run by members of self-help groups who have been similarly bereaved. It also provides information for the bereaved and for health professionals and support for the next pregnancy.

Tommy's: The Baby Charity
Nicholas House
3 Lawrence Poutney Hill
London EC4R 0BB
Tel. 0870 770 7070
www.tommys-campaign.org

Tommy's offers support to parents-to-be, those who are trying for a baby and for those who have had difficulties related to pregnancy. It also provides specific information to health care professionals who care for pregnant women.

Traumatic injury and death

ASSIST – Assistance Support & Self-help in Surviving Trauma
11 Albert Street
Rugby

Warwickshire CV21 2RX
Helpline: 01788 560 800
www.traumatic-stress.freeserve.co.uk

ASSIST provides a confidential counselling service and offers support, understanding and friendship to anyone affected by post-traumatic stress disorder.

Brakecare
Helpline: 01484 421611
Tel. 0845 603 8570
www.brake.org.uk

Brakecare is a charity caring for people who have been bereaved, injured or affected by a road crash. It campaigns for greater road safety. It also provides information on erecting roadside memorials.

CADD – Campaign Against Drinking and Driving
PO Box 62
Brighouse
West Yorkshire HD6 344
Tel. 0845 123 5541
www.cadd.org.uk

CADD provides support for the families of victims killed and injured by drunk and irresponsible drivers. It also campaigns for greater awareness of the risks involved in drinking and driving.

Disaster Action
Tel. 01483 799 066
www.disasteraction.org

Disaster Action is a charity set up and run by survivors and bereaved from UK and overseas disasters. Founded in 1991, it provides an independent advocacy and advisory service that represents the interests of those directly affected by disaster.

FoMC – Families of Murdered Children
Tel. 01698 336646
www.fomc.org.uk

FoMC offers practical and emotional support to families and friends of murdered victims. It has close links with Victim Support.

Inquest
89–93 Fonthill Road
London N4 33H
Tel. 020 7263 1111
www.inquest.org.uk

Inquest provides information and advice for those who are bereaved after a death in custody – in prison, in a police station, in psychiatric detention and in immigration. They offer a casework service. It is a national service and will work with the bereaved throughout the UK.

Medical Foundation for the Care of Victims of Torture
11 Isledon Road
London N7 7JW
Tel. 020 7697 7777
www.medicalfoundation.org.uk

The Medical Foundation is a national charity that supports those who have been affected by torture, including refugees and asylum seekers. It offers one to one counselling, medical treatment, legal and psychotherapeutic support.

Papyrus
Lodge House
Thompson Park
Omerod Road
Burnley
Lancashire BB11 2RU
Tel. 01282 432 555
Hopeline UK: 0870 170 4000
www.papyrus-uk.org

Papyrus offers support and resources for anyone dealing with suicide, depression and distress, particularly teenagers and young adults. The Hopeline is a telephone service for anyone concerned about a young person who might be thinking of suicide.

POMC – Parents of Murdered Children
100 East Eighth Street
Suite 202
Cincinnati
Ohio 45202
www.pomc.com

POMC provides ongoing emotional support, education and advocacy for children who are murdered, and their family and friends. They offer online support, guidelines for victims and support for survivors as well as giving advice to professionals who are working with the family of a child who has been murdered.

Roadpeace
PO Box 2579
London NW10 3PW

Helpline: 0845 450 0355
General: 020 8838 5102
www.roadpeace.org.uk

This is a national charity which supports road traffic victims and their families. Trained volunteers offer emotional and practical support and information about legal aspects. Roadpeace volunteers can arrange for contact with others similarly affected by injury or bereavement following a road traffic accident.

Shadow of Suicide
www.tcf.org.uk

The Compassionate Friends offers support to parents who have been bereaved by a child's suicide. It is a self-help organisation which provides individual, one to one support as well as support in groups.

SOBS – Survivors of Bereavement by Suicide
SOBS Centre
88 Saner Street
Hull HU3 2TR
Helpline: 0870 241 3337
www.uk-sobs.org.uk

This is a self-help voluntary organisation which offers telephone support, practical advice, home visits and group sessions and has a bereavement pack. It also strives to raise public awareness about suicide, and training for both professionals and volunteers.

Sudden Death Support Association
Dolphin House
Part Lane
Swallowfield
Reading RG7 1TB
Tel. 0118 988 9797
Helpline: 0118 988 8099 (24 hour answerphone)
www.patient.co.uk

This listening-only service offers support to relatives and friends of people who have died suddenly. It is run by people who have experienced a sudden loss and offers practical as well as emotional support.

Sudden Trauma Information Service Helpline
Tel. 0845 367 0998
www.stish.org

The Sudden Trauma Information Helpline provides a confidential service for survivors of all kinds of sudden trauma.

Support After Murder and Manslaughter (SAMM)
Cranmer House
39 Brixton Road
London SW9 6DZ
Tel 020 7735 3838
www.samm.org.uk

A national self-help support group, SAMM offers support and advice to those bereaved through murder or manslaughter. There are local groups and volunteers and the national office provides details of local representatives.

SAMM Abroad offers support to those who have been bereaved by murder or manslaughter while abroad.

Support & Care after Road Death & Injury (SCARD)
PO Box 62
Brighouse
West Yorkshire HD6 3YY
Tel. 0845 123 5541
www.scard.org.uk

Works to help those who have been injured, bereaved or affected by road death or injury. There is access to free practical and legal help as well as counselling. SCARD also provides one to one visits, accompanying people to court, liaising with police, and providing support at inquests, as well as offering educational input for schools and youth groups.

Victim Support
Cranmer House
39 Brixton Road
London SW9 6DZ
Tel. 020 7735 9166
www.victimsupport.org.uk

Practical advice and support is offered to victims of crime and their families. This includes those who have been bereaved through crime and violence. Victim Support operates throughout the UK.

Victim's Voice
PO Box 110
Chippenham SN14 7QB
Tel. 07984 078 918
www.victimsvoice.co.uk

Victim's Voice is a campaigning charity. It is an umbrella organisation which provides a voice for organisations and individual members, to raise issues that arise when people are bereaved by traumatic sudden death or suffer serious assaults. It will offer one to one support but generally signposts people to relevant organisations according to the nature of the sudden death.

Glossary

Advance Directive

A living will in which a mentally competent person states in writing their wishes in the event of needing terminal care. The directive comes into effect when the person is no longer able to make decisions about their health care during the course of terminal care or if the person is in a permanent coma.

Anniversary response

An 'anniversary response' is an increase in memories, intense feelings and feelings of grief in the days leading up to and after the anniversary of a traumatic event. Also known as 'Anniversary reaction' it may involve physical as well as emotional reactions.

Anticipatory grief

Anticipatory grief happens with the impending loss of a significant person or an important aspect of the person's life. It takes place prior to the loss and may apply to the dying person as well as to those who love and care for him. It can be just as painful and stressful as the actual death of a person and may have the same symptoms as grief after loss.

Autopsy

An examination of the organs and/or tissues of the body after death. Though it is often used to determine the cause of death, it may also be used to facilitate research into fatal diseases to bring about improved treatment and prevention strategies.

Beneficence

Beneficence is the principle that counsellors must prevent harm, not cause harm and promote the good of another person. It is the founding rule of counselling. In bioethics, it refers to the obligation of those working in health care to seek the well-being or benefit of the patient.

Bereavement

'Bereavement is an event: grief is the emotional process following the death of a significant person and mourning is the cultural process' (Oliviere et al. 1998: 121). Bereavement relates to the loss of a loved one through death. From the root meaning 'to be robbed', the word originates in the border raids between Scotland and England, where the 'reivers' crossed the borders to kill and kidnap their enemy. To be 'bereived' was to be the subject of such an event.

Bereavement refers to the fact, the event, without implying an emotional state.

Bereavement support groups

Bereavement support groups work with people who have been bereaved in order to address their specific losses: for example, a group for parents who have each experienced the loss of a child. The groups help to break down feelings of isolation and can show how others have coped; in addition, being able to offer support to others can be part of the healing process following bereavement. These may be self-help groups or run by a bereavement counsellor or grief support worker.

Cemetery

A place where people are buried other than a churchyard.

Complicated grief

Complicated grief is usually defined as grief which does not diminish over time; the intensity of emotions remain high and it interferes with normal functioning. It may be accompanied by depressed mood, high anxiety, substance abuse and suicidal ideation.

Coroner

A coroner is a person employed by the government to investigate any death in which there is doubt about the cause of death. The coroner conducts an inquest to discover the facts about the death and to reach a verdict. Violent, sudden or suspicious deaths are investigated, as are deaths where there may be indications of medical malpractice.

Cremation certificates

These are forms which have to be completed before a cremation can take place. A funeral director will arrange for these to be signed and delivered to the crematorium.

Crematorium

A place where a dead body is burned or cremated. This practice is not acceptable to some religious groups such as Muslims and Orthodox Jews.

Death:

Physical death refers to the cessation of life, when all vital functions and signs have stopped.

Personal death: In this state the person is still technically alive but unable to function without the assistance of others or is reliant on machinery to keep her alive. The person has no autonomy and no control over basic physical and emotional functions.

Social death: The person is physically alive but has lost the ability to interact socially. Others may treat such a person as being dead although he is still breathing. Also called a psychosocial death, it includes those who have lost the essence of their personality because of a coma, irreparable brain damage or stroke. The social death may not be recognised by others in the wider society, which makes grieving difficult.

Death certificate

This is an official document issued by the Registrar of Births, Marriages and Deaths when the death is registered at the Register Office. There is a small fee for the service.

Death notice

A death notice, also known as a funeral notice, is an advertisement paid for by the family of the deceased which is published in a newspaper. It provides details of the death and information about arrangements regarding the funeral or cremation. It often states whether the family wish flowers to be sent, or sometimes specifies a charity where people can donate money rather than give flowers.

Disenfranchised grief

Disenfranchised grief is the grief that people cannot openly acknowledge or display in public. It is not socially supported so that the disenfranchised griever's feelings are not validated. This may happen when a person's family member has been imprisoned because of a vicious crime: others judge his behaviour but often do not recognise the pain and loss of the family.

Elegy

Elegies are laments for the dead.

Eulogy

A eulogy is a speech or piece of writing in praise of a person, usually at a funeral or memorial service.

Euthanasia

Euthanasia is bringing about the death of someone with an incurable terminal illness in as painless a manner as possible. It originates in the

Greek word *eu* meaning 'well' and *thanatos,* 'death'. It should be carried out for the benefit of the person who is about to die.

Passive euthanasia: letting a person die by forgoing or withdrawing treatment or switching off life support. It is sometimes called a 'mercy killing'.

Active euthanasia: causing the death of a person by administering a lethal dose of a drug. In America this is sometimes referred to as 'Physician Assisted Dying' (PAD) or medically enabled suicide (Costello 2006).

Funeral

A public ceremony at which a dead person is buried or cremated. This may be a religious or a non-religious event.

Funeral Director – also known as an Undertaker

The funeral director prepares the dead body for burial or cremation and takes care of the arrangements for the funeral, usually including the transportation of the body and the family or leading mourners to the place of interment or cremation.

Grief

The term grief incorporates the complex range of feelings, cognitions and behaviour of an individual in reaction to a loss. It is the sorrow following the loss of a significant person or possession (such as an animal) or position, such as expectations about the future, life-changing illness and so on. It is the subjective experience of loss. From the root meaning, 'heavy', It commonly includes feelings of guilt, anger and despair and may involve physical reactions including changes in sleep patterns and appetite.

Grief work

This describes the process in which a person adjusts to the loss of a loved one and the life that continues without that person. Stroebe (1992–93) describes it as the process of confronting loss, going through what happened before and at the time of death, focusing on memories and shared events and working towards detachment from the deceased. It involves active work to come to terms with the loss and be fully aware of it rather than suppressing feelings or denying the impact of the loss.

Gurdwara

A gurdwara is a Sikh temple. After a body has been cremated the friends and relatives usually return to the temple to offer a service of prayers and hymns for the deceased.

Hospice

First introduced in Britain by Dame Cecily Saunders, the hospice is designed to care for terminally ill people and to enable them to be pain free. It offers home-like comfort, high-quality emotional, spiritual and physical support to both the dying person and their families and friends. Its literal meaning is 'a place of shelter'.

Life-limiting illness

An illness that no longer responds to medical interventions to cure the condition which has afflicted the person.

Mortality

The word originates in the Latin *Mors*, meaning death. Immortality means the opposite: the person lives on for ever, perhaps in works she has created. Mortality figures reflect death rates.

Mosque

A Muslim holy place of worship.

Mourning

Formal practices of an individual or group after a death. Some regard mourning as a visible reaction to a loss. Socially defined responses to loss reflect the culture in which the death takes place and include death rituals and specific behaviours and activities. The root meaning is 'remembering with care and sorrow'.

The expression 'to be in mourning' refers to the period customary in the culture or society in which the bereaved lives and is defined by the clothes they wear, as well as the activities and events that take place during the mourning period.

Obituary

An obituary is published after the death of a person and is usually printed in a newspaper. It includes a biography of the person with specific details of major life events. Normally it is written by a journalist, though some newspapers print obituaries written by friends of the deceased.

Palliative care or Palliative treatment

Palliative care relieves symptoms, such as pain, but it is not expected to cure the illness. It is directed at making the patient's quality of life as good as it can possibly be and should include physical, emotional and spiritual care.

Post-mortem examination

This is an examination of the dead body to establish the cause of death. It takes place if the death was sudden and unexpected, or caused by criminal interference, such as foul play, or by criminal neglect.

Post-traumatic stress

Post-traumatic stress is an anxiety disorder that occurs following a traumatic experience, such as murder or a close brush with death, such as being in a place where a bomb exploded. Initially the person's reaction may be a feeling of numbness, which gives way to depression, heightened fear, flashbacks, nightmares, sleep disturbance, irritability and over-reaction to sudden noises.

Secondary losses

Secondary losses accompany all types of loss and death. The death of a husband, for example, may bring about financial loss, loss of future plans, loss of social contacts and loss of position as a partner, to his widow, who is no longer part of a couple.

Synagogue

A place of Jewish worship.

Thanatology

Thanatology is the study of everything that has to do with dying, death and grief.

Trauma

In medical terms trauma is a severe injury, wound or shock. Emotionally, trauma pertains to an experience which is shocking, extremely distressing, overwhelming and which threatens the person's resources. Trauma is manifest both physically and emotionally and can have lasting effects on the individual.

Undertaker – see Funeral director

Wake

A wake is a vigil or watch held over the body of a dead person before burial or cremation. It is mainly an Irish tradition though it is also practised by some Caribbean communities.

Will

A legal declaration by the dead person prior to death, which states how they wish their possessions and property to be distributed following their death. It may also include their wishes regarding their funeral and burial or cremation.

Appendix: Assessments and Scales

The reason for an assessment at your first meeting with a client is to establish a shared understanding of how you will work together, to allow your client to feel heard and understood and to explain the boundaries of the support or counselling you are offering (Milner and O'Byrne 2003).

Assessment scales may have to be adapted to reflect the culture of the person with whom you are working, as the grief process is tightly bound up with the beliefs and norms of each person (Benoliel 1971). However, many assessment scales measure grief according to the industrialised Western model, which may not be appropriate for some of the bereaved people you support. In my work as bereavement counsellor I prefer to work in an open-ended way relying on the core issues raised by William Worden (1991). These allow me to ask further questions about areas which may seem more problematic for the client.

The essential aspects to establish at the first meeting are the following:

- The nature of the relationship to the deceased;
- The nature of the attachment – strong, ambivalent, long term, new and so on;
- Mode of death – anticipated, unexpected, pain free, painful, traumatic;
- History of other losses – including any bereavement in childhood;
- Personality variables – vulnerable, resilient, generally positive or generally negative;
- Social variables – is the bereaved part of a strong social network of family and friends? Does she feel isolated? Is she a member of a faith group that offers companionship? (Walker et al. 1977)

There are a number of instruments for measuring grief and depression following bereavement; however, these are usually administered by professionals who have been trained in their use. These include the Texas Revised Inventory of Grief and the Inventory of Complicated Grief Revised. The MM Caregiver Grief Inventory is designed for use with people who are supporting those with progressive dementia, such as Alzheimer's Disease. It is in the public domain, though its designers,

Thomas Meuser and Samuel Marwit, would appreciate feedback on how the scale is used.

The Adult Attitude to Grief (AAG) Scale

Devised by Linda Machin, Honorary Research Fellow, Keele University, UK, the scale comprises nine attitudinal statements which reflect whether the bereaved feels overwhelmed (statements 2, 5, 7), balanced/resilient (statements 1, 3, 9) or controlled (statements 4, 6, 8) (Machin 2006). Respondents rate their responses to the questions on a scale of 1–5, where 1 is strongly agree. The AAG is a six-stage process of 'Mapping Grief' which offers a structured approach to working with grief and is likely to gain widespread use once it is more familiar to practitioners.

Attitudinal statements

1   I feel able to face the pain which comes with loss.
2   For me, it is difficult to switch off thoughts about the person I have lost.
3   I feel very aware of my inner strength when faced with grief.
4   I believe I must be brave in the face of loss.
5   I feel that I will always carry the pain of grief with me.
6   For me, it is important to keep my grief under control.
7   I believe that nothing will ever be the same after an important loss.
8   I think it is best to just get on with life after loss.
9   It may not always feel like it but I do come through the experience of grief.

The AAG scale can be administered more than once and the change in scoring may indicate change within the grieving process. In scoring you may find contradictions – for example the bereaved are aware of their inner strength yet also feel they will always carry the pain of grief. This reflects the inner confusion that can be so debilitating for bereaved people, whose world has shifted; at this time they are still in the process of adapting to their new status.

Using the scale will also allow you to engage in a dialogue based on the person's responses. For example, you might explore:

* the persistence of the pain of grief;
* the intrusion of grief;
* awareness of personal resources;
* the need to seem fine in public;
* the sense of being overwhelmed and utterly transformed.

A full account of Linda Machin's scale and its use is published by Sage (Machin 2008).

Assessment

The Death

What is the person's understanding of how the death happened? This is important because in the shock of bereavement, particularly in unexpected, traumatic bereavement, facts may become unclear and misunderstandings prevail, causing further grief. Clarification through the counselling process as the client tells her story can ease the emotions of loss.

Previous history of loss

Has she experienced previous bereavements?
Has she experienced other losses, secondary losses such as loss of health, job, home?
Is she experiencing concurrent losses following the bereavement, such as financial difficulties, change of social status or having to move in with another member of his family?

Relationship

What was the person's relationship to the person who died?
How long had they known each other?
Was the bereaved a carer for the deceased?

Complicating factors

Was she excluded from being with the person prior to or at death?
Was she excluded from the funeral?
Was the relationship one which was kept secret?

Social factors

Does the person have a supportive social network? Family, friends, neighbours, faith group etc.?
Does she have a special friend who is supportive at present?

Other factors

Are there any mental health difficulties?
Are drugs or alcohol an issue?
What experience of counselling or befriending has the person had previously?
Does she feel a sense of the presence of the deceased?

Self-assessment of grief

Please take as long as you need to answer these questions. Your answers may help you to decide if you would like to have additional support. It doesn't matter whether your loss was recent or a long time ago.

1   I feel I need more support from my family and friends.

     Yes   Not sure   No

2   Are you concerned about your eating or sleeping patterns?

     Yes   Not sure   No

3   Do you feel that your energy levels have decreased so that you don't have enough energy to spend time with friends, or at work, doing the things you enjoyed before your bereavement ?

     Yes   Not sure   No

4   Have you increased your use of alcohol, drugs or medication or are you using more medication than your prescription calls for?

     Yes   Not sure   No

5   I feel, since the death of my loved one, that the intensity of my grief has got worse.

     Yes   Not sure   No

6   Are you having more financial, health, work or relationship problems since the death of your loved one ?

     Yes   Not sure   No

7   I have had more than one significant loss in the last year

     Yes   No

8   I feel my life has lost its purpose since my bereavement.

     Yes   Not sure   No

Are there any other things you are concerned about which are not covered here? If so, please add them here:

If you have answered 'Yes' to any of these questions and would like some help, you might find it helpful to talk to someone at the Centre, where we have befrienders and counsellors who are trained and experienced in working with grief following bereavement.

Spiritual assessment

The spiritual aspects of dying, death and bereavement are important and need to be taken into account when offering support. Obviously, your own beliefs (or lack of beliefs), may influence your own practice; however, in maintaining beneficence, non-judgmental positive regard and empathy you can support those who have beliefs that are different from your own. Where you feel this is not possible you should refer the person on to someone whose approach is more sympathetic to their faith.

Doug Smith (2006) devised a simple, spiritual assessment for his work with terminally ill patients and the bereaved. He emphasises the person's feeling about their strength and their peace. In brief, regarding strength he asks:

What is strength to you?
Where can you get it from?
Who gives it to you?
How can you get more?

Regarding peace, he asks:

What is peace for you?
Where can you get it from?
Who gives it to you?
How can you get more?

The replies he receives give the basis for the ensuing conversation and enable the formation of a sense of the person's beliefs and values. As he said, 'Our terminally ill clients, as well as those who are grieving, are searching and struggling over spiritual things. We need to be ready for conversation, and we cannot have a conversation if we do not know what language our clients speak' (2006: 8).

References

Abdesselem, M. (1991) 'Mawt' (Death), in C. E. Bosworth et al. (eds), *The Encyclopedia of Islam*, new edn, Vol. VI. Leiden: E.J. Brill. pp. 910–11.

Ainsworth, M., Blehar, M., Waters, E. and Wall, S. (1978) *Patterns of attachment: A Psychological Study of the Strange Situation*. Hillsdale, NJ: Lawrence Erlbaum.

Al-Awwal, J. (2007) Salaam advice: Death at home or hospital: Instructions for Muslims in the UK. File://Users/ibook/Desktop/Salaam%20Advice.html; 06/07/2007

Alexander, H. (2002) *Bereavement: A Shared Experience*, 3rd edn. Oxford: Lion.

Allen, N. H. (1991) 'Survivor-victims of homicide: murder is only the beginning', in D. Leviton (ed.), *Horrendous Death: Health and Well-being*. New York: Hemisphere. pp. 5–23.

Alvarez, A. (1972) *The Savage God*. London: Weidenfield & Nicolson.

Anderson, C. (1949) 'Aspects of pathological grief and mourning', *International Journal of Psycho-analysis*, 30: 48.

Anderson, S. (2006) 'Five months pregnant and my baby was dead', *Guardian Weekend*, 7 January: 12.

Antoni, M. H., Schneiderman, N., Fletcher, M. A., Goldstein D. A., Ironson, G. and Lapierre, A. (1990) 'Psychoneuroimmunology and HIV-1', *Journal of Consulting and Clinical Psychology*, 58: 38–49.

Ardelt, M. (2003) 'Effects of religion and purpose in life on elders' subjective well-being and attitudes towards death', *Journal of Religious Gerontology*, 14: 55–77.

Armstrong, K. (2000) *Islam: A Short History*. London: Weidenfeld & Nicolson.

Artemidorus (1975) *The Interpretation of Dreams*, in *Oneirocritica*, trans. Robert J. White. Park Ridge, NJ: Noyles Press.

Ashby, M. (2004) Editorial: 'The weight of this sad time', *Grief Matters. The Australian Journal of Grief and Bereavement*, Autumn: 3.

Attig, T. (1991) 'The importance of conceiving of grief as an active process', *Death Studies*, 15: 385–93.

Attig, T. (1996) *How We Grieve: Relearning the World*. New York: Oxford University Press.

Attig, T. (2000) *The Heart of Grief: Death and the Search for Lasting Love*. New York: Oxford University Press.

Averill, J (1968) 'Grief: its nature and significance', *Psychological Bulletin*, 70: 721–48.

Awooner- Renner, S. (1993) 'I desperately needed to see my son', in D. Dickenson and M. Johnson (eds), *Death, Dying and Bereavement*. London: Sage.

Bacon, F. (1604) 'Thoughts on the nature of things', in *The Times Book of Quotations*. London: HarperCollins, 2000 p. 115.

Bailey, P. H. (1996) 'Assuring quality in narrative research', *Western Journal of Nursing Research*, 18: 186–94.

Barrett, D. (1992) 'Through a glass darkly: images of the dead in dreams', *Omega: Journal of Death and Dying*, 24: 97–108.

Barrett, D. (1996) *Trauma and Dreams*. Cambridge, MA: Harvard University Press.

Bartrop, R. W. (1977) 'Depressed lymphocyte function after bereavement', *Lancet*, 16: 834–6.

Batten, M. and Oltjenbruns, K. (1999) 'Adolescent sibling bereavement as a catalyst for spiritual development: a model for understanding', *Death Studies*, 23: 529–46.

Bawden, N. (2005) *Dear Austen*. London: Virago.

Bawden, N. (2006) 'Nina Bawden', *Observer Magazine*, 12 November: 10.

Bayliss, 1 (1999) *Supporting Loss and Grief*. Cambridge: National Extension College.

BBC News (2002) 'Spiritual belief "helps grieving process"', http://news.bbc.co.uk/1/hi/health/2070378.stm

Bearison, D. J. (1991) *They Never Want To Tell You*. Cambridge, MA: Harvard University Press.

Becker, S. H. and Knudson, R. M. (2003) 'Visions of the dead: imagination and mourning', *Death Studies*, 27: 691–716.

Bedard, K. (2006) *Compassion and Courage in the Aftermath of Traumatic Loss*. Binghamton, NY: Haworth Press.

Belicki, K., Gulko, N., Ruzycki K. and Aristotle, J. (2003) 'Sixteen years of dreams following spousal bereavement', *Omega: Journal of Death and Dying*, 47 (2): 93–106.

Bell, D. (2007) 'In the name of the law', *Guardian*, 14 June: 10–13.

Bell, T. (1961) *In the Midst of Life*. New York: Atheneum, quoted in Imara (1975), p. 149.

Bennett, G. and Bennett, K. M. (2000) 'The presence of the dead: and empirical study', *Mortality*, 5 (2): 139–57.

Benoliel, J. Q. (1971) 'Assessments of loss and grief', *Journal of Thanatology*, 1: 182–94.

Benoliel, J. Q. (1999) 'Loss and bereavement: perspectives, theories, challenges', *Canadian Journal of Nursing Research*, 30 (4): 263–72.

Berder, J. (2004–2005) 'Loss of the assumptive world: how we deal with death and loss', *Omega: Journal of Death and Dying*, 50 (4): 255–65.

Berkman, L. F. and Syme, S. L. (1979) 'Social networks, host resistance, and mortality: a nine-year follow-up study of Alameda County residents', *American Journal of Epidemiology*, 109: 186–204.

Bertman, S. L. (ed.) (1999) *Grief and the Healing Arts: Creativity as Therapy*. Amityville, NY: Baywood.

Berzoff, J. and Silverman, P. R. (eds) (2004) *Living with Dying: A Handbook for End-of-life Healthcare Practitioners*. New York/Chichester: Columbia University Press.

Bissler J. V. (2002) 'Identification of processes that have been helpful during the bereavement process for mothers and fathers who have experienced the sudden deaths of their 15–28-year-old biological children'. Doctoral dissertation, Kent State University, Kent, Ohio.

Bissler, J. V. (2005) 'Group counselling with bereaved parents', *The Forum*, Association for Death Education and Counselling (ADEC), July–September: 4–5.

Black, A. (2004) 'Traumatic grief in the children of a Northern Irish police officer', *Bereavement Care*, 3 (1): 11–13.

Black, D. (2005) Quote from her presentation with Dr D. Trickey, 'Children bereaved by murder and manslaughter', 7th International Conference on Grief and Bereavement in Contemporary Society, 12–15 July. King's College, London.

Blackman, N. (2003) *Loss and Learning Disability*. London: Worth.

Bloom, Archbishop, A. (1969) The David Kissen Memorial Lecture, 26 March, quoted in J. Bowlby (1975) *Attachment and Loss*, Vol.1. Harmondsworth: Penguin, pp. 317–40.

Boerner, K. and Heckhausen, J. (2003) 'To have and have not: adaptive bereavement by transforming mental ties to the deceased', *Death Studies*, 27: 199–226.

Bolton, G. (1999) *The Therapeutic Potential of Creative Writing*. London: Jessica Kingsley.

Bonnano, G. A., Wortman, C. B. and Nesse, R. M. (2004) 'Prospective patterns of resilience and maladjustment during widowhood', *Psychology and Aging*, 19: 260–71.

Bonnell-Pascual, E., Huline-Dickens, S., Hollins, S., Esterhuyzen, A., Sedgwick, P., Abdelnoor, A. and Hubert, J. (1999) 'Bereavement and grief in adults with learning difficulties: a follow-up study', *British Journal of Psychiatry*, 175: 348–50.

Boss, P. (1999) *Ambiguous Loss*. Cambridge, MA: Havard University Press.

Boss, P. (2006) *Loss, Trauma, and Resilience: Therapeutic Work with Ambiguous Loss*. New York: W.W. Norton.

Bowlby, J. (1975) *Attachment and Loss*, Vol. 2. Harmondsworth: Penguin.

Bowlby, J. (1980) *Attachment and Loss*, Vol. 3: *Loss, Sadness and Depression*. London: Hogarth.

Bowlby, J. and Parkes, C. M. (1970) 'Separation and loss within the family', in C. J. Anthoney and C. J. Koupernik (eds), *The Child in his Family*. New York/Chichester: Wiley.

Boyd-Franklin, N. (1989) 'Therapists' use of self and value conflicts with black families', in N. Boyd-Franklin (ed.), *Black Families in Therapy: a Multisystems Approach*. New York: Guilford Press.

Boyles, J. (2004) Medical Foundation for the Care of the Victims of Torture, Northwest Presentation. Manchester Area Bereavement Forum Conference, Sedgley Park, Manchester, 9 September 2004.

Bragg, M. (date unknown) 'Best of times, worst of times', *Sunday Times*, p. 15

Braun, M. J. and Berg, D. H. (1994) 'Meaning reconstruction in the experience of parental bereavement', *Death Studies*, 18: 105–29.

Bregman, L. (2003) *Death and Dying, Spirituality and Religions*. New York: Peter Lang.

Bregman, L. (2006) 'The roles of religions in the Death Awareness Movement: hidden legacies', *The Forum*, Association for Death Education and Counselling (ADEC), April/May/June: pp. 4–5.

Brimacombe, M. (1996) 'The emotional release of writing', *GP*, 13 December: 9.

Bringa, T. (1995) *Being Muslim the Bosnian Way*. Princeton, NJ: Princeton University Press.

Brockes, E. (2005) 'Emma Brockes interview: Joan Didion', *Guardian*, 16 December: 14–17.

Bruner, J. (1990) *Acts of Meaning*. Cambridge, MA: Harvard University Press.

Bucholz, J. A. (2002) *Homicide Survivors: Misunderstood Grievers*. Amityville, NY: Baywood.

Bulkeley, K. (1995) *Spiritual Dreaming: a Cross-cultural and Historical Journey*. New York: Paulist Press.

Bulkeley, K. (2000) *Transforming Dreams: Learning Spiritual Lessons from the Dreams You'll Never Forget*. New York: Paulist Press.

Bulkeley, K. (2002) 'Reflections on the dream traditions of Islam', *Sleep & Hypnosis*, 4: 1–11.

Burch, W. E. (2004) 'The healing cocktail', *DreamTime*, Winter (International Association for the Study of Dreams).

Burns, L. H. and Convington, S. H. (eds) (1999) *Infertility Counselling: A Comprehensive Handbook for Clinicians*. New York: Parthenon.

Busch, C.J. (2001) 'On creating a healing story: one chaplain's reflections on bereavement, loss and grief', *Innovations in End-of-Life Care*, 3 (3), www.edc.org/lastacts

Bynum, E.B. (1993) *Families and the Interpretation of Dreams*, Binghamton, NY: Harrington Park Press.

Caleb, R. (1998) 'An "ultimate situation"', *Counselling News*, November: 7–9.

Calhoun, L. G., Cann, A., Tedeschi, R. G. and McMillan, J. (2000) 'A correlational test of the relationsip between posttraumatic growth, religion and cognitive processing', *Journal of Traumatic Stress*, 13: 521–7.

Campbell, J. (1972) *Myths To Live By*. New York: Viking.

Caring Connections (2006) Culture and its Relationship to Grief, retrieved from www.caringinfo.org/i4a/pages/index.cfm?pageid+3494 on 30/08/06

Carlisle, D. (2005) 'Clinical Management – end-of-life care', *Health Service Journal*; retrieved from www.hsg.co.uk/nav?Page=hsj.news.story.21.11.2005: pp. 1–6.

Carmichael C. and Roig, M. (2003) 'The art of remembering: creative expression of grief', *Epilogue*, Duke Community Bereavement Centre, Spring: 5–6.

Carroll B. (2001) 'A phenomenological exploration of the nature of spirituality and spiritual care', *Mortality*, 6: 1.

Carswell, C. (2003) 'Where are the grieving men?' *Counselling and Psychotherapy Journal*, May: 24–7.

Cartwright, R. and Lambert, L. (1992) *Crisis Dreaming: Using Your Dreams to Solve Your Problems*. New York: HarperCollins.

Caserta, M. S. and Lund, D. A. (1992) 'Bereavement stress and coping among old people: expectations versus the actual experience', *Omega*, 25: 33–45.

Cassidy, S. (1988) *Sharing the Darkness: The Spirituality of Caring*. London Darton, Longman & Todd.

Caverhill, P. A. (2002) 'Qualitative research in thanatology', *Death Studies*, 26: 195–207.

Cecil, D. (1969) *Visionary and Dreamer*. London: Constable.

Chadwick, H., trans. (1991) *St Augustine's Confessions*. Oxford: World Classics.

Chang, C. and Sofka, C. (2006) 'Coping with loss in Chinese and North American "cyberspace" communities: e-temples and virtual cemeteries', *The Forum, Association of Death Education and Counselling*, 32 (4): 7.

Chittik, W. C. (1992) '"Your sight today is piercing": the Muslim understanding of death and afterlife', in H. Obayashi (ed.), *Death and Afterlife: Perspectives of World Religions*. New York: Praeger.

Chodoff, P., Friedman, S. B. and Hamburg, D. (1964) 'Stress, defenses and coping behaviour: observations in parents of children with malignant disease', *American Journal of Psychiatry*, 120 (8): 743–9.

Clare, S. Sr. (2000) 'Spiritual values in nursing care', *Fairacres Chronicle*, the magazine of the Sisters of the Love of God, Oxford, Spring.

Clark, J. and Franzmann, M. (2006) 'Authority from grief: presence and place in the making of roadside memorials', *Death Studies* 30 (6): 579–99.

Clark, S. E. and Goldney, R. (2000) 'The impact of suicide on relatives and friends', in K. Hawton and K. Van Heeringen (eds), *The International Handbook of Suicide and Attempted Suicide*. Chichester: Wiley. pp. 467–84.

Cleiren, M. (1999) Guest editorial: 'The complexity and simplicity of grief', *Mortality*, 4 (2): 109–10.

Cleiren, M. and Diekstra, R. (1995) 'After the loss: bereavement after suicide and other types of death', in B. Mishara (ed.), *The Impact of Suicide*. New York: Springer. pp. 7–39.

Cleiren, M., Grad, O., Zavasnik, A. and Diekstra, R. F. W. (1996) 'Psychosocial impact of bereavement after suicide and fatal traffic accident: a comparative two-country study', *Acta Psychiatrica Scandinavia*, 94: 37–44.

Cobb, M. (2001) *The Dying Soul: Spiritual Care at the End of Life*. Buckingham: Open University Press.

Coleman, N. (2007) 'The day my dad floored me', *Guardian*, 'Family Section', 13 January: 1–2.

Connor, K. (2005) 'A terrible question', *Counselling and Psychotherapy Journal*, 16 (4): 19–21.

Conrad, B. H. (1998) *When a Child Has Been Murdered: Ways You Can Help the Grieving Parents*. Amityville, NY: Baywood.

Corr, C. (1992) 'A task-based approach to coping with dying', *Omega*, 24 (2): 81–94.

Costello, J. (2006) 'Euthanasia and physician-assisted suicide: who makes the choice?' Presentation at 'Death with Dignity conference. Living before dying: contemporary issues at the end of life.' 12 July 2006. Manchester, UK.

Costello, J. and Trinder-Brook, A. (2000) 'Children's nurses' experiences of caring for dying children in hospital', *Paediatric Nursing*, July, 12 (6): 28–32.

Cottington, E. M., Matthew, K. A., Talbott, E. and Kuller, L. H. (1980) 'Environmental events preceding sudden death in women', *Psychosomatic Medicine*, 42 (6): 567–74.

Cowper, W. (1782) 'Charity', in *The Times Book of Quotations*, London: HarperCollins 2000. p. 324.

Cox, G., Bendiksen, R. and Stevenson, R. (2003) *Making Sense of Death: Spiritual, pastoral and personal aspects of death, dying and bereavement*. Amityville, NY: Baywood.

Cox, P. and Camp Weave-A-Hope (2005) 'Family bereavement camp: re-knitting the fabric of torn lives in contemporary society'. Presentation at Cruse International Conference, London, July.

Cruse (2005) 'The last thing we talk about', *Counselling and Psychotherapy Journal*, May, 16 (4): 5–7.

Culliford, L. (2002) 'Spirituality and clinical care', *British Medical Journal*, 325: 1434–5.

Culliford L. and Powell W. (2005) *Spirituality and Mental Health*. Leaflet of the Spirituality and Psychiatry Special Interest Group, Royal College of Psychiatrists, London.

Currer, C. (2001) *Responding to Grief; Dying: Bereavement and Social Care*. New York: Palgrave.

Dahlen, E. R. and Canetto, S. S. (2002) 'The role of gender and suicide precipitants in attitudes toward nonfatal suicidal behaviour', *Death Studies*, 26: 99–116.

Dale, N. (2007) *What Colour Is Grief? A Journey*. Slynedales, Lancaster: Different Sky, CancerCare.

Dannemillar, H. C. (2002) 'The parent's response to a child's murder', *Omega*, 45 (1): 1–21.

Darwin, C. (1872) *The Expression of Emotion in Man and Animals*. London: John Murray.

Davidson, J., Lee-Archer, S. and Sanders, G. (2005) 'Dream, imagery and emotion', *Dreaming: Journal of the Association for the Study of Dreams*, 15 (1): 33–47.

Davidson, K. (2000) 'Gender, age and widowhood: gender differences in adaptation in the medium and long term', *Bereavement Care*, 19 (2) Summer: 25–7.

Deeken, A. (2004) 'A nation in transition: bereavement in Japan', *Bereavement Care*, 23 (3), Winter: 35–7.

Despelder, L. and Barrett, R. (1997) 'Developing multicultural competency', *The Director*, 69: 66–8.

Deutsch, H. (1937) 'The absence of grief', *Psychoanalytical Quarterly*, 6: 12–22.

Devers, E. (1997) *After-death Communications: Experiences with Departed Loved Ones*. London: Robert Hale.

Didion, J. (2005a) *The Year of Magical Thinking*. London: Fourth Estate.

Didion, J. (2005b) 'A year of magical thinking', review, *Guardian*, 24 September: 4–6.

Dietrich, D. R. and Shabad, P. C. (1989) *The Problem of Loss and Mourning*. Madison, CT: International University Press.

Dijkstra, I. C. and Stroebe, M. S. (1998) 'The impact of a child's death on parents: a myth (not yet) disproved', *Journal of Family Studies*, 4 (2): 159–85.

Dinesen, I. (1938) *Out of Africa*. New York: Random House.

Dixon, R. (2001) 'SAMM – support after murder and manslaughter', *Bereavement Care*, 20 (2), Summer: 21.

Doka, K. (ed.), (1989) *Disenfranchised Grief: Recognizing Hidden Sorrows*. Lexington, MA: Lexington Books.

Doka, K. J. (ed.) (2002a) *Disenfranchised Grief: New Directions, Challenges and Strategies for Practice*. Champaign, IL: Research Press.

Doka, K. (ed.) (2002b) *Living with Grief: Loss in Later Life*. Washington, DC: Hospice Foundation of America.

Domar, A. D., Broome A., Zuttermeister, P. C., Seibel, M. M. and Friedman, R. (1992) 'The prevalence and predictability of depression in infertile women', *Fertility and Sterility*, 58: 1158–63.

Doss, E. (2002) 'Death, art and memory in the public sphere: the visual and material culture of grief in contemporary America', *Mortality*, 7: 63–82.

Driscoll, M. (2007) 'Benn and the woman he can't forget', *Sunday Times*, 30 September: 10.

Dunblane (1996) 'In Dunblane ten years on', *Observer*, 12 February: 26–8.

Duncan, S. (2006) *Salvation Creek*. Sydney: Random House Australia.

Dunn, A. A., Oyebode, J. R. and Howard, R. A. (2005) 'Emotional reactions to continuing bonds in spousal bereavement'. *Presentation at the 7th International Conference on Grief and Bereavement in Contemporary Society*, 12–15 July, King's College, London.

Dutta, S. (2006) 'Backwards and forwards', *Therapy Today*, 17 (9): 13–16.

Dyregrov, A. and Dyregrov, K. (1999) 'Long-term impact of sudden infant death: a 12- to 15-year-old follow-up', *Death Studies*, 23: 635–61.

Dyregrov, K. (2003–2004) 'Micro-sociological analysis of social support following traumatic bereavement: unhelpful and avoidant responses from the community', *Omega*, 48 (1): 23–44.

Dyregrov, K., Nordanger, D. and Dyregrov, A. (2003) 'Predictors of psychosocial distress after suicide, SIDS and accidents', *Death Studies*, 27: 143–65.

Edwards, K. (2002) 'Bereavement counselling in the hospice movement', *Counselling and Psychotherapy Journal*, July/August: 14–17.

Effiace, F. and Marrone, R. (2002) 'Spiritual issues and quality of life assessment in cancer care', *Death Studies*, 26 (9): 743–56.

Egan, G. (1994) *The Skilled Helper: A Problem-management Approach to Helping*. Pacific Grove, CA: Brookes/Cole.

Eisenbruch, M. (1990) 'Cultural bereavement and homesickness', in S. Fisher and C. L. Cooper (eds), *On the Move: The Psychology of Change and Transition*. Chichester: Wiley.

Eliot, T. S. (1963) *Collected Poems, 1909–1962*. London: Faber & Faber.

Elliott, J. L. (1999) 'The death of a parent in childhood: a family account', *Illness, Crisis and Loss*, 7 (4): 360–75.

Ellis, C. (1998) 'Epistotherapy', *British Medical Journal*, 299: 1230.

Ellison, J. and McGonigle, C. (2003) *Liberating Losses: When Death Brings Relief*. Cambridge, MA: Perseus.

Emblen, J. D. (1992) 'Religion and spirituality defined according to current use in nursing literature', *Journal of Professional Nursing*, 8: 41–47.

Engel, G. L. (1961) 'Is grief a disease?', *Psychosomatic Medicine*, 23: 18–22.

Erikson, E. H. (1963) *Childhood and Society*. New York: W.W. Norton.

Etherington, K. (2003) *Trauma, the Body and Transformation: A Narrative Enquiry*. London: Jessica Kingsley.

Evans, W. (2003) 'Emerging from bereavement – altered but alive', *Counselling and Psychotherapy Journal*, July: 22–3.

Farrell, J. J. (1982) 'The dying of death: historical perspectives', *Death Education*, 6: 105–23.

Feynman, R. (2005) 'To Arline Feynman, October 17, 1946', in *Perfectly Reasonable Deviations from the Beaten Track: The Letters of Richard P. Feynman*. New York: Basic Books.

Figley, C. R. (1988) 'Post-traumatic family therapy', in F. M. Ochberg (ed.), *Post-traumatic Therapy and Victims of Violence*. New York: Brunner/Mazel. pp. 83–109.

Figley, C. R., Mazza, N. and Bride B. (eds) (1997) *Death and Trauma: The Traumatology of Surviving*. Washington, DC: Taylor & Francis.

Filak, V. F. and Abel, S. (2004) 'Boys don't cry: cartooning, grieving strategies and gender-based stereotypes in the aftermath of September 11', *Grief Matters. Australian Journal of Grief and Bereavement*, 7 (1): 12–17.

Firth, S. (2003) 'Changing Hindu attitudes to cremation in the UK', *Bereavement Care*, 22 (2): 25–8.

Forte, J. A., Barrett, A. V. and Campbell, M. H. (1996) 'Patterns of social connectedness and shared grief work: a symbolic interactionist perspective', *Social Work with Groups*, 19 (1): 29–51.

Forte, A., Hill, M., Pazder, R. and Feudtner, C. (2004) 'Bereavement care interventions: a systematic review', *BMC Palliative Care* 3 (3). www.biomedcentral.com/1472–684X-3-3.

Frampton, D. R. (1986) 'Restoring creativity to the dying patient', *British Medical Journal*, 293 (6562): 1593–5.

Franks, H. (1990) 'Mummy Doesn't Live Here Anymore'. London: Doubleday.

Frayley, R. C. and Shaver, P. R. (1999) 'Loss and bereavement: attachment theory and recent controversies concerning "grief work" and the nature of detachment', in J. Cassidy and P. R. Shaver (eds), *Handbook of Attachment: Theory, Research and Clinical Applications*. New York: Guildford Press. pp. 735–59.

Freud, S. (1917) 'Mourning and Melancholia', in J. Strachey (ed. and trans.), *The Standard Edition of the Complete Psychological Works of Sigmund Freud*, Vol. 14. London: Hogarth Press, 1957. pp. 243–58.

Freud, S. (1960) 'Letter to Binswanger (letter 239)', in E. L. Freud (ed.), *Letters of Sigmund Freud*. New York: Basic Books.

Frude, N. (2005) 'Prescription for a good read', *Counselling and Psychotherapy Journal* February: 28–31.

Fuchel, J. (1985) 'Writing poetry can enhance the psychotherapeutic process: observations and examples', *The Arts in Psychotherapy*, 12: 89–93.

Galanter, M. (2005) *Spirituality and the Healthy Mind: Science, Therapy, and the Need for Personal Meaning*. Oxford: Oxford University Press.

Gamino, L. A., Easterling, L. W., Stirman, L. S. and Sewell, K. W. (2000) 'Grief adjustment as influenced by funeral participation and occurrence of adverse funeral events', *Omega*, 41: 79–92.

Gannon, K., Glover, L. and Abel, P. (2004) 'Masculinity, stigma and media reports', *Social Science and Medicine*, 59 (6): 1169–75.

Garfield, P. (1991) *The Healing Power of Dreams*, New York: Fireside Press.

Garfield, P. (1996) 'Dreams in bereavement', in D. Barrett (ed.), *Trauma and Dreams*. Cambridge, MA: Harvard University Press.

Garfield, P. (1997) *The Dream Messenger: How Dreams of the Departed Bring Healing Gifts*. New York: Simon & Schuster.

Gay, G. M. (2006) 'Ziggy Marley sounding a spiritual tone', *Arizona Daily Star*, 8 October. www.axstarnet.com

Gerhardt, S. (2004) *Why Love Matters: How Affection Shapes a Baby's Brain*. London: Brunner-Routledge.

Gerner, M. (1991) 'The grief of the newly bereaved', *The Compassionate Friend's Newsletter*, Summer.

Gersie, A. (1997) *Reflections on Therapeutic Storymaking: the Use of Stories in Groups*. London: Jessica Kingsley.

Gibson, M. (2006) *Order from Chaos: Responding to Traumatic Events*, 3rd edn. Bristol, UK: Policy Press.

Giddens, A. (1991) *Modernity and Self-identity*. Cambridge: Polity Press.

Gilbert, K. R. (1996) '"We've had the same loss, why don't we have the same grief?" Loss and differential grief in families', *Death Studies*, 20: 269–83.

Gilbert, K. R. (2002) 'Taking a narrative approach to grief research: finding meaning in stories', *Death Studies*, 26 (3): 222–39.

Gilbert, K. R. (2005) Traumatic Loss and Grief. Retrieved 01/15/2007; www.indiana. edu/~familygrf/units/traumatic.html

Gilbert, K. R. and Smart, L. S. (1992) *Coping with Infant or Fetal Loss: the Couple's Healing Process*. New York: Brunner/Mazel.

Gilbert P. and Nicholls V. (2003) *Inspiring Hope: Recognising the Importance of Spirituality in a Whole Person Approach to Mental Health*. London: National Institute for Mental Health in England.

Giljohann, B. A., Hansen, M. and Wilkens, K. (2000) 'Building relationships between loss and grief self-help organisations and health professionals', *Grief Matters*, 3 (1), Autumn: 7–11.

Gingell, S. (2005) 'A widow's tale', *Independent on Sunday*, 23 October: 58.

Ginsburg, G. D. (2004) *Widow to Widow*, rev. edn. Cambridge, MA: Da Capo Press.

Glassock, G. (2006) 'Coping with uncertainty: the grieving experience of families of missing people', *Bereavement Care*, 25 (3), Winter: 43–6.

Goelitz, N. (2001) 'Nurturing life with dreams: therapeutic dreamwork with cancer patients', *Clinical Social Work Journal*, 29: 375–85.

Goelitz, N. (2007) 'Exploring dream work at end of life', *Dreaming*, 17 (3): 159–71.

Gogar, A. and Hill, C. (1992) 'Examining the effects of brief individual dream interpretation', *Dreaming*, 2: 239–48.

Golden, T. (2005) 'Why do men avoid support groups?' *The Forum, Association of Death Education and Counselling*, 31 (3): 1–2.

Golden, T. (2006) 'Healing and the internet', *The Forum, Association of Death Education and Counselling*, 32 (4): 8.

Goldenberg, S. (2007) 'We are so sorry, we feel helpless and lost', *Guardian*, 21 April: 13.

Gordon, C. (2004) 'Counsellors' use of reflective space', *Counselling and Psychotherapy Research*, 4 (2): 40–4.

Gordon, R. (1978) *Dying and Creating: A search for meaning*, Vol. 5. London: The Society of Analytical Psychology.

Gorer, G. (1965) *Death, Grief and Mourning in Contemporary Britain*. London: Cresset Press.

Grubbs, G. (2004) *Bereavement Dreaming and the Individuating Soul*. Berwick, ME: Nicolas-Hays.

Guo, K. (2006) '"Online tomb sweeping" becomes popular: thirty-thousand worship ancestors through the internet', *People Daily*, 6 April. Retrieved 19/07/06 from http:media.people.com.cn/BIG5/40606/427487.html

Handzo, R. (1996) 'Chaplaincy: a continuum of caring', *Oncology*, 10 (9): 45–7.

Hansen, A. (2004) *Responding to Loss: A Resource for Caregivers*. Amityville, NY: Baywood.

Hanson, T. (2005) 'Finding a path to healing'. Presentation at the 7th International Conference on Grief and Bereavement in Contemporary Society, 12–15 July, King's College, London.

Hargrave, A. (2003) 'Fit to Work', *Counselling and Psychotherapy Journal*, 14 (2): 28–9.

Harris, T. (2006) 'Volunteer befriending as an intervention for depression: implications for bereavement care', *Bereavement Care*, 25 (2): 27–30.

Harrison, R. (1999a) 'The impact of stranger murder', *The Therapist*, 6 (1): 32–8.

Harrison, R. (1999b) 'The impact of murder on families and the need to work in partnership'. Presentation at the 6th International Bereavement and Loss Conference, Challenges in Bereavement into the 21st Century, CIS Manchester, 4 September 1999.

Hartmann, E. and Basile, R. (2003) 'Dream imagery becomes more intense after 9/11/01', *Dreaming: the Journal of the Association for the Study of Dreams*, 13 (2): 61–6.

Hawton, K. and Simkin, S. (2003) 'Helping people bereaved by suicide: their needs may require special attention', *Bereavement Care*, 22 (3): 41–2.

Hedtke, L. and Winslade, J. (2004) *Re-membering Lives: Conversations with the Dying and Bereaved*. Amityville, NY: Bywood.

Helmrath T. A. and Steinitz, E. (1978) 'Death of an infant: parental grieving and the failure of social support', *Journal of Family Practice*, 6: 785–90.

Henderson, A. R. (2008) 'Unexplained infertility: psychotherapy work that precedes fertility treatment may eliminate difficulty in conceiving', *Therapy*, 2008 (February): 29–31.

Henderson, A. S. (1974) 'Care-eliciting behaviour in man', *Journal of Nervous and Mental Disease*, 159: 172–81.

Hennezel, M. de (1995) *An Intimate Death: How the Dying Teach Us to Live*, trans. Carol Janeway. London: Warner.

Herford, K. Neycha (2004) *White Noise: the Underbelly of Traumatic Loss*, Brooklyn, NY: Sunday Rising Publishing. p. 1. A Guided Journal Companion to White Noise CD, associated with The White Noise Project (WNP) – helping co-victims of homicide and other tragically bereaved persons penetrate the silence. www.tobearwitness.org.

Herman, J. L. (1992) *Trauma and Recover: the Aftermath of Violence*. New York: Basic Books.

Hinton, J. M. (1967) *Dying*. Harmondsworth: Penguin Books.

Hobson, J. A. (1989) 'The Dreaming Brain. New York: Basic Books.

Hofer, M., Wolff, C., Friedman, S. and Mason, J. W. (1977) 'A psychoendocrine study of bereavement', *Psychosomatic Medicine*, 39: 481–504.

Hollin, S. and Esterhuyzen, A. (1997) 'Bereavement and grief in adults with learning difficulties', *British Journal of Psychiatry*, 170: 497–501.

Houben, L. M. (2006) 'Reflecting on culture, religion and mourning', *The Forum*, Association for Death Education and Counselling (ADEC), April–June: 9.

House, J. S., Landis, K. R. and Umberson, D. (1988) 'Social relationships and health', *Science*, 241: 540–4.

Howarth, G. (2000) 'Dismantling the boundaries between life and death', *Mortality*, 5 (2): 127–38.

Huertas, P. (2005) 'Are we hard wired for love and grief?' *Healthcare Counselling and Psychotherapy* Journal, 5 (3): 14–15.

Humphrey, G. M. and Zimpfer, D. G. (1996) *Bereavement and Support: Healing in a Group Environment*. London: Taylor & Francis.

Hunt, J. and Monach, J. H. (1997) 'Beyond the bereavement model: the significance of depression for infertility counselling', *Human Reproduction*, 12 (Suppl. 2): 188–94.

Imara, M. (1975) 'Dying as the last stage of growth', in E. Kubler-Ross, *Death: The Final Stage of Growth*. Touchstone, Simon & Schuster. pp. 147–64.

Imperial War Museum London (2007–2008) 'My Boy Jack'. Exhibition about Jack Kipling, including his last letter to his parents, at the Imperial War Museum, London, 6 November 2007 – 24 February 2008.

Ironstone-Catterall, P. (2004–2005) 'When Isaak was gone: an auto-ethnographic meditation on mourning a toddler', *Omega*, 50 (1): 1–21.

Irwin, M., Daniels, M. and Weiner, H. (1987) 'Immune and neuroendocrine changes during bereavement', *Psychiatric Clinics of North America*, 10: 449–65.

Jacobs, S. (1999) *Traumatic Grief: Diagnosis, Treatment and Prevention*. Philadelphia, PA: Brunner/Mazel.

Janoff-Bulman, R. (1992) *Shattered Assumptions: Towards a New Psychology of Trauma*. New York: The Free Press.

Janoff-Bulman, R. and Berge, M. (1998). *Perspective on Loss: a Sourcebook. Death, Dying and Bereavement*. New York: The Free Press.

Janoff-Bulman, R. and Franz, C. (1997) 'The impact of trauma on meaning: from meaningless world to meaningful life', in M. Power and C. Brewin (eds), *The Transformation of Meaning in Psychological Therapies*. New York: Wiley. pp. 91–106.

Jaspers, K. (1954) *Way to Wisdom*, trans. Ralph Manheim. New Haven: Yale University Press.

Jenkins, C. and Merry, J. (2005) *Relative Grief*. London: Jessica Kingsley.

Jenkins, P. (2002) *Legal Issues in Counselling and Psychotherapy*. London: Sage.

Jenkinson, K. and Bodkin, C. (1996) 'Sudden death – a personal journey', *Lifeline*, 19 (Winter/Spring): 12–14.

Jennings, I. and Shovholt, T. M. (1999) 'The cognitive, emotional and relational characteristics of master therapists', *Journal of Counselling Psychology*, 46 (1): 3–11.

Jerrom, C. (2004) 'Death without respect', *Community Care*, 2004 (16–22 September): 30–3.

Jones, S. (2005) 'Disenfranchised grief and non-finite loss as experienced by the families of death row inmates'. Presentation at the 7th International Conference on Grief and Bereavement in Contemporary Society, 12–15 July King's College, London.

Jones, W. (2007) 'I came home to find my boyfriend dead', *Guardian Weekend*, 24 March: 15.

Jonker, G. (1997) 'The many facets of Islam: death, dying and disposal between orthodox rule and historical convention', in C. M. Parkes, P. Laungani and B. Young (eds), *Death and Bereavement Across Cultures*. Hove and New York: Brunner-Routledge.

Jordan J. R. (2001) 'Is suicide bereavement different? A reassessment of the literature', *Suicide and Life-Threatening Behavior*, 31: 91–102.

Jordan, J. R. and Neimeyer, R. A. (2003) 'Does grief counselling work?' *Death Studies*, 27: 765–86.

Jordan, J. R., Kraus, D. R. and Ware, E. S. (1993) 'Observations on loss and family development', *Family Process*, 32: 425–39.

Jordan, L. E. (2003) 'Suviving a suicide', *Epilogue*, Duke Community Bereavement Centre, USA, Summer.

Jordan, L. E. (2006) Quoted in *Epilogue, Duke Community Bereavement Journal*, Spring: 1 and 8.

Jung, C. G. (1973) *Memories, Dreams, Reflections*, recorded and edited by A. Jaffe, trans. R. and C. Winston. New York: Random House.

Jurgensen, G. (1999) *The Disappearance: How Do You Live When Your Children Live No More?* trans. Adriana Hunter. London: Flamingo/HarperCollins.

Kalischuk R. G. and Hayes, V. E. (2003–2004) 'Grieving, mourning, and healing following a youth suicide: a focus on health and well being in families', *Omega*, 48 (1): 45–67.

Kasher, A. (2003) 'Life in the heart', *Journal of Loss and Trauma*, 8 (4): 247–60.

Katz, I. (2007) Obituary of Dina Rabinovitz, *Guardian*, 1 November: 39.

Kellaway, K. (2005) 'Cicely Saunders', *Observer Magazine*, 5 December: 37.

Keller J. W., Brown, G., Maier, K., Steinfurth, K., Hall, S. and Pietrowski C. (1995) 'Use of dreams in therapy: a survey of clinicians in private practice', *Psychology Reports*, 76: 1288–90.

Kenney, J. S. (2002) 'Metaphors of loss: murder, bereavement, gender and presentation of "victimised" self', *International Review of Victimology*, 9 (3): 219–51.

Khalid, S. (2007) 'Counselling from an Islamic perspective', *Therapy Today*, 18 (2): 34–7.

Killick, J. (1996) 'Communicating as if your life depended on it: life history work with people with dementia', in T. Heller et al. (eds), *Mental Health Matters*. London: Macmillan.

Kilmartin, C. T. (2004) 'Men, anger and rage', in: J. Lynch (ed.), *Anger Avoiders: The Hidden Face of Anger*. Oakland, CA: New Harbinger. pp. 146–70.

Kilmartin, C. (2005) 'Depression in men: communication, diagnosis and therapy', *Journal of Men's Health and Gender* 2 (1): 95–9.

King, M. (2002) 'Spiritual Belief helps grieving process', *British Medical Journal*, June: 324.

King and Norgard (1999) in *Florida State University Law Review*, 26, cited by Sarah Jones (2005).

Kirschenbaum, H. and Hendersin, V. L. (1992) *The Carl Rogers Reader*. London: Constable.

Kissane, D. and Bloch, S. (2003) *Family Focussed Grief Therapy*. Buckingham: Open University Press.

Klass, D. (1988) *Parental Grief: Solace and Resolution*. New York: Springer.

Klass, D. (1999a) 'Developing a cross-cultural model of grief: the state of the field', *Omega: Journal of Death and Dying*, 39: 153–78.

Klass, D. (1999b) *The Spiritual Lives of Bereaved Parents*. Philadelphia, PA: Brunner/Mazel.

Klass, D. (2000) 'How self-help and professional help helps', *Grief Matters, The Australian Journal of Grief and Bereavement*, 3 (1): 3–6.

Klass, D. (2001) 'The inner representation of the dead child in the psychic and social narratives of bereaved parents', in R. A. Neimeyer (ed.), *Meaning Reconstruction and the Experience of Loss*. Washington, DC: American Psychological Association. pp. 77–94.

Klass, D., Silverman P. R. and Nickman, S. L. (eds) (1996) *Continuing Bonds: New Understandings of Grief*. Washington, DC: Taylor & Francis.

Koenig, B. A. and Gates-Williams, J. (1995) 'Understanding cultural differences in caring for dying patients', *Western Journal of Medicine*, 163: 244–9.

Koenig, H., McCullogh M. and Larson D. (2001) *Handbook of Religion and Health*. Oxford: Oxford University Press.

Kubler-Ross, E. (1970) *On Death and Dying*. London: Tavistock.

Kubler-Ross, E. (1975) *Death: the Final Stage of Growth*. New York: Prentice-Hall.

Kushner, H. (1982) *When Bad Things Happen to Good People*. London: Pan.

Lager, E. and Wagner. S. (1997) *Knowing Why Changes Nothing: Diary of Sorrow and Survival*. Dianella, WA, Australia: Options Publishing.

Larsen, D., Edey, W. and Lemay, L. (2007) 'Understanding the role of hope in counselling: exploring the international uses of hope', *Counselling Psychology Quarterly*, 20 (4): 401–16.

Laungani, P. (1996) 'Death and bereavement in India and England: a comparative analysis', *Mortality*, 1: 191–212.

Laungani, P. (1997) 'Death in a Hindu family', in C. M. Parkes, P. Laungani and B. Young (eds), *Death and Bereavement across Cultures*. London: Routledge.

Laungani, P. (2004) 'East meets west', *Counselling and Psychotherapy Journal*, October: 21–3.

Lawrence, D. (2006) *And Still I Rise*. London: Faber & Faber.

Lehman, D. R., Wortman, C. B. and Williams, A. F. (1987) 'Long-term effects of losing a spouse or child in a motor vehicle crash', *Journal of Personality and Social Psychology*, 52: 218–31.

Lehman, D. R., Lang, E. L., Wortman, C. B. and Sorenson, S. B. (1989) 'Long-term effects of sudden bereavement: marital and parent–child relationships and children's reactions', *Journal of Family Psychology*, 2: 344–67.

Lehman, L. Jimerson, S. R. and Gaasch, A. (2000) *Counselling for Grief and Bereavement*. London: Sage.

Leichtentritt, R. D. and Rettig, K. D. (2002) 'Family beliefs about end-of-life decisions: an interpersonal perspective', *Death Studies*, 26 (7): 567–94.

Lemkau, J. P., Mann, B., Little, D., Whitecar, P., Hershberger, P. M. and Schumm, J. A. (2000) 'A questionnaire survey of family practice physicians' perceptions of bereavement care', *Archives of Family Medicine*, 9 (9): 822–9.

Lendrum, S. and Syme, G. (1992) *Gift of Tears: a Practical Approach to Loss and Bereavement Counselling*. London: Routledge.

Levine, S. (1982) *Who Dies?* New York: Anchor Books.

Leviton, D. (1991) *Horrendous Death: Health and Well-being*. New York: Hemisphere.

Lewis, C. S. (1961) *A Grief Observed*. London: Faber & Faber.

Lilford, R. J., Stratton, P., Godsil, S. and Prassed, A. (1994) 'A randomised trial of routine versus selective counselling in perinatal bereavement from congenital disease', *British Journal of Obstetrics and Gynaecology*, 101 (4): 291–6.

Lindemann, E. (1944) 'Symptomatology and management of acute grief', *American Journal of Psychiatry*, 101: 141–8.

Littlewood, J. L., Cramer, D., Hockstra. J. and Humphrey, G. B. (1991) 'Gender differences in parental coping following their child's death', *British Journal of Guidance and Counselling*, 19 (2): 139–48.

LoConto, D. G. (1998) 'Death and dreams: a sociological approach to grieving and identity', *Omega*, 37: 171–85.

London Foundation for the Study of Infant Death (FSID) (2001) *When My Baby Died ... Thirty Parents Tell Their Stories*. London: FSID.

Lopez, B. (2003) Quoted in *Epilogue, Duke Community Bereavement Journal*, Spring: 5.

Lovell, A. (2001) 'The changing identities of miscarriage and stillbirth: influences on practice and ritual', *Bereavement Care*, 20 (3): 37–40.

Ludman, B. L. (2000) Jewish Burial – A study of the psychology of healing, www.adec.org/pubs/jewishburial.htm. Downloaded 29/09/2000

Lyons, P. (1997) 'Creative writing and healing', *Lapidus News*, 4: 4–5.

Lyons, T. (2003) 'Transforming the cancer experience through embodying the dream'. Paper presented to the Association for the Study of Dreams International conference June–July, Berkeley, California.

Mabey, R. (2006) *Nature Cure*. London: Pimlico.

McCormick, E. W. (1997) *Living on the edge*. Shaftesbury: Element.

McDermott, M. Y. and Ahsan, M. M. (1980) *The Muslim Guide for Teachers, Employers, Community Workers and Social Administrators in Britain*. Leicester: Islamic Foundation.

McDermott, M. and Moore, O. (2004) 'Post-traumatic Stress Disorder and Bereavement', *Bereavement Care*, 3 (3) Winter: 41–2.

McGahern, J. (2005) Memoir. London: Faber & Faber.

McGoldrick, M. (2004) 'Gender and mourning', in F. Walsh and M. McGoldrick (eds), *Living beyond Loss: Death in the Family*. New York: W. W. Norton. pp. 99–118.

McGrath, P. (2003) 'Religiosity and the challenge of terminal illness', *Death Studies*, 27 (10): 881–99.

Machin, L. (2006) 'The landscape of loss', *Bereavement Care*, 25 (1): 7–11.

Machin, L. (2008) *Working with Loss and Grief: A New Model for Practitioners*. London: Sage.

Machin, L. and Spall, R. (2004) 'Mapping grief: a study in practice', *Counselling and Psychotherapy Research*, 4 (1): 9–17.

McKissock, M. and McKissock, D. (1985) *Coping with Grief*. Sydney: ABC Books.

McKissock, D., McKissock, M. and Williams, P. (1994) *Bereavement Support Groups: a Handbook for Group Leaders*. Sydney: Bereavement Care Centre.

McLeod, J. (1997) *Narrative and Psychotherapy*. London: Sage.

McLoughlin, D. (1985) 'Creative writing in a hospice', *Hospice Bulletin*, October: 8–9.

McNiff, S. (1992) *Art as Medicine: Creating a Therapy of the Imagination*. Boston: Shambhala.

Maddison, D. C. and Walker, W. L. (1967) 'Factors affecting the outcome of conjugal bereavement', *British Journal of Psychiatry*, 113: 1057–67.

Mahoney, M. J. and Graci, G. M. (1999) 'The meanings and correlates of spirituality. Suggestions from an exploratory survey of experts', *Death Studies*, 23: 521–8.

Mallon, B. (1987) *An Introduction to Counselling Skills for Special Educational Needs: Participant's Manual*. Manchester: Manchester University Press.

Mallon, B. (2000a) *Dreams, Counselling and Healing*. Dublin: Gill & Macmillan.

Mallon, B. (2000b) 'The guiding spirit in dreams', *The Churches' Fellowship for Psychical & Spiritual Studies*, Summer (184): 5–7.

Mallon, B. (2001) *Venus Dreaming: A Guide to Women's Dreams and Nightmares*. Dublin: New Leaf.

Mallon, B. (2005) 'Dreams and bereavement', *Bereavement Care*, 24 (3): 43–6.

Mallon, B. (2006) 'Dreams and bereavement', *DreamTime, International Association for the Study of Dreams*, Winter: 8–11.

Mallon, B. (2007) *The Mystic Symbols*. London: Godsfield/Octopus.

Mallon, B., Tufnell, M. and Rubidge, T. (2005) *When I Open My Eyes: A Report on a Three Year Project Exploring Body, Imagination and Health*. Cumbria: Body Stories.

Malone, L. (2007) 'Supporting people bereaved through homicide', *Bereavement Care*, 26 (3): 51–3.

Mander, G. (2005) 'Bereavement talk', *Therapy Today*, 16 (9): 42–5.

Maqsood, R. W. (1998) *After Death, Life!* Birmingham: Goodword Books.

Marie Curie Cancer Care (2003) *Spiritual and Religious Care Competencies for Specialist Palliative Care*. London: Marie Curie Cancer Care, October.

Marks, A. (1988–89) 'Structural parameters of of sex, race, age and education and their influence on attitudes toward suicide', *Omega*, 19: 327–36.

Martin, D. (2000) 'Internet support for bereaved people', *Bereavement Care*, 19 (3): 38–40.

Martin, T. and Doka, K. (1996) 'Masculine grief', in K. Doka (ed.), *Living with Grief after Sudden Loss*. Washington, DC: Hospice Foundation of America.

Martin, T. and Doka, K. (2000) *Men Don't Cry … Women Do: Transcending Gender Stereotypes of Grief*. Philadelphia, PA: Brunner Mazel.

Maultsaid, D. (2007) 'Epiphanies: writing for compassion', *Spirituality and Health International*, 8 (3): 157–9.

Mehrabian, A. (1981) *Silent Messages: Implicit Communications of Emotions and Attitudes*. 2nd edn. Stamford, CT: Wadsworth.

Mendel, G. (2006) 'The Memory Box project', *Guardian*, 29 November: 6–15.

Meuser, T. M. and Marwit, S. J. (2001) 'A comprehensive, stage-sensitive model in dementia caregiving', *The Gerontologist*, 4 (5): 658–770.

Mezey, G., Evans, C. and Hobdell, K. (2002) 'Families of homicide victims: psychiatric responses and help seeking', *Psychology and Psychotherapy: Theory, Research*, 75 (1): 65–75.

Miller, B. and McGown, A. (1997) 'Bereavement: theoretical perspectives and adaptation', *American Journal of Hospice and Palliative Medicine*, 14 (4): 156–77.

Milner, J. and O'Byrne, P. (2003) 'How do counsellors make client assessments?' *Counselling and Psychotherapy Research*, 3 (4): 139–45.

Mitchell, Stephen (ed.) (2004) *Gilgamesh*. New York: Free Press.

Moffitt, A., Kramer, M. and Hoffman, R. (eds) (1993) *The Functions of Dreaming*. Albany, NY: State University of New York Press.

Monach, J. (2006) 'Stresses and distresses', *Therapy Today*, 17 (8): 24–7.

Montaigne, M. (1533–92), *Essays*, 'Of Experience'.

Montaigne, Mde. (1603) 'Of sadness and sorrowes', in *The Essayes, or Morall, Politike, and Militarie Discourses of Michael, Lord of Montaign*, trans. John Florio. London: V. Sims.

Moody, R. (1993) *Reunions: Visionary Experiences with Departed Loved Ones*. New York: Villamy.

Morgan, J. and Laungani, P. (eds) (2002) *Death and Bereavement around the World*, Vol. 1: *Major Religious Traditions*, Amityville, NY: Baywood.

Morrice, J. K. W. (1983) 'Poetry as therapy', *British Journal of Medical Psychology*, 56: 367–70.

Mount, B. M. (2003) 'The existential moment', *Palliative and Supportive Care*, 1: 94.

Mowll, J. (2007) 'Reality and regret: viewing or not viewing a body after sudden death', *Bereavement Care*, 26 (1): 3–6.

Muggeridge, M. (2007) 'Half in love with death': article of 22 February 1970 reprinted in *Guardian* Sunday Best, 4 November: 22–3.

Murphy, S. A. and Johnson, C. (2003) 'Finding meaning in a child's violent death: a five year prospective analysis of parents' personal narratives and empirical data', *Death Studies*, 27 (5): 381–404.

Murray, J. A., Terry, D. J., Vance, J. C., Battistutta, D. and Connolly, Y. (2000) 'Effects of a program of intervention on parental distress following infant death', *Death Studies*, 24: 275–305.

Murray, R. and Zentner, J. (1989) *Nursing Concepts for Health Promotion*. London: Prentice-Hall.

Nadeau, J. W. (1998) *Families Making Sense of Death*. Thousand Oaks, CA: Sage.

Neimeyer, R. (1998) *Lessons of Loss: a Guide to Coping*. New York: McGraw-Hill.

Neimeyer, R. (ed.) (2001) *Meaning Reconstruction and the Experience of Loss*. Washington, DC: American Psychological Association.

Neimeyer, R. (2005) 'Grief, loss and the quest for meaning: narrative contributions to bereavement care', *Bereavement Care*, 24 (2): 27–30.

Neimeyer, R. A., Prigerson, H. and Davies, B. (2002) 'Mourning and meaning', *American Behavioural Scientist*, 46: 235–51.

Neuberger, J. (2004) *Caring for Dying People of Different Faiths*. Abingdon: Radcliffe Medical Press.

Newman, M. (2002) 'Bereavement and trauma', *Bereavement Care*, 21 (2): 27–9.

NHS (2007) NICE Guidance on Cancer Services: Improving supportive and palliative care for adults with cancer. Downloaded 02/19/2007 from www.nice.org.uk/guidance/csgsp

Norbury, E. (2004) 'Meaning in life and faith after death', *Spirituality and Health International*, 5 (1): 813.

Norman, R. (2004) *On Humanism*. London: Routledge.

Nuland, S. B. (1994) *How We Die*. London: Chatto & Windus.

Observer (1998) 'The *Observer* Special Report: *Cries Unheard: the Story of Mary Bell*, by Gitta Sereny', *Observer*, 3 May 1998, pp. 3–5.

O'Connor, M. and Russell, A. (2003) 'Working with the Legacy of Trauma', *Bereavement Care*, 22 (2): 22–4.

Oldham, A. and Nourse, C. (2006) '"Forgotten victims"? – adults look back on their childhood bereavement by homicide', *Bereavement Care*, 25 (1) Spring: 12–15.

Oliviere, D., Hargreaves, R. and Monroe, B. (1998) *Good Practices in Palliative Care*. Aldershot: Ashgate.

Olshansky, S. (1962) 'Chronic sorrow: a response to having a mentally defective child', *Social Casework*, 43 (4): 190–3.

Oltjenbruns, K. A. and James, L. (2006) 'Adolescents' use of the internet as a modality of grief support', *The Forum, Association of Death Education and Counselling*, 32 (4): 5–6.

Orbach, A. (1999) *Life, Psychotherapy and Death*. London: Jessica Kingsley.

Osterfield, J. (2002) 'Volunteers working in a bereavement service', in D. Doyle (ed.), *Volunteers in Hospice and Palliative Care: A Handbook for Volunteer Service Managers*. Oxford: Oxford University Press.

Papadopoulos, R. (1997) 'Individual identity and collective narratives of conflict', *Journal of Jungian Studies*, 43 (2): 7–26.

Papadopoulos, R. (2001) 'Refugees, therapists and trauma: systemic reflections', *Context*, 54: 5–8.

Parch, H. (2005) Edited extract from *Last Post: the Final Words from Our First World War Soldiers*. London: Weidenfeld & Nicolson.

Pargament, K. I. and Park, C. L. (1997) 'In times of stress: the religion-coping connection', in B. Spilka and D. M. McIntosh (eds), *Psychology of Religion: Theoretical Approaches*. Boulder, CO: Westview Press. pp. 43–53.

Parker, S. (1993) 'Writing yourself towards wholeness: the creative journal', *International Journal of Complementary Medicine*, November: 27–8.

Parkes, C. M. (1971) 'Psycho-social transitions: a field for study', *Social Science and Medicine*, 5: 101–15.

Parkes, C. M. (1972) *Bereavement: Studies of Grief in Adult Life*. New York: International Universities Press.

Parkes, C. M. (1986) 'Orienteering the caregiver's grief', *Journal of Palliative Care*, 1: 5–7.

Parkes, C. M. (1988) 'Bereavement as a psychosocial transition: processes of adaptation to change', *Journal of Social Issues*, 44 (3): 53–65.

Parkes, C. M. (1996) *Bereavement: Studies of Grief in Adults*, 3rd edn. Harmondsworth: Penguin.

Parkes, C. M. (2000) 'Counselling bereaved people – help or harm?' *Bereavement Care*, 19 (2): 19–21.

Parkes, C. M. (2002) 'Grief: lessons from the past, visions for the future', *Death Studies*, 26 (5): 367–85.

Parkes, C. M. (2007) 'Dangerous words', *Bereavement Care*, 26 (2): 23–5.

Parkes, C. M. and Weiss, R. S. (1983) *Recovery from Bereavement*. New York: Basic Books.

Parkes, C. M., Benjamin, B. and Fitzgerald, R. G. (1969) 'Broken Heart: a statistical study of increased mortality among widowers', *British Medical Journal*, 1: 740–3.

Parkes, C. M., Laungani, P. and Young, B. (eds) (1997) *Death and Bereavement across Cultures*. London: Routledge.

Parkes, K. R. (1986) 'Coping in stressful episodes: the role of individual differences, environmental factors, and situational characteristics', *Journal of Personality and Social Psychology*, 51: 1277–92.

Paul, C. (2006) 'Guilt and blame in the grieving process', *Bereavement Care*, 25 (3): 50–2.

Payne, M. (2006) *Narrative Therapy*, 2nd edn. London: SAGE.

Payne, S., Horn, S. and Relf, M. (1999) *Loss and Bereavement*. Buckingham: Open University Press.

Peltier, L. (2006) 'Spirituality and sudden loss: a personal story', *The Forum*, ADEC, 32 (2) April–June: 8.

Penson, J. (1990) 'Teaching bereavement care', *Bereavement Care*, 9 (2): 22–4.

Peppers, L. G. and Knapp, R. J. (1980) *Motherhood and Mourning*. New York: Praeger.

Perkins, J. (2006) 'The psychological impact of infertility', *Therapy Today*, October 17 (8): 17–19.

Persaud, S. and Persaud, M. (2003) 'Does it hurt to die: bereavement work to help people with learning difficulties', *Bereavement Care*, 22 (1): 9–11.

Phillip, R. (1996) 'The links between poetry and healing', *The Therapist*, 3 (4): 15.

Picardie, J. (2001) *If the Spirit Moves You*. London: Picador.

Picardie, R. (1998) *Before I Say Goodbye*, London: Penguin.

Pierce, B. (2003) *Miscarriage and Stillbirth: the Changing Response*. Dublin: Veritas.

Pointon, C. (2006) 'On the starting blocks', *Therapy Today*, March: 34–6.

Pollack, C. E. (2003) 'Intentions of burial: mourning, politics, and memorials following the massacre at Sebrenina', *Death Studies*, 27: 125–42.

Pollock, G. H. (1971) 'Temporal anniversary manifestations: hour, day, holiday', *Psychoanalytic Quarterly*, 40: 435–6.

Pook, S. (2006) 'Betrayed mothers set up relatives' help group', *Daily Telegraph*, 1 February: 5.

Post, S., Puchalski, C. and Larson, D. (2000) 'Physicians and patient spirituality: professional boundaries, competency and ethics', *Annals of Internal Medicine*, 132: 578–83.

Potts, S. (2005) *Everylife*. Wiltshire: APS Publishing.

Poussaint, A. F. (1984) 'The grief response following homicide'. Paper presented at the 92nd Annual Convention of the American Psychological Association, Toronto, Ontario, 24–8 August.

Prigerson, H. (2004) 'Complicated grief: when the path of adjustment leads to a dead-end', *Bereavement Care*, 23 (3): 38–40.

Purnell, C. (1996) 'An attachment-based approach to working with clients affected by HIV and AIDS', *British Journal of Psychotherapy*, 12 (4): 521–50.

Rando, T. A. (ed.) (1986) *Parental Loss of a Child*. Champaign, IL: Research Press.

Rando, T. A. (1984) *Grief, Dying and Death: Clinical Interventions for Caregivers*. Champaign, IL: Research Press.

Rando, T. A. (1993) Treatment of Complicated Mourning. Champaign, IL: Research Press.

Raphael, B. (1977) 'Preventive intervention with the recently bereaved', *Archives of General Psychiatry*, 34: 1450–4.

Raphael, B. (1980) 'Primary prevention: fact and or fiction?', *Australian and New Zealand Journal of Psychiatry*, 14: 163–74.

Raphael, B. (1984) *An Anatomy of Bereavement: a Handbook for the Caring Professions*. London: Unwin Hyman.

Raphael, B. (2005) 'After the tsunami – harnessing Australian expertise for recovery'. Presentation at the Shrine Dome, Canberra, 31 March.

Raphael, B. and Martinek, N. (1997) 'Assessing traumatic bereavement and posttraumatic stress disorder', in J. P. Wilson and T. M. Keane (eds), *Assessing Psychological Trauma and PTSD*. New York: Guildford.

Raphael, B. and Minkov, C. (1999) 'Abnormal grief', *Psychiatry*, 12: 99–102.

Read, S. (2006) 'Living in the shadow of grief: bereavement and people with learning difficulties'. Presentation at Manchester Area Bereavement Forum's 13th International Conference on Bereavement and Loss, 14 September.

Redfield Jamieson, K. (2002) *Night Falls Fast: Understanding Suicide*. New York: Vintage Books.

Redwood, D. (2002) 'Dr Redwood Interviews: Rachel Naomi Remen Living in the Post-9/11 World. Retrieved from file:///Users/ibook/Desktop/Interview – Rachel Naomi Remen. 10/22/2007 07.10 pm.

Reed, M. L. (2000) *Grandparents Cry Twice: Help for Bereaved Grandparents*. New York: Baywood.

Rees, D. (1971) 'The hallucinations of widowhood', *British Medical Journal*, 4: 37–41.

Reid, J. (1979) 'A time to live, a time to grieve: patterns and processes of mourning among the Yolngu of Australia', *Cultural Medical Psychiatry*, 3 (4): 319–46.

Relf, M. (1998) 'Involving volunteers in bereavement counselling', *European Journal of Palliative Care*, in Osterfield (2002) above.

Relf, M. (2000) 'The effectiveness of voluntary bereavement care: an evaluation of a palliative care bereavement service', Doctoral thesis, University of London.

Ribbens, McCarthy, J. (2005) 'The meaning of "meaning": towards an inter-disciplinary and multi-method approach to bereavement.' Presentation at the 7th International Conference on Grief and Bereavement in Contemporary Society, 12–15 July, King's College, London.

Riches, G. and Dawson, P. (1998) 'Spoiled memories: problems of grief resolution in families bereaved through murder', *Mortality*, 3 (20): 143–59.

Riches, G. and Dawson, P. (2000) *An Intimate Loneliness: Supporting Bereaved Parents and Siblings*. London and Buckingham: Open University Press.

Riches, G. and Dawson, P. (2002) 'Shoestrings and bricolage: some notes on researching the impact of a child's death on family relationships', *Death Studies*, 26 (3): 209–22.

Richie, D. (2000) 'Fateful moments and the discourses of grief', *Grief Matters*, Autumn 7 (1): 8–11.

Richie, D. (2003) Death: Mortality and religious diversity. Exhibition at the Immigration Musuem, Melbourne, November 2003–February 2004. www. immigration. museum.vic.gov.au

Rilke, R. M. (1992) *Duino Elegies*, trans. S. Mitchell. Boston, MA: Shambala Publications Inc.

Riordan, R. J. (1996) 'Scriptotherapy: therapeutic writing as a counsellor adjunct', *Journal of Counselling and Development*, 74: 263–9.

Roberts, P. (2006) 'From My Space to our space: the functions of web memorials in bereavement', *The Forum, Association for Death Education and Counselling*, 32 (4): 1–3.

Rogers, C. (1974) *On Becoming a Person*. London: Constable.

Rogers, J., Sheldon, A., Barwick, C. et al. (1982) 'Help for families of suicide: survivors' support program', *Canadian Journal of Psychiatry*, 27: 444–9.

Roos, S. (2002) *Chronic Sorrow: a Living Loss*. New York: Brunner-Routledge.

Rose, J. (2001) *From a 'Bundle of Joy' to a Person of Sorrow: Disenfranchised Grief in the Donor-conceived Adult*. Queensland University of Technology Applied Ethics Seminar Series.

Rosen, M. (2002) *Carrying the Elephant: a Memoir of Love and Loss*. Hardmondsworth: Penguin.

Rosenblatt, P. C. (1993) 'Cross-cultural variation in the experience, expression and understanding of grief', in D. P. Irish, K. F. Lindquist, V. J. Nelsen (eds), *Ethnic Variations in Dying Death and Grief: Diversity in Universality*. Washington, DC: Taylor & Francis. pp. 13–19.

Rosenblatt, P. C. (2000a) 'Parents talking in the present tense about their dead child', *Bereavement Care*, 19 (3): 35–7.

Rosenblatt, P. C (2000b) *Help Your Marriage Survive the Death of a Child*. Philadelphia, PA: Temple University press.

Rosenblatt, P. C. (2001) 'A social constructivist perspective on cultural differences in grief', in M. Stroebe, R. Hasson, W. Stroebe and H. Schut (eds), *Handbook of Bereavement Research*. Washington, DC: American Psychological Association. pp. 285–300.

Rosenblatt, P. C., Walsh, R. P. and Jackson, A. (1976) *Grief and Meaning in Cross Cultural Perspective*. New Haven: HRAF Press.

Rothschild, B. (2005) 'Applying the Brakes', *Counselling and Psychotherapy Journal*, February: 12–16.

Rubin, S. S. (1984) 'Mourning distinct from melancholia: the resolution of bereavement', *British Journal of Medical Psychology*, 57: 339–45.

Rubin, S. S. (1999) 'The Two Track Model: overview, retrospect and prospect', *Death Studies*, 23: 681–714.

Rubin, S. S. and Malkinson, R. (2001) 'Parental response to child loss across the life cycle: clinical and research perspectives', in M. Stroebe, R. Hansson, W. Stroebe and H. Schut (eds), *Handbook of Bereavement Research: Consequences, Coping and Care*. Washington, DC: American Psychological Association. pp. 219–40.

Rubin, S. S. and Yasien-Esmael, H. (2004) 'Loss and bereavement among Israel's Muslims: acceptance of God's will, grief, and the relationship to the deceased', *Omega*, 49 (2): 149–62.

Rubin, S. S., Malkinson, R. and Witztum, E. (2003) 'Trauma and bereavement: conceptual and clinical issues revolving around relationships', *Death Studies*, 27 (8): 667–90.

Saari, S. (2005) *A Bolt from the Blue: Coping with Disasters and Acute Traumas*. London: Jessica Kingsley.

Sajid, Imam, A. (2003) 'Death and bereavement in Islam'. Lecture given at St Christopher's Hospice, 2 July.

Sanders, C. M. (1993) *Grief: The Mourning After: Dealing with Adult Bereavement*. Chichester: Wiley.

Schoenberg, B., Carr, A. C., Kutscher, A. H., Peretz, D. and Goldberg, I. K. (eds) (1974) *Anticipatory Grief*. New York: Columbia University Press.

Schredl, M. (2000) Book review: '*Dreams and Nightmare*: the new theory of the origins and meaning of dreams', *Dreaming*, 2 (4): 247–50.

Schut, H. (2005) 'Balancing research and counselling'. Presentation at the 7th International Conference on Grief and Bereavement in Contemporary Society, 12–15 July, King's College, London.

Schwab, R. (1992) 'Effects of a child's death on the marital relationship: a preliminary study', *Death Studies*, 16: 141–54.

Schwab, R. (1996) 'Gender differences in parental grief', *Death Studies*, 20: 103–14.

Seaton, J. (2006) 'The Old Black', *Guardian*, 3 January: 24–5.

Sebold, A. (2002) *The Lovely Bones*. London: Picador.

Sereny, G. (1998) *Cries Unheard: The Story of Mary Bell*. London: Macmillan.

Shalev, R. (1999) 'Comparison of war bereaved and motor vehicle accident bereaved parents'. Master's thesis, University of Haifa, Haifa, Israel.

Shapiro, E. R. (1994) *Grief as a Family Process: A Developmental Approach to Clinical Practice*. New York: Guildford Press.

Shapiro, E. R. (1996) 'Family bereavement and cultural diversity: a social development perspective', *Family Process*, 35: 313–32.

Shear, M. K., Frank, E., Houck, P. R. and Reynolds, C. F. (2005) 'Treatment of complicated grief: a randomized controlled trial', *Journal of American Medical Association*, 293: 2601–8.

Shuchter, S. R. and Zisook, S. (1993) 'The course of normal grief', in M. Strobe, W. Stroebe and R. O. Hanson (eds), *Handbook of Bereavement*. Cambridge: Cambridge University Press. pp. 23–43.

Silverman, P. R. (2001) 'Living with grief, rebulding a world', *Innovations in End-of-Life Care*, 3 (3). www.edc.org/lastacts

Silverman, P. R. (2004) *Widow to Widow*, 2nd edn. New York: Routledge.

Smith, D. (2006) 'Spiritual assessments: keep them simple but not too simple', *The Forum*, ADEC, 32 (2): 8.

Smith, J. I. and Haddad, Y. Y. (1981) *The Islamic Understanding of Death and Resurrection*. Albany: State University of New York Press.

Socrates (2000) attr. in Plato 'Apology', in *The Times Book of Quotations*. London: HarperCollins 2000. p. 186.

Sophocles (1963) *The Antigone*, translated by G. Murray. London: George Allen & Unwin.

Spall, B., and Callis, S. (1997) *Loss, Bereavement and Grief: a Guide to Effective Caring*. Cheltenham: Nelson Thorne.

Speck, P. W. (2000) 'Spiritual issues in pallaitive care', in D. Doyle, G. Hanks and M. MacDonald (eds), *Oxford Textbook of Palliative Medicine*, 16, Oxford: Oxford University Press.

Spiegel, D. (1993) *Living beyond Limits*. London: Vermilion.

Spiegel, D. and Glafkides, M. S. (1983) 'Effects of group confrontation with death and dying', *International Journal of Group Psychotherapy*, 33: 433–47.

Spiegel, D. and Yalom, I. D. (1978) 'A support group for dying patients', *International Journal of Group Psychotherapy*, 28: 233–45.

Standal, S. (1954) 'The need for positive regard: a contribution to client-centred theory'. Ph.D. dissertation, University of Chicago.

Stanworth, R. (2004) *Recognizing Spiritual Needs in People Who Are Dying*. Oxford: Oxford University Press.

Stebbins, J. and Stebbins, S. (1999) 'The contribution of the self-help support-group experience to the survival of the suicide-bereaved', *Grief Matters, Australian Journal of Grief and Bereavement*, 2 (3): 52–4.

Steele, R. L. (1977) 'Dying, death and bereavement among Maya Indians of Mesoamerica', *American Psychologist*, 32 (12): 10060–8.

Stephens, S. (1972) *Death Comes Home*. London: Mowbrays.

Stroebe, M. (1992–93) 'Coping with bereavement: a review of the grief work hypothesis', *Omega*, 26 (1): 19–42.

Stroebe, M. and Schut, H. (1999) 'The dual model of coping with bereavement: rationale and description', *Death Studies*, 23: 197–224.

Stroebe, M., Gergen, M. M., Gergen, K. J. and Stroebe, W. (1992) 'Broken hearts or broken bonds: love and death in historical perspective', *American Psychologist*, 7: 1205–12.

Stroebe, M., Gergen, M., Gergen, K. L. and Stroebe, W. (1993) 'Hearts and bonds: resisting classification and closure', *American Psychologist*, 48 (9): 991–2.

Stroebe, M., Schut, H. and Finkenauer, C. (2001) 'The traumatisation of grief: a conceptual framework for understanding the trauma-bereavement interface', *Israel Journal of Psychiatry*, 30: 185–201.

Sulmasy, P. D. (1997) *The Healer's Calling: A Spirituality for Physicians and Other Health Care Professionals*. New York: Paulist Press.

Sulmasy, P. D. (1999) 'Is medicine a spiritual practice?' *Academic Medicine: Journal of the Association of American Medical Colleges*, 74: 1002–5.

Swinton, J. (2002) 'Spirituality and the lives of people with learning disabilities', *The Tizard Learning Disability Review*, 7 (4): 29–35.

Talbot, K. (2002) *What Forever Means after the Death of a Child*. New York: Brunner & Routledge.

Taylor, S. E. (2003) *The Tending Instinct: Women, Men and the Biology of our Relationships*. New York: Henry Holt.

Taylor, S. F. (2005) 'Between the idea and the reality: a study of the counselling experiences of bereaved people who sense a presence of the deceased', *Counselling and Psychotherapy Research*, 5 (1): 53–61.

Teel, C. S. (1991) 'Chronic sorrow: analysis of the concept', *Journal of Advanced Nursing*, 16: 1311–19.

Thomas, P. (1996) 'Big boys don't cry? Mental health and the politics of gender', *Journal of Mental Health*, 5: 107–10.

Thompson, R. (2006a) 'Dear Charlie First Person', *Observer Magazine*, 22 October: 22–31.

Thompson, R. (2006b) *Dear Charlie: Letters to a Lost Daughter*. London: John Murray.

Traylor, E. S., Hayslip, B., Zaminski, P. I. and York, C. (2003) 'Relationships between grief and family system characteristics: a cross lagged longitudinal analysis', *Death Studies*, 27: 575–601.

Trickey, D. (2005) 'The impact of traumatic bereavement on families'. Presentation at the 12th International Bereavement and Loss Conference, Manchester 8 September.

Tschudin, V. (1997) *Counselling for Loss and Bereavement*. London: Bailliere Tindall in association with Royal College of Nurses.

Turp, M. (2004) *Hidden Self-Harm*. London: Jessica Kingsley.

Valdes-Dapena, M. (1995) 'The post mortem examination', *Paediatric Annals*, 24 (7): 365–72.

Vance, J., Foster, W., Najman, J., Thearle, J., Embleton, G. and Boyle, F. (1993) 'Parental responses to different types of infant death', *Bereavement Care*, 12: 18–21.

Van der Hart, O. (1983) *Rituals in Psychotherapy*. New York: Irvington.

Van der Kolk, B. A., McFarlane, A. C. and Weisaeth, L. (eds) (1996) *Traumatic Stress: The Effects of Overwhelming Stress on Mind, Body and Society*. New York: The Guildford Press.

Van der Wal, J. (1989) 'The aftermath of suicide: a review of the empirical evidence', *Omega: Journal of Death and Dying*, 20: 149–71.

Verlaine, P. (1874) 'Romances sans paroles', in *The Times Book of Quotations*. London: HarperCollins 2000. p. 682.

Versalle, A. and McDowell, E. E. (2004–2005) 'The attitudes of men and women concerning gender differences of grief', *Omega, Journal of Death and Dying*, 50 (1): 53–67.

Vickio, C. J. (1998) 'Together in spirit: keeping our relationship alive when loved ones die', *Death Studies*, 21: 134–86.

Victim Support (2006) *In the Aftermath: the Support Needs of People Bereaved by Homicide: a Research Report*. London: Victim Support National Office.

Volkan, V. D. (1981) *Linking Objects and Linking Phenomena*. New York: International Universities Press.

Vollman, R. R., Ganzert, A., Richer, L. and Williams, W. V. (1981) 'The reactions of family systems to sudden and unexpected death', *Omega*, 2: 101–6.

VonDras, D. D. and White, J. L. (2006) 'Spirituality and death: a transformation into a new life', *The Forum*, ADEC: 1–3.

Von Franz, M. L. (1986) *On Dreams and Death*. London: Shambhala.

Von Goethe, J. W. (1828), in G. Almansi and C. Beguin, *Theatre of Sleep*. London: Picador 1986. p. 279.

Waines, A. (2004) *The Self-Esteem Journal: Using a Journal to Build Self-esteem*. London: Sheldon Press.

Walker, G., Bradburn, J. and Maher, J. (1996) *Breaking Bad News*. London: King's Fund.

Walker, K. N., McBride, A. and Vachon, M. L. (1977) 'Social support networks and the crisis of bereavement', *Social Science and Medicine*, 11: 35–41.

Wallbank, S. (1992) *The Empty Bed: Bereavement and the Loss of Love*. London: Darton, Longman & Todd.

Walsh, K., King, M., Jones, L., Tookman, A. and Blizard, R. (2002) 'Spiritual beliefs may affect outcome of bereavement: prospective study', *British Medical Journal*, 324: 1551–4.

Walsh, N. (2007) 'My dad died when I was 47 but he's now my best friend. I speak to him all the time', Family section, *Guardian*, 17 March: 4–5.

Walsh-Burke, K. (2005) *Grief and Loss: Theories and Skills for Helping Professionals*. Boston, MA: Allyn & Bacon.

Walter, T. (1996a) *The Eclipse of Eternity: a Sociology of the Afterlife*. Basingstoke: Macmillan.

Walter, T. (1996b) 'A new model of grief: bereavement and biography', *Mortality*, 1 (1): 7–25.

Walter, T. (1999) *On Bereavement: the Culture of Grief*. Buckingham: Open University Press.

Walter, T. (2003) 'Historical and cultural variants on the good death', *British Journal of Medicine*, 26 July: 218–20.

Walter, T. (2006) 'Telling the dead man's tale: bridging the gap between the living and the dead', *Bereavement Care*, 25 (2): 23–6.

Wellman, M. M. and Wellman, R. J. (1986) 'Sex differences in peer responsiveness to suicide ideation', *Suicide and Life Threatening Behaviour*, 16: 360–78.

Wertheimer, A. (1999) *A Special Scar: The Experiences of People Bereaved by Suicide*, 5th edn. London: Routledge.

Wertheimer, A. (2001) *A Special Scar: the Experiences of People Bereaved by Suicide*. London: Routledge.

Wheeler, J. (2001) 'Parental bereavement: the crisis of meaning', *Death Studies*, 25 (1): 51–66.

Whitaker, A. (ed.) (1984) *All in the End is Harvest: An Anthology for those who Grieve*. London: Darton, Longman & Todd Ltd.

Wickie, S. K. and Marwit, S. J. (2000–2001) 'Assumptive world views and the grief reactions of parents of murdered children', *Omega*, 42 (2): 101–3.

Wiener, H. (1989) 'The dynamics of the organism: implications of recent biological thought for psychosomatic theory and research', *Psychosomatic Medicine*, 51: 608–35.

Wijngaards-de Meij, L., Stroebe, M., Schut, H., Stroebe, W., van den Bout, J., van der Heijden, P. G. M. and Dijkstra, I. (2007) 'Patterns of attachment and parents' adjustment to the death of their child', *Personality and Social Psychology Bulletin*, 33 (4): 537–48.

Wilkinson, M. (2006) *Coming into Mind. The Mind–Brain Relationship: a Jungian Clinical Perspective*. London: Routledge.

Wimpenny, P. (2007) 'A literature review on bereavement and bereavement care: developing evidence-based practice in Scotland', *Bereavement Care*, 26 (1): 7–10.

Witztum, E. and Roman, I. (2000) 'Psychotherapeutic intervention in complicated grief: metaphor and leave-taking ritual with the bereaved', in R. Malkinson, S. Rubin and E. Witztum (eds), *Traumatic and Nontraumatic Loss and Bereavement: Clinical Theory and Practice*. Madison, CT: Psychosocial Press.

Worden, J. W. (1991) *Grief Counselling and Grief Therapy. A Handbook for the Mental Health Practitioner*, 2nd edn. London: Routledge.

Wortman, C. B. and Silver, R. C. (2001) 'The myths of coping with loss revisited', in M. S. Stroebe, R. O. Hansson, W. Stroebe and H. Schut (eds), *Handbook of Bereavement Research: Consequences, Coping, and Care*. Washington, DC: American Psychological Association Press. pp. 405–30.

Wortman, C. B., Silver, R. C. and Kessler, R. C. (1993) 'The meaning of loss and adjustment to bereavement', in M. S. Stroebe, W. Stroebe and R. O. Hansson (eds), *Handbook of Bereavement*. New York: Cambridge University Press. pp. 349–66.

Wright, M. C. (2002) 'The essence of spiritual care: a phenomenological enquiry', *Palliative Medicine*, 16: 125–32.

Yalom, I. D. (1980) *Existential Psychotherapy*. New York: Basic Books.

Yalom, I. D. (2000) 'Religion and psychiatry'. Speech on receiving the 2000 Oscar Pfister prize delivered at the American Psychiatric Association's annual meeting, May, New Orleans. Retrieved from Internet 06/09/2006, www.yolam.com/pfister.html

Yalom, I. D. and Greaves, C. (1977) 'Group therapy with the terminally ill', *American Journal of Psychiatry*, 134: 396–400.

Yamamoto, J. (1970) 'Cultural factors in loneliness, death and separation', *Medical Times*, 98: 177–83.

Youqing, L. (2000) 'Last Testament', *Guardian*, 9 December.

Yule, W. (ed.) (1999) *Post-traumatic Stress Disorders: Concepts and Therapy*. London: John Wiley and Sons.

Zisook, S., Chentsova-Dutton, Y. and Shuchter, S. R. (1998) 'PTSD following bereavement', *Annals of Clinical Psychiatry*, 10: 157–63.

Index